CHAUCER

HERE AND NOW

CHAUCER

HERE AND NOW

EDITED BY
MARION TURNER

BODLEIAN
LIBRARY
PUBLISHING

A Good wyf ther was of beside bathe
And she was somdeel deef & that was scathe
Of cloth makynge had she suche an haunt
She passyd them of ypre and of gaunt
In al the parisshe wyf was ther non
That to the offrynge before hyr sholde goon
And yf ther dyd certayn wroth was she
Than was she oute of al charyte
Her kercheuys ful fyn were of grounde
I durste swere they weyed thre pounde
That on a sonday were on hyr hede
Hyr hosyn were of fyne scarlet reede
Ful streyte I teyd and shoos ful moyst and newe
Bold was her face fayr and rede of hewe
She was a worthy womman al hyr lyue
Husbondys at the chyrche dore hadde she fyue
Wythoute other companye in youthe
But her of nedyth not to speke as nowthe

CONTENTS

Venus

Compleynt of Mars and Venus

Gladeth ye lovers on the morowe gray
Loo Venus rysen amonge yow rowes rede
And flowres fressh honouren the this day
For when the sune uprist then wol they sprede
But ye lovers that lye in eny drede
Fleeth lest wikked tonges yow espye
Loo yonde the sune the candel of Ialosye

Wyth teres blew and with a wounded hert
Taketh your leve and with sent John to borowe
Apeseth sumwhat of your sorowes smert
Tyme cometh ofte that ese shal your sorowe
The glad nyght ys worthe an hevy morowe
Seynt Valentyne a foule thus herd I synge
Vpon your day er sune gan vp sprynge

Yet sange this foule I rede yow al a wake
And ye that han not chosen in humble wyse
Yet at this fest renoveleth your servyse
With out repentyng cheseth your make
And ye that han ful chosen as I devise
Conferneth hyt perpetuely to dure
And paciently taketh your aventure

And for the worship of this high fest
Yet wol I in my briddes wise synge
The sentence of the compleynt at the lest
That woful Mars made atte departyng
Fro fressh Venus in a morwnyng
Whan Phebus with his firy torches rede
Ransaked hath every lover in hys drede

Whilom the thrid hevenes lord a bove
As wel by hevenysh revolucion
As by desert hath wonne Venus his love
And she hath take hym in subieccion
And as a maistresse taught hym his lesson

FOREWORD

The Bodleian Library's collections include a wide range of Chaucerian material, from lavishly illustrated fifteenth-century manuscripts to William Morris's beautiful Arts and Crafts inspired Kelmscott Chaucer; from early copies of the seventeenth-century ballad *The Wanton Wife of Bath* to translations of *The Canterbury Tales* into Hebrew, Chinese and even Esperanto.

Chaucer's writings have had enormous cultural power since he first put pen to parchment in the second half of the fourteenth century. He was a boldly experimental poet who expanded the range of what the English language and English poetry could do, inventing new forms and genres inspired by the writings of his French and Italian contemporaries. Across time, he has been seen in wildly varying ways. John Dryden wrote that when he read Chaucer's work, he immediately knew that 'I had a soul congenial to his'. Countless readers have felt the same way. Precisely because Chaucer's work is so diverse, and because he was so interested in depicting multiple perspectives and points of view, readers can always find themselves and their own concerns in Chaucer's texts.

In different eras, different Chaucers have been popular. While fifteenth-century readers preferred dream visions and serious tales, more modern readers liked the bawdy fabliaux stories about sex in trees and misdirected kisses. During some centuries Chaucer has been heavily censored, in others he has been very

pp. 6–7 One of Chaucer's lesser-known short poems, *The Complaint of Mars* appears in MS. Fairfax 16, accompanied by one of the most accomplished of all illustrations of Chaucer's works. The image depicts Mars and Venus, with Jupiter suspended above. The elaborate flower-and-spray border motifs include the arms of John Stanley of Hooton, Cheshire (d. *c*.1469). The artist has been identified as the Abingdon Missal Master, who was working in the mid-fifteenth century. Oxford, Bodleian Library, MS. Fairfax 16, fols 14v–15r.

Image of the 'author' figure speaking to the audience in Zadie Smith's *The Wife of Willesden*. Like the Chaucer narrator in *The Canterbury Tales*, Smith's avatar is introduced to us in a London pub, and she concludes by 'retracting' – disavowing – any parts of the text that offend her audience. Unlike Chaucer, she has a MacBook – and cites Chaucer himself as the authority behind her text.

freely adapted for film and television. At times, many different Chaucers have jostled for prominence: the Victorians promoted imperial Chaucer, domestic Chaucer and children's Chaucer, for instance. Recently, postcolonial responses to Chaucer by writers such as Patience Agbabi and Zadie Smith have placed his texts in new contexts – and translations have made his poetry available all over the world, from Brazil to Japan.

Chaucer Here and Now explores the different 'Chaucers' that readers, writers and artists have imagined across time. This collection of essays, which complements an exhibition held at the Bodleian, explores manuscripts and books, plays and films, translations and cartoons, pop-up books and fortune-telling cards.

Many different kinds of readers have responded to Chaucer's texts. Although the vast majority of his early readers were English, and most writers creating new versions of his poetry between 1400–1800 were male, that has changed in recent centuries. In the last 200 years we have seen more and more women writing new versions of Chaucer's texts. Translations and adaptations have been crafted by people from all around the world over the last century and, in the last few decades in particular, Black women have been at the forefront of Chaucerian reception and adaptation.

Through illustrated examples of beautiful – and scruffy! – manuscripts, early printed books, multilingual translations, innovative rewritings and visual adaptations, this book tells many different tales about Chaucer across time, around the world, and in multiple forms and genres. Like *The Canterbury Tales*, the stories of Chaucer's afterlives are varied and surprising. Together, the essays demonstrate the influence that Chaucer has had in many heres and nows – and which he continues to have today.

I would like to express thanks to the Bodleian's Public Engagement team, led by Madeline Slaven, for their staging of the exhibition, and to colleagues at Bodleian Publishing for producing such a beautiful book – combining stimulating scholarship with stunning illustration. Finally, profound thanks to Marion Turner, Tolkien Professor of English, and the library's guest curator for this exhibition, and editor of this volume. It has been a great pleasure for the Bodleian to work with Professor Turner, one of the world's leading scholars on Chaucer.

Richard Ovenden OBE, Bodley's Librarian

INTRODUCTION

Every century invents its own Chaucer.[1] One of the most famous of all canonical poets, Geoffrey Chaucer has occupied a central place in literary history since his death in 1400. However, what he stands for has changed dramatically across time, as readers shape him according to their own interests and preoccupations. There is a Chaucer for every *here* and every *now* – from the here and now of sixteenth-century England, when readers turned him into an enthusiastic Protestant, to the here and now of 1970s Italy, when Pasolini imagined him as an earthy enthusiast for male proletarian sexuality; from the here and now of England's nineteenth-century empire, when Chaucer was described as a keen footballer whose works were destined to spread English values across the globe, to the here and now of London in 2021, when Zadie Smith reimagined the Wife of Bath as a contemporary Londoner of Caribbean heritage. He has been seen as conservative and radical, misogynist and feminist, serious and comic, Catholic and Protestant. And, as we shall see, just as he wrote in an exceptionally – almost incredibly – wide range of genres and forms, so he has inspired a dizzying range of interpretations and responses. These include children's adaptations, grime mixes, translations into many languages, propagandist films, scandalous ballads, Victorian wedding cabinets, and cartoons.

0.1
This cabinet, painted by Edward Burne-Jones as a wedding present to William and Jane Morris in 1859, is a fascinating – and disturbing – example of Pre-Raphaelite medievalism. It is decorated with an image of Chaucer and scenes from 'The Prioress's Tale', an antisemitic story about a Christian boy murdered by Jews who miraculously continues singing to the Virgin Mary after his death. Ashmolean Museum, University of Oxford, WA1939.2.

In the 650 years since Chaucer started writing poetry, he has always occupied a prominent position in English letters. From early on in his reception history, his texts were being read and appropriated in other parts of the British Isles, and since the seventeenth and eighteenth centuries he has enjoyed great cultural capital in many other countries. While his texts first spread to Europe and to Britain's colonies, more recently his texts have been read, studied, translated and interpreted in countries including Mongolia, Soviet Russia and Brazil. This is an author who has long had global appeal, from Voltaire's version of 'The Wife of Bath's Tale' in the eighteenth century to a Chinese version of 'The Nun's Priest's Tale' in the early twentieth century.

Although in every era we can see diversity in how people respond to Chaucer, we can also trace broad trends in different periods, particularly in terms of the materiality of the texts and of the genres that dominate. The first chapter of this book explores Chaucer in the manuscript culture of the fifteenth century, while the second focuses on what happened when he emerged into print in the late fifteenth, sixteenth and early seventeenth centuries. We then turn to the later seventeenth and eighteenth century as an era of translation and adaptation (Chapter 3), before examining Victorian responses to Chaucer, which ranged from the domestic to the imperial. Chapters 5 and 6 are thematic in approach. 'Women Reading Chaucer' ranges across time, but takes the nineteenth century as a case study, while 'Chaucerian Multilingualism' compares Chaucer's own multilingualism with multilingual responses to his writings, especially in the twentieth century and up to the present day. The last two chapters turn to modernity: first to Chaucer on film and television from the 1940s to the twenty-first century, and then to twenty-first-century poetic responses by contemporary authors. As a whole, the book demonstrates both the richness of readers' responses to Chaucer and the ongoing centrality of Chaucer in cultural history. It also reveals astonishing variety in how readers, editors, scribes, playwrights, cartoonists, film-makers, translators, artists, scriptwriters and poets have used Chaucer's texts.

Within this exceptional range, we can see some continuities. In general, *The Canterbury Tales* has occupied a far larger space in readers' imaginations than any of Chaucer's other texts – although those texts have not been ignored; *Troilus and Criseyde*, for instance, has spawned many fascinating imitations, translations and sequels, from Shakespeare's *Troilus and Cressida* to Lavinia Greenlaw's 2014 *A Double Sorrow*.[2] Within the *Tales*, the Wife of Bath has proved much more magnetic than any other character. We see this in scribes' annotations, as discussed in the first chapter, and in the work of contemporary writers including Jean 'Binta' Breeze, Caroline Bergvall and Zadie Smith, the focus of the last chapter. The Wife of Bath's hold on readers' imaginations is unique. A good example of this is John Skelton's late-medieval poetic summary of *The Canterbury Tales*: he allocates four lines in total to all the other tales, and then ten to the Wife of Bath. Chapter 3 discusses the hugely popular seventeenth-century ballad about the Wife of Bath – a text that caused printers to be imprisoned, and that was itself burnt – as well as John Gay's play about the character.[3]

The second continuity that we can see across time is in Chaucer's association with nation. Chaucer himself was a multilingual man, a much-travelled diplomat whose major poetic influences were written in French, Italian and Latin, and who developed new poetic forms by drawing closely on Continental models. He was married to a woman from a Hainault family, and was associated with a cosmopolitan social and political group. Throughout his life, he was immersed in the politics of trade, travelling to Genoa to negotiate treaties relating to the wool trade, working for many years as the customs' officer in charge of the Wool Quay in London, and, for much of his life, watching the ships come into the Thames, laden with products from as far afield as Indonesia, and leaving again, heavy with English wool. England was a multilingual country in the fourteenth century, and the idea of a 'nation' was flexible and developing.[4] Chapter 6 demonstrates how appropriate it is that multilingual responses to this multilingual poet have spread to every corner of the world.

Chaucer's English and British readers, however, have tended to see him as the Father of English Literature, a national – even nationalist – figure who embodies Englishness. In Chapter 2 we shall see how he was constructed by early printers as the founder of the canon. Chaucer was held up as an example of a particular kind of cultural identity as medievalism became a key part of an imperial, Victorian idea of nation (Chapter 4). This tendency reaches its apogee in G.K. Chesterton's astonishing opening to his 1932 book: 'If I were writing this in French, as I should be if Chaucer had not chosen to write in English…'. He adds that 'Chaucer was the Father of his Country, rather in the style of George Washington' and that 'He made a national language, he came very near to making a nation… Chaucer made not only a new nation but a new world'.[5] Nation, patriarchy and empire (the new world) are bound up together in this idea of Chaucer. A decade later, *The Canterbury Tales* was to be the inspiration for a very odd wartime film, *A Canterbury Tale*, that paints an evocative picture of the English landscape and English culture that

0.2
A page from a Russian translation of *The Canterbury Tales*, illustrated with a striking lithograph. This is the opening of 'The Pardoner's Tale', and the image shows the three rioters who, while seeking to kill Death, meet a mysterious old man who tells them where they can find him. The text is translated by Ivan Kashkin and Osip Rumer with lithographs by Sergey Barkhin, and dates from 1980. *Kenterberiĭskie rasskazy*, 1980, Oxford, Bodleian Library, 27976 g.2, pp. 194–5.

РАССКАЗ
ПРОДАВЦА
ИНДУЛЬГЕНЦИЙ

Здесь начинается рассказ
Продавца индульгенций

Так вот: в Брабанте некогда жила
Компания повес; тенета зла
Их всех опутали, они в борделе
Иль в кабаке за ночью ночь сидели.
Тимпаны, лютни, арфы и кифары
Их горячили, и сплетались пары
В греховной пляске. Всю-то ночь игра,
Еда и винопийство до утра.
Так тешили маммона в виде свинском
И в капище скакали сатанинском.
От их божбы власы вставали дыбом,
Они распять спасителя могли бы,
Когда бы не был он за нас распят.
  Был нечестив и самый их наряд.
И с ними были юные блудницы,
Цветочницы, нагие танцовщицы,
Певцы, кондитеры, коты и сводни,
Которые как встарь, так и сегодня
Слугами дьявольскими состоят.
Огонь разжегши, в нем они горят,
И похотью костер тот разжигают,
И боль вином напрасно заливают.

194

the Allies were fighting for (Chapter 7). While these ideas of nationalism have usually been decidedly patriarchal and male, women have always read Chaucer's texts (Chapter 5), and indeed the heroine of *A Canterbury Tale* offers something of a counter-narrative – as well as herself being a radical recreation of the Wife of Bath.

In more recent decades Chaucer has been associated with nation and place in a different way. He has become the poet of journeying, refugees, displacement and postcolonial understandings of British history and culture. Many writers, including Black British and Black American poets, as well as scriptwriters for the BBC *Canterbury Tales*, and a very wide range of writers in the *Refugee Tales* project, have taken Chaucer's texts as an inspiration for writing about the journeys and identities of the Windrush generation, of slaves, and of refugees. The issues of travel, desire, identity, landscape, displacement and the past that dominate parts of *The Canterbury Tales*, especially the opening, remain of central importance to writers today. Chapter 8 examines how contemporary poets have used *The Canterbury Tales* to explore border crossings and nation in new literary experiments.

The history of Chaucerian reception is a vast topic and this book does not, of course, aim to be comprehensive. We have not attempted to say much about the history of academic criticism of Chaucer's texts, for example. The main foci have been on how Chaucer is presented to a wider public through particular kinds of manuscripts, editions, translations or adaptations; on specific major trends in attitudes to Chaucer's writings; and on some prominent new versions of his works (e.g. Dryden's translations, Victorian children's editions, modern television adaptations, and Zadie Smith's recent play).

This book also aims to demonstrate visually the range of ways in which readers or viewers might encounter Chaucer across time and around the world. The materiality of the text makes a dramatic difference to how we understand it. Today, many of us first encounter Chaucer in a school edition of an individual tale, and then in a collected works edition – in the UK usually *The Riverside Chaucer*. Each edition provides a version of Chaucer curated by an editor – or rather a team of editors across time.

0.3
The opening of the 'General Prologue' of *The Canterbury Tales*, from a mid-fifteenth century manuscript. The beautifully decorated initial 'W' spans eight lines, introducing the famous opening: 'Whan that Aprille with his shoures soote'. Above that, in red, you can read 'Here beginneth the prolog of the tales of Caunterbury'. Oxford, Bodleian Library, MS. Hatton donat. 1, fol. 1r.

Here beginneth the prolog of the tales of Caunterbury

Whan that Aprill with his shoures swote
The drought of Marche hath perced þe rote
And bathed every veyn in suche licoure
Of which vertu engendered is the floure
Whan zepherus eke with his swete brethe
Enspired hath in every holt and hethe
The tendre croppes and the yong sonne
Hath in the Ramme his half cours yronne
And smale foules maken melodye
That slepen all night with open ye
So priken hem nature in here corage
Than longen folk to go on pilgrymage
And palmers to sechen strange strondes
And halowes couth in many londes
And specialli from every shires ende
Of Engelond to Caunterbury thei wende
To seche the blisfull martir that is meke
That hem hath holpen whan þei were seke
It befell þat in þat seson on a day
In Southwerk atte Tabard as I lay
Redi to wende on my pilgrimage
To Caunterbury with devoute corage
And night was comyn in that herbary
Well xxix in a company
Of sondri folk be aventure I fall
In felaship as pilgrymes were thei all
That toward Caunterbury wold ride
The chambres and hall were wide
And well were þei esed atte best
And shorteli whan the son was gon to rest
So had I spoken with hem everich oon
That I was of here felaship anoon
And made forward erli for to rise
To make oure wei ther as I yow devise
But nathelese while I have tyme and space
Or that I ferther in this tale pase
Me thenk it accordyng to resoun
To tell you al þe condicion
Of eche oon of hem so as it semed me
And which þei were and of what degre
And in what arai þei were yn
And atte a knight I will begyn
knight þere was and þat a worthi man

Reading Chaucer in the Hengwrt manuscript is a very different experience to reading Chaucer in MS Hatton donat. 1 – which is different again to Speght's 1602 edition, or a modern collected works. If you encounter Chaucer first in a translation into another language, in Jonathan Myerson's animations, or in Patience Agbabi's *Telling Tales*, your experiences will be even more varying – but each version captures something of what Chaucer was doing. And there is no 'original' for us to read at all. The images in this book illustrate not only the various ways in which Chaucer's texts can be experienced, but also the extraordinary art that his texts have inspired.

Chaucer was a poet of the later fourteenth century. Many aspects of his time might seem similar to our own – he grew up in a pandemic and in a time of social and cultural change, witnessing tension between England and other parts of Europe, chaotic parliaments and cost-of-living crises. But his era was also profoundly different to our own, a time of universal religious belief, little medical knowledge, no real democracy, and a much more extreme patriarchal system. Some parts of his poetry seem startlingly relevant to modern readers while others are disturbingly alien. For a whole host of reasons, his writings continue to enthral readers. While some might be fascinated by Chaucer's poetic and formal experiments, others focus on his characters; some are interested in his narrative power, others in his engagement with theories of literature and authorship; some are moved by his philosophical poetry, others prefer his razor-sharp humour. His texts remain alive to readers precisely because of his kaleidoscopic, virtuoso abilities. Chaucer's time is, and has always been, here and now.

0.4
Thomas Speght's influential editions of Chaucer (1598 and 1602) included a great deal of textual apparatus usually reserved for classical authorities. This elevated Chaucer, but also emphasized the difference between his English and that of his readers. This page is the beginning of Speght's glossary, 'The old and obscure words in Chaucer explaned', with references to analogy and etymology. *The Workes of our ancient and learned English poet, Geffrey Chaucer*, 1602, Oxford, Bodleian Library, A 2.5 Art.Seld., fol. 378.

The old and obscure words in Chaucer explaned, whereof either by nature, or deriuation,

Some are Arabicke, Some Greeke, Some Latine, Some Italian, Some French, Some Dutch, — Noted with *a.* *g.* *l.* *i.* *f.* *d.*

Some Dialects within this our Country of Brittain, and many of them deriued from the Saxon tongue, — Noted with *b.*

The rest are explaned by way of Analogie.

Annotations also vpon some words and places, with direction to the Folio and Page.

ABandon, *f.* libertie.
abandon, *f.* giue ouer.
abandoning, *f.* rejectment.
abawed, *b.* daunted, abashed.
abet, *b.* setting on.
abedge, *b.* abye.
abying, *b.* state.
abit, *b.* abideth, dwelleth.
abidst, *b.* suffred.
abode, receiued.
abode, *b.* tarrying.
abrayde, *b.* arose, recouered.
abrayde, *b.* brake of, vpstart.
abreding, vpbraiding.
ablusions, *l.* clensings.
abyme, *l.* from below.
acale, *d.* cold.
accesse, *b.* ague.
accidie, *l.* wanhope.
accoy, *f.* assuage.
acoyed, *f.* pampered, made quiet.
achecked, *b.* stayed.
acheked, *b.* choked.
ackele, *b.* coole.
acloyeth, *b.* ouerchargeth.
acroke, *b.* awrie.
acquite, *f.* match, to dispatch.
adassed, *b.* abashed.
adawed, *b.* awaked.
adiacent, *l.* adjoyning.
aduertence, *l.* audience: also mind, or thought.
aduert, *l.* marke.
aduentaile, *f.* coat of Armour.
afare, *f.* a noyse, a businesse.
afyne, *f.* fined.
affi, *f.* haue trust.
affray, *b.* feare, stirre, assault.
affrey, *f.* sturdinesse, also feare.
agasteth, *b.* skarreth.
agiler, *f.* a marker of men.
agilted, *b.* offended.
agilt, *b.* committed, offended.
agre, to please, to content.
agredge, *f.* aggrauate, to gather together.
agrise, *b.* afraid.
agrisen, *b.* afearde.
agrise, *b.* faint, terrifie, greeue.
agriseth, *b.* beginneth to quake.
agramed, *d.* greeued.
agrose, *b.* was greeued, daunted.
agroted, *d.* cloyed, made bigge, swelled.
agrutched, abridged.
aiust, *b.* remooue.
alayes, *b.* wayes: also temperance.
(**Alnath**, fol. 50. page. 1.) Alnath is a fixed starre in the hornes of Aries, from whence the first mansion of the Moon taketh his name, and is called Alnath.
alledgement, *i.* ease.
alledged, *i.* diminished.
Alderan, *a.* a starre in the neck of the Lion.
algate, *b.* notwithstanding, euer, forsooth, euen now, altogether.
alcali, *a.* Nightshade, salt wort.
(**Algezer**) Algezira, a Cittie in Spaine, neere the streights of Gibralter.
als, *d.* also: as well.
alestake, *d.* Maypole.
Almagist, *a.* a worke of Astronomie, written by Ptolomie.
alembic, *a.* a stillitorie.
alures, *f.* walkes, alleyes.
algomisa, *a.* (*Canis minor*) the lesse dog starre.
alder, *b.* all alone, onely, cheefe.
alhabor, *a.* (*Canis maior*) the greater dog starre.
alswa, *d.* also.
ally, *f.b.* kin.
alien, *f.* allie.
(**Alisandre**) Alexandria in Ægypt, now called Scanderia.
almurie, *a.* the denticle of Capricorne.
algrim, *a.* (*algebra.*) The art of figurate numbers.
alterate, *l.* chaunged.

¶ Heere bigynneth the prologe of the tale of the wyf of Bathe

Experience though noon auctoritee
Were in this world is right ynogh for me
To speke of wo that is in mariage
For lordynges sith þt I twelf yeer was of age
Thonked be god that is eterne on lyue
Housbondes atte chirche dore I haue had fyue
If I so ofte myghte han wedded be
And alle were worthy men in hir degree
But me was told certeyn noght longe agon is
That sith þt Crist ne wente neuere but onys
To weddyng in the Cane of Galilee
That by the same ensample taughte he me
That I ne sholde wedded be but ones
¶ Herke eek lo which a sharp word for the nones
Bisyde a welle Jhesus god and man
Spak in repreeue of the Samaritan
¶ Thow hast yhad fyue housbondes quod he
And that ilke man which that now hath thee
Is nat thyn housbonde thus he seyde certeyn
What that he mente ther by I kan nat seyn
But þt I axe why þt the fifthe man
Was noon housbonde to the Samaritan
How manye myghte she han in mariage
Yet herde I neuere tellen in myn age
Vp on this nombre diffynycioun
Men may dyuyne and glosen vp and doun
But wel I woot expres withouten lye
God bad vs for to wexe and multiplye
That gentil text kan I wel vnderstonde
¶ Eek wel I woot he seyde þt myn housbonde
Sholde lete fader and moder and take to me
But of no nombre mencion made he
Of bigamye or of Octogamye
Why sholde men thanne speke of it vileynye
¶ Lo heere the wise kyng daun Salomon
I trowe he hadde wyues many oon

1

COLLABORATION AND CHAOS: CHAUCER'S EARLY READERS

Marion Turner

When Chaucer died in 1400, he did not leave a neatly bound and packaged 'complete works'. Nor did he even leave a finished *Canterbury Tales*. He left some complete poems, often in more than one version, such as *Troilus and Criseyde* and the *Prologue to the Legend of Good Women*, some incomplete poems, such as the *House of Fame* and *Anelida and Arcite*, and a mass of 'fragments' (sections of the text, mainly in very polished form) that together formed the unfinished *Canterbury Tales*. 'The Cook's Tale' was abandoned after fifty lines and some pilgrims, including the Plowman, did not tell a tale at all. Chaucer changed his mind about whether the Wife of Bath or the Shipman would tell the story of the cuckolded merchant, and about whether the Man of Law would tell a tale in prose or in rhyme royal. Some tales had originally been written as stand-alone texts and reworked for the tale collection. It was clear that what we call Fragment I – the 'General Prologue', and the Knight's, Miller's, Reeve's and Cook's Prologues and Tales – was supposed to come first, and that Fragment X – 'The Parson's Prologue and Tale' – should come last, but the 'best' order of the rest of the fragments was not obvious. Scribes, editors and patrons had to make major interventions to create a readable *Canterbury Tales*, and these interventions were driven by a wide range of interests and agendas.[1]

1.1
The opening of 'The Wife of Bath's Prologue' from the earliest *Canterbury Tales* manuscript, the Hengwrt Chaucer, which dates from around Chaucer's death in 1400. The running title at the top of the page 'The Wyf of Bathe' helps readers to navigate the manuscript if they are looking for a particular tale. The only decoration on the page is centred around the letter 'E' at the beginning of 'Experience' – the first word of the Prologue. Aberystwyth, National Library of Wales, Peniarth MS. 392D, fol. 58r.

The earliest manuscript of the *Tales* is the Hengwrt Chaucer (National Library of Wales Peniarth MS 392D) (FIGURE 1.1). This was probably produced in the few years immediately after Chaucer died, although it is just possible that it was put together in the last years of his life. Most critics think it is an early-fifteenth-century production, and agree that someone knowledgeable must have had editorial control. That person made decisions about which tale followed which, and they may have been informed by personal knowledge of Chaucer's intentions. Candidates for this overseer or editor figure include Thomas Chaucer, the wealthy and clever eldest son of the poet; Thomas Hoccleve, the poet and scribe who saw himself as a kind of literary heir to Chaucer; and Adam Pynkhurst, suggested in 2004 as 'Chaucer's scribe', and the target for a great deal of discussion and scholarly controversy ever since.[2]

The same scribe was also responsible for the Ellesmere Chaucer (Huntington Library, mssEL 26 C 9), the most famous *Canterbury Tales* manuscript, written hot on Hengwrt's heels (FIGURE 1.2). By the time he wrote Ellesmere, this scribe had got hold of another tale ('The Canon's Yeoman's Tale', which does not appear in Hengwrt), and he (or his master) also had a different idea about the best tale order. Ellesmere is a more luxurious manuscript, presumably produced for someone who was willing to pay well for a text complete with beautiful miniatures of the pilgrims (FIGURE 1.3). Indeed, Chaucer manuscripts are very variable in their production costs and value: at one end of the spectrum we have gorgeously illustrated manuscripts such as MS Fairfax 16 and Corpus Christi Cambridge MS 61, while on the other we hear in 1394 of a relatively cheap copy of *Troilus* being used to pay off a debt for 20 shillings (the price of two cows).[3]

1.2
The opening of the 'General Prologue' from the Ellesmere Chaucer, the most famous Chaucer manuscript (dating from the early fifteenth century). The first letter is very elaborately decorated, and new ideas or sections are marked with decorated capitals. The scribe has written 'knyght' on the right to indicate to readers where a character description begins. San Marino, Huntington Library, MS. EL 26 C 9, fol. 1r.

Whan that Aprill with hise shoures soote
The droghte of March hath perced to the roote
And bathed euery veyne in swich licour
Of which vertu engendred is the flour
Whan zephirus eek wt his sweete breeth
Inspired hath in euery holt and heeth
The tendre croppes and the yonge sonne
Hath in the Ram his half cours yronne
And smale foweles maken melodye
That slepen al the nyght with open eye
So priketh hem nature in hir corages
Thanne longen folk to goon on pilgrimages
And Palmeres for to seken straunge strondes
To ferne halwes kowthe in sondry londes
And specially fram euery shires ende
Of Engelond to Caunterbury they wende
The holy blisful martir for to seke
That hem hath holpen whan þt they were seeke
Bifil that in that seson on a day
In Southwerk at the Tabard as I lay
Redy to wenden on my pilgrymage
To Caunterbury with ful deuout corage
At nyght were come in to that hostelrye
Wel nyne and twenty in a compaignye
Of sondry folk by auenture yfalle
In felaweshipe and pilgrymes were they alle
That toward Caunterbury wolden ryde
The chambres and the stables weren wyde
And wel we weren esed atte beste
And shortly whan the sonne was to reste
So hadde I spoken wt hem euerichon
That I was of hir felaweshipe anon
And made forward erly for to ryse
To take oure wey ther as I yow deuyse
But nathelees whil I haue tyme and space
Er that I ferther in this tale pace
Me thynketh it acordaunt to resoun
To telle yow al the condicion
Of ech of hem so as it semed me
And whiche they were and of what degree
And eek in what array that they were Inne
And at a knyght than wol I first bigynne
A knyght ther was and that a worthy man
That fro the tyme that he first bigan
To ryden out he loued chiualrie
Trouthe and honour fredom and curteisie
Ful worthy was he in his lordes werre
And ther to hadde he riden no man ferre

Sol in Ariete

Knyght

If the editor of Hengwrt knew Chaucer, then the comment 'Of this cokes tale maked Chaucer na moore' (Chaucer wrote no more of this Cook's Tale) may reflect an honest desire to make clear to readers that there is no more to come for the 'Cook's Tale'; that the ending has not been lost – it never existed (FIGURE 1.4). It also discourages anyone from adding extra lines to try to finish off the tale. In contrast another, slightly later, manuscript, Christ Church 152, adds another tale at this point for the Cook – the 'Tale of Gamelyn' – without telling the reader that this tale has nothing to do with Chaucer whatsoever (FIGURE 1.5). Indeed, in contrast to Hengwrt, at the point where the 'Cook's Tale' peters out, rather than saying that Chaucer made no more of this tale, the scribe writes: 'Here begynnyth the Cokys tale', before launching into 'Gamelyn'. One possibility is that some scribes did indeed believe that the tale was by Chaucer, as many other manuscripts also used 'Gamelyn' as a 'Cook's Tale'. Another manuscript – MS. Bodl. 686 – expanded and then finished off Chaucer's own 'Cook's Tale' (FIGURE 1.6). Whoever wrote the additional lines was either extraordinarily inept, or had no interest in trying to imitate Chaucer's style. Chaucerian lines, such as the opening couplet, 'A prentys whilom dwelled in our cite, / And of a crafte of vitellers was he' (An apprentice once lived in our city / and belonged to a food-providing guild), written in iambic pentameter, sound very different from lines such as 'With Rech-never and Recheles this lessoun he lerys / With Waste and with Wranglere, his owne pley-ferys' (He learns this lesson with Never-care and Careless / With Waste and with Quarreller, his own play-fellows). The new lines are written in alliterative long lines with four stresses. This metrical style along with the inclusion of multiple allegorical personifications makes the text seem much more like William

1.3
The end of 'The Wife of Bath's Prologue' and the beginning of her 'Tale', from the Ellesmere Chaucer. The page is strikingly decorated, and features a famous miniature image of the Wife of Bath. She appears here riding her horse, carrying a whip, with red clothes, a large hat and a determined expression on her face. San Marino, Huntington Library, MS. EL 26 C 9, fol. 72r.

Quod this Somonour and I bishrewe me
But if I telle tales two or thre
Of freres er I come to Sidyngborne
That I shal make thyn herte for to morne
For wel I woot thy pacience is gon
Oure hoost cride pees and that anon
And seyde lat the womman telle hire tale
Ye fare as folk that dronken were of ale
Do dame telle forth youre tale and that is best
Al redy sire quod she right as yow lest
If I haue licence of this worthy frere
Yis dame quod he tel forth and I wol heere

Heere endeth the wyf of Bathe hir prologe and bigynneth hir tale

In th'olde dayes of kyng Arthour
Of which that Britons speken greet honour
Al was this land fulfild of fayerye
The Elf queene with hir joly compaignye
Daunced ful ofte in many a grene mede
This was the olde opinion as I rede
I speke of manye hundred yeres ago
But now kan no man se none elues mo
For now the grete charitee and prayeres
Of lymytours and othere hooly freres
That serchen euery lond and euery streem
As thikke as motes in the sonne beem
Blessynge halles chambres kichenes boures
Citees burghes castels hye toures
Thropes bernes shipnes dayeryes
This maketh that ther been no fayeryes
For ther as wont to walken was an elf
Ther walketh now the lymytour hym self
In vndermeles and in morwenynges
And seyth his matyns and his hooly thynges
As he gooth in his lymytacioun
Wommen may go saufly vp and doun
In euery bussh or vnder euery tree
Ther is noon oother incubus but he
And he ne wol doon hem but dishonour
And so bifel that this kyng Arthour
Hadde in hous a lusty bachiler
That on a day cam ridynge fro ryuer
And happed that allone as he was born
He saugh a mayde walkynge hym biforn

Langland's *Piers Plowman* than a Canterbury Tale. The author of the continuation also tries to make Chaucer's text less bawdy: the verb 'swyved', used in the context of declaring that the wife of the apprentice's friend 'swyved for hir sustenaunce' (had sex for her occupation) is changed to the less explicit 'pleyed'. Different editors and scribes dealt with the problem of the ostentatiously unfinished 'Cook's Tale' in varying ways – and with varying success.[4]

Christ Church 152 presents a more complete *Canterbury Tales* in other ways too. For instance, it includes a 'Plowman's Tale' (FIGURE 1.7). There is no evidence that Chaucer ever wrote a tale for this pilgrim, the most socially unimportant person in his group. But in Christ Church 152, after the unfinished 'Squire's Tale' – most manuscripts depict the Franklin interrupting the Squire to prevent his tale going on too long – the scribe inserts 'The Plowman's Prologue and Tale', before 'The Second Nun's Tale' (here called the first nun's tale!).

This 'Plowman's Tale' is, in fact, a poem by Thomas Hoccleve. It is a religious text, an entirely orthodox poem devoted to the Virgin Mary. The text was inserted into blank pages in the manuscript by a second scribe, filling in space that the first scribe had left empty, perhaps because he was hoping that the rest of the 'Squire's Tale' would turn up. Whoever made the decision to give the decent, impoverished Plowman a voice, and a strikingly orthodox voice, was making a particular decision about how to position virtuous pilgrims in the atmosphere of the early or middle fifteenth century, when Lollard heretics were a particular target of suspicion and persecution. (Lollardy developed from the writings of John Wycliffe in Chaucer's lifetime and advocated for a reformed church, focused on the Bible rather than sacraments. In the fifteenth century some Lollards were persecuted and

1.4
The end of the unfinished 'The Cook's Tale', from the early Hengwrt Chaucer. The scribe – who may have known Chaucer personally – has written on the left 'Of this Cokes tale maked Chaucer na moore', making it clear that there is no more to come. Aberystwyth, National Library of Wales, Peniarth MS. 392D, fol. 57v.

His maister shal it in his shoppe abye
Al haue he no part of the mynstralcye
ffor thefte and riot they been conuertible
Al konne he pleye on Giterne or Rubible
Reuel and trouthe as in a lowe degree
They been ful wrothe al day as men may see
This ioly prentys with his maister bood
Til he were neigh out of his prentishood
Al were he snybbed bothe erly and late
And somtyme lad with reuel to Newegate
But atte laste his maister hym bithoghte
Vp on a day whan he his papir soghte
Of a prouerbe that seith this same word
Wel bet is roten appul out of hoord
Than þt it rotte al the remenaunt
So fareth it by a riotous seruaunt
It is ful lasse harm to lete hym pace
Than he shende alle the seruantz in the place
Ther fore his maister gaf hym acquitaunce
And bad hym go with sorwe and with meschaunce
And thus this ioly prentys hadde his leue
Now lat hym riote al the nyght or leue
And for ther nys no theef with oute a lowke
That helpeth hym to wasten and to sowke
Of that he brybe kan or borwe may
Anon he sente his bed and his array
Vn to a compeer of his owene sort
That loued dees and reuel and disport
And hadde a wyf that heeld for contenaunce
A shoppe and swyued for hir sustenaunce

Of this Cokes tale
maked Chaucer na
moore

Wele bette is roten appul out of horde
Than that he rote all the remenaunt
So fareth it by a ryotous servaunt
It is full lesse harme to lete hym pace
Than he shende all the servauntes in the place
Therfore his maister yaf hym acquitaunce
And badde hym goo with sorwe and myschaunce
And thus this joly prentise hadde his leve
Now lete hym ryote all the nyght or leve
And for ther is no theef with oute a lowke
That helpeth hym to waste and to souke
Of that he brybe kan or borowe may
Anone he sente his bedde and his array
Un to a compere of his owne sorte
That loved dyse ryot and disporte
And hadde a wife that helde for contenaunce
A shoppe and swyved for sustenaunce

Here begynnyth the Cokes tale &c

Lithen & lystonyth & herkenyth a right
And ye shul heren of a doughty knyght
Syr John of Boundis was his name
he coude of norture and mochell of game
Thre sones the knyght had & with his body he hem wan
The eldest was a moche shrewe & sone he began
his brethren loved wele her ffader & of hym were agast
The eldest deserved his ffaders curs & had it at last
The good knyght his ffader loved so yore
That deth was comen hym & handled hym full sore
The good knyght cared sore sike there he lay
how his children shuld lyven after his day
he hadde ben wyde where but non husbond he was
Alle the londe that he had it was verrey purchas
ffayn he wolde it were dressed amonge hem alle

Better ys betyme to voyde suche a clerke
The lenger he abydeth ye wors is his werke
He yat his Maister no profite wolle wynne
I holde hym better out of ye hous yan with ynne
And thus ye Joly Prentys had leve
Now let hym ryott alle ye nyght or leve
Ther ys no thiffe with out alowke
That helpeth hym to waste & to sowke
Or that he bryle can or oght borowe may
Anon he sent his bedde and alle his aray
Unto a compere of his owne sorte
That loved welle ye Dyse Ryot & disporte
A wife he hadde that helde her contenaunce
A shoppe and ever she pleyed for his sustenaunce
What thorowe hym selfe and his felawe yat sought
Unto a myschefe bothe yey were broght
The tone y dampned to preson perpetually
The tother to deth for he couthe not of clergye
And therfore yonge men lerne while ye may
That with mony dyvers thoghtes beth prycked al ye day
Remembre you what myschefe cometh of mysgovernaunce
Thus mowe ye lerne worshep & come to substaunce
Thenke how grace and governaunce hath broght he a boune
Many pore mannys son chefe state of ye towne
Ever rewle the after ye beste man of name
And god may grace ye to come to ye same

Here endeth the Cokes tale

Oure hoste

p.30 **1.5**
The end of Chaucer's 'The Cook's Tale' in a fifteenth-century manuscript, Christ Church 152. After Chaucer's unfinished tale, the scribe has written 'Here begynneth the Cokes Tale' and has added a second (non-Chaucerian) tale – the story of the Tale of Gamelyn. Oxford, Christ Church MS. 152, fol. 58v.

p.31 **1.6**
The end of Chaucer's 'The Cook's Tale' in a fifteenth-century manuscript, Bodley 686. The scribe has replaced 'swyved' (had sex) with the more neutral 'pleyed'. He interpolated various extra lines earlier in the tale and has also added another twelve lines at the end to 'finish off' Chaucer's incomplete tale, concluding with 'Here endeth the Cokes tale'. Oxford, Bodleian Library, MS. Bodl. 686, fol. 55v.

right **1.7**
After 'The Squire's Tale' breaks off, a different scribe has added a Prologue and Tale for the Plowman, a pilgrim who appears in the 'General Prologue', but for whom Chaucer did not write a tale. 'The Plowman's Tale' that appears in this manuscript is a poem by Thomas Hoccleve, an early-fifteenth-century writer and admirer of Chaucer. Oxford, Christ Church, MS. 152, fol. 228v.

even burnt at the stake.) The Parson (the Plowman's brother) is jokingly accused of Lollardy in the endlink to 'The Man of Law's Tale' that exists in some manuscripts, and the second scribe of Christ Church 152 is keen (in contrast) to align the *Tales* and its 'good' pilgrims with orthodox Catholicism. In sixteenth-century Protestant England, the opposite happened, and a Lollard (anti-Catholic) text was repackaged as a tale for the Plowman, and inserted into early print editions of *The Canterbury Tales*. This was part of an attempt to present Chaucer as a proto-Protestant himself, an acceptable antecedent for sixteenth-century writers.[5]

This insertion of Hoccleve's poem into Christ Church 152 illustrates two very common trends in the way that Chaucer's texts were treated in diverse manuscripts. First, poems by his successors such as Hoccleve and John Lydgate (another important fifteenth-century poet) were often jumbled up with Chaucer's own texts. Often, either no attempt was made to point out different authorship or the texts by other authors were in fact marked as being by Chaucer. Second, collections of Chaucer's poems were often driven by a specific agenda, a desire to present Chaucer within a particular context or for a particular audience.

Scottish Chaucer

MS. Arch. Selden. B. 24 reveals both of these tendencies. Poems by Chaucer copied in this manuscript include *Troilus and Criseyde, The Parliament of Fowls, The Legend of Good Women, The Complaint of Mars* and *The Complaint of Venus*. The manuscript also contains many texts by other authors, some of which are spuriously associated with Chaucer. John Lydgate's *Complaint of the Black Knight*, for example, is termed at the end 'The maying and disport of Chaucere' (The May-time

And after wole I speke of Algarsyf
how that he wan Theodora to his wyf
ffor whom ful ofte in grete peril he was
Ne hadde he ben holpen by the stede of bras
And after wole I speke of Camballo
That faught in lystes with the brethern two
ffor Canace er that he myght hir wynne
And ther I lefte I wole ayayn begynne

Explicit secunda pars. Incipit tercia pars

Apollo whyrleth up his chaar so hye
Til that the god Mercurius hous the slye

The prologe of the Ploughman

As the pylgrymys fforth dede ryde
Oure host gan to loke abowte
And seyd ffelawys we most prvyde
Who that best of alle this route
Kan telle hys tale as lot comyth abowte
Ploughman tylyer drawe the nere
And telle thy tale and we wyl here
Syr he seyde y shalle telle as y can
A tale of Crystys modyr dere
Mary that bere bothe god and man
How to a monk she dod a prayere
That ony day seyde here sautere
And hevenis blysse had to hys mede
Who servyth oure lady the bet shalle spede

Here he gynnyth the tale

playing and entertainment of Chaucer) (FIGURE 1.8). Similarly, at the end of Hoccleve's 'Mother of God' the text is attributed to Chaucer with the words 'Oracio Galfridi Chaucere' (the prayer of Geoffrey Chaucer) (FIGURE 1.9). Sometimes the agenda of the scribe is obvious. An anonymous, antifeminist lyric, 'Deuise proues and eke humylitee' (Consider nobility and also humility) is assigned to Chaucer's authorship with the words 'Quod Chaucere quhen he was rycht auisit' (This is what Chaucer said when he was thinking correctly). Chaucer is being shaped into the authority that the scribe – and/or an overseer or patron – wants to see.

MS. Arch. Selden. B. 24 (*c.* 1490) also sets out to construct a Chaucer for Scotland. The manuscript contains the only copy of the Scottish King James I's poem *The Kingis Quair*. This poem is heavily influenced by a number of Chaucer's poems, is written in a rhyme scheme (rhyme royal) invented by Chaucer, and is dedicated to Chaucer, along with Gower, as poets laureate. In one way, then, we could see this particular manuscript collection as implying that Scottish poetry can be Chaucerian, rather than the other way round. Other aspects of the manuscript, however, construct a Scottish version of Chaucer himself, a Chaucer more varied and complex than the 'Father of *English* Literature'. Chaucer's poems are transposed into a Scottish context by the scribe's replacing of English spellings with Scottish conventions: 'what' becomes 'quhat'; 'whiche' becomes 'quhiche'; 'hem'/'hym'/'them' become 'thame'; 'erly' becomes 'airly'; 'noght' becomes 'nocht', and so on. For a Scottish reader, Chaucer's poems are made more familiar, more local in their tone, and he might seem to be 'their' poet, rather than the poet of the English – especially as he is associated with a Scottish king in this manuscript.[6]

1.8
In the 'Scottish Chaucer', a poem by a fifteenth-century poet, John Lydgate's *Complaint of the Black Knight* is attributed to Chaucer. At the end of the poem, the scribe has written 'Here endeth the maying and disport of Chaucere' (Here ends the May-time playing and entertainment of Chaucer). Oxford, Bodleian Library, MS. Arch. Selden. B. 24, 129v.

And quhen þt sche was gane unto hir rest
I roos anan and hame to bed I went
For werely me thoᵗ it for the best
Prayand thus in all my best entent
That all trewe that bene wt dangere schent
With mercy may in relesche of thair payne
Recouerit be or May cum eft agayne

And for þt I may now no langer wake
Farewele ze lovers all þt bene trewe
Prayand to god and thus my leve I take
That or the sonne tomorowe be rysen newe
And or he haue agayne rose hewe
That eche of zow may have such a grace
His awne lady in armes to enbrace

I mene thus þt in all honeste
Withouten more ze may with other speke
Quhare so zow list at good liberte
That eche may to other thair hert breke
On jelousie only for to wreke
That hath so long of his malice and envye
Werreyed treuth with his tyrannye

Princes plesith to zour benignite
This litill dyte for to have in mynd
Off womanhede also for to se
That zour trewe man may sum mercy fynd
And pitee eke þt hath long ben behind
Lett thame agayne be prouoked to grace
For treuly it is agayne is kynd
Fals dangere for to occupy his place

Go lytill quare/ go to my lyvis quene
And to my verray hertis soverayne
And be rycht glad for sche sall the sene
Such is thy grace bot I alace in payne
Am left behynd and not to quham to playne
For mercy treuth grace and eke pitee
Exiled ben þt I may nocht attayne
Recure to fynd of my adversitee

here endith the maying and disport
of Chaucere

The treatment of Chaucer's dream vision poem *The Parliament of Fowls* is particularly important in MS. Arch. Selden. B. 24. It omits the last hundred lines of the poem, instead substituting a completely new ending, which both turns the poem into something different and emphasizes its Scottish credentials. While Chaucer's version ends in stasis and deferral for the female bird, who is able to put off choosing a suitor, the Selden version pairs her off with her most socially important suitor. This version may be linked to James IV of Scotland's marriage to Margaret Tudor, sister of Henry VIII of England, and it also seems to be influenced by a Scottish poem, *The Buke of the Howlat* (The Book of the Young Owl). Both the vocabulary and the spelling of this added section are decidedly Scottish too, further bringing Chaucer and his poem into a Scottish cultural world.

Courtly Chaucer

Other manuscripts construct Chaucer as a poet of the English court. Evidence from Chaucer's lifetime suggests a city rather than a courtly environment for his great poem *Troilus and Criseyde*. Chaucer himself dedicated the poem to London lawyers and city officials – John Gower and Ralph Strode – and early readers and manuscript owners that we know of include the minor political player and scribe Thomas Usk and the scribe and brothel-keeper Thomas Spencer, both figures associated with London and its suburbs. *Troilus and Criseyde* may well have been read by more important figures too, but the evidence is sketchy. However, the posthumous 'Troilus frontispiece', in Cambridge, Corpus Christi College, MS. 61, depicts Chaucer in a far more elevated environment, reading to the royal court (FIGURE 1.10). This lavish illumination was instrumental in creating the image

1.9
The 'Scottish Chaucer' attributes many poems not by Chaucer to the poet. Here, at the end of the fifteenth-century poet Thomas Hoccleve's poem 'Mother of God', the scribe has noted 'Explicit oracio Galfridi Chaucere', (Here ends the prayer of Geoffrey Chaucer). Oxford, Bodleian Library, MS. Arch. Selden. B. 24, 131v.

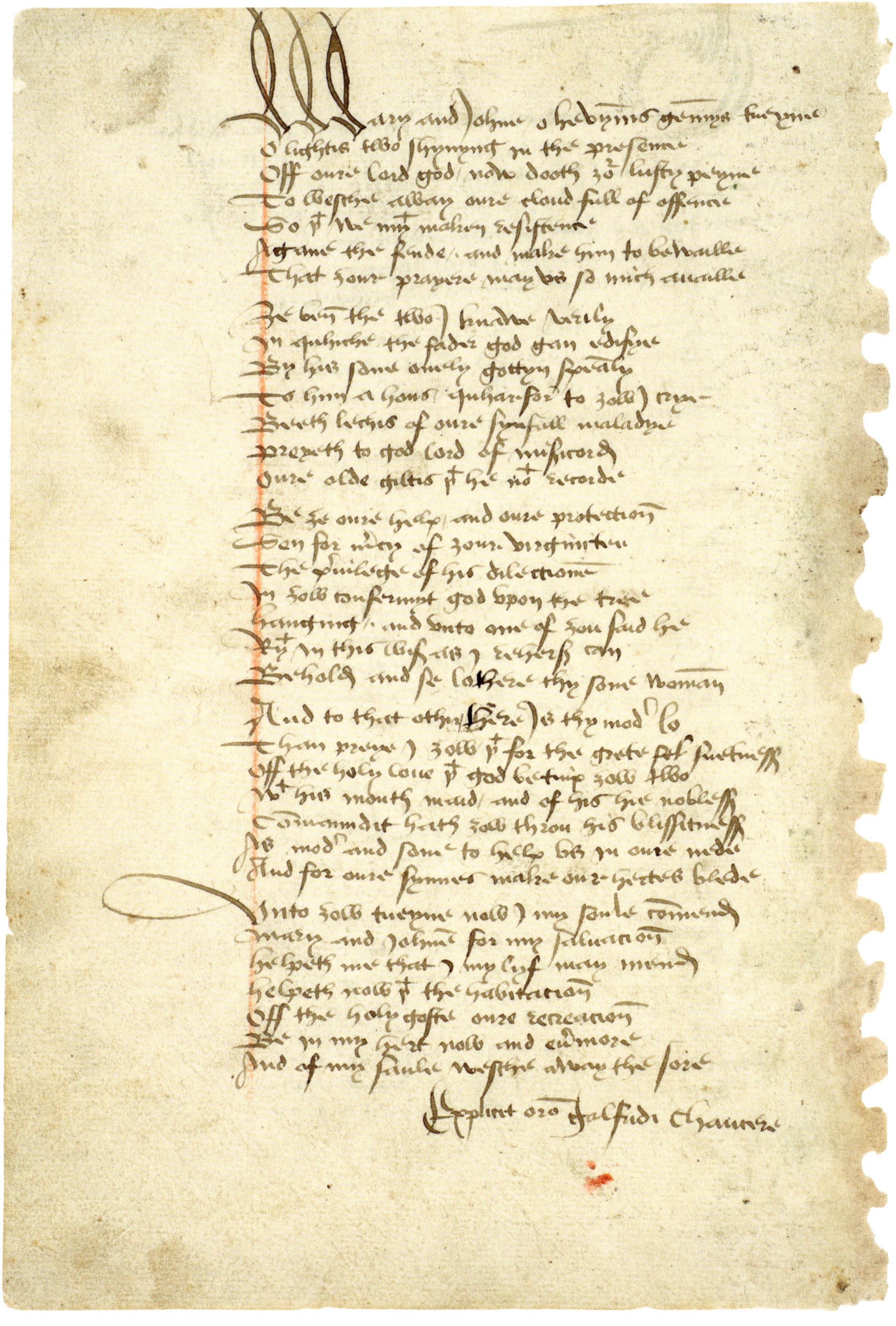

Mary and Johne o hevynly gemmys tweyne
O lightis two shynyng in the presence
Off oure lord god now dooth youre besy peyne
To weshe away oure cloud full of offence
So that we mowe maken resistence
Agayne the fende and make him to bewaille
That youre prayere may so moch availle

Ye ben the two I knawe verily
In whiche the fader god gan edifye
By his sone only gotyn specialy
To him a hous ewharsor to yow I cry-
Beseth lechis of oure synfull maladye
Preyeth to god lord of misericorde
Oure olde giltis that he not recorde

Be ye oure help and oure protection
Sen for meryt of youre virginite
The privilege of his dilectione
In yow conferrmyt god upon the tree
Hangynge and unto one of yow said he
Right in this wise as I reherse can
Behold and se lo here thy sone woman

And to that other here is thy moder lo
Than praye I yow that for the grete swetnesse
Off the holy love that god betwix yow two
With his mouth maad and of his hie noblesse
Commendit hath yow throu his blissidnesse
His moder and sone to help us in oure nede
And for oure synnes make oure hertis blede

Unto yow tweyne now I my saule commend
Mary and Johne for my salvacion
Helpeth me that I my lyf may mend
Helpeth now that the habitacion
Off the holy goste oure recreacion
Be in my hert now and evermore
And of my saule weshe away the sore

Explicit oracio Galfridi Chaucer

of Chaucer as a court poet, perhaps even a poet patronized by the king, although there is no evidence from his lifetime to suggest that he occupied this kind of position. We might see this image as part of the fifteenth-century promotion of Chaucer as a patriarch, an Author with a capital A, associated with didactic authority, the poet of kings.[7]

Other manuscripts suggest that we could instead view him as the poet of queens, or more generally of wealthy, adventurous, confident women. Both MS. Bodl. 638 and MS. Fairfax 16 package Chaucer's texts, specifically *The Legend of Good Women*, with texts that encouraged privileged women to play erotic games. MS. Bodl. 638 includes *Ragman Roll*, a text voiced by a phallic figure, King Ragman Holly, associated with medieval gender debates between the holly and the ivy. The text involves women receiving a 'character', some of which are explicitly sexually suggestive. Both manuscripts also include the *Chaunce of Dice*, a text addressed to a mixed-sex audience in which each person receives a 'fortune', some of which are obscene. The *Chaunce of Dice* also refers to Chaucerian texts such as the *Legend* and to Chaucerian characters including the Wife of Bath and Griselda (the heroine of 'The Clerk's Tale').[8] These manuscripts reveal that one context in which Chaucer's poems were read in the fifteenth century was sophisticated, sexually adventurous, mixed-sex groups – the kind of group that might anticipate the atmosphere of the Tudor court in which poets such as Wyatt were to write their sonnets.

1.10
This gorgeous illumination, from the Corpus *Troilus*, is generally known as the Troilus frontispiece. It seems to depict Chaucer reading to, or addressing, a beautifully dressed courtly circle, with a castle in the background. This is a posthumous depiction of Chaucer – there is no evidence that he actually held this kind of 'court poet' role. Cambridge, Corpus Christi College, MS. 61, fol. 1v.

The Wife of Bath

Some scribes, however, emphatically did not want Chaucer's texts to be read by adventurous women, and even worried that his texts might encourage women in rebellious behaviour.

This can be seen particularly clearly in scribes' treatment of 'The Wife of Bath's Prologue'.

One of the ways in which scribes most obviously collaborate with authors in a manuscript context is through glossing, or adding explanations and commentary alongside the texts. Of the eighty-three manuscripts of *The Canterbury Tales* dating from before 1500, only twelve have no glosses.[9] Looking across the manuscripts, it is evident not only that 'The Wife of Bath's Prologue' is particularly heavily glossed, but also that the kind of commentary that she attracted was often noticeably intense and passionate. Even when the glossing is neutral or supportive – as in the case of Ellesmere, for instance, where the glossator tends to add partial quotations that support Alison's case – the fact that the gloss is so extensive, is written in a script as large as the text itself, and is penned in the more authoritative Latin language, gives the impression that this female teller stands in more need than male tellers do of the validation of male, Latinate, textual authority.[10]

In some other manuscripts, the scribe's attitude to the Wife of Bath is aggressive and outraged, verging on the hysterical. London, British Library, Add. MS. 5140 and London, British Library, Egerton MS. 2864 share an extensive set of glosses to 'The Wife of Bath's Prologue', glosses that clearly demonstrate that the scribe (unlike most of his fellows) was not simply trying to give relevant sources, explain difficulties or highlight key parts of the text.[11] Rather, he saw himself as an interpreter of the text and tried to direct the reader's understanding of the Wife of Bath. Specifically, he seems to be angry with the Wife, and wants readers too to dislike her, and to see how wrong she is (FIGURE 1.11).

1.11
Scribes often wrote comments – glosses – next to Chaucer's text. 'The Wife of Bath's Prologue' was particularly heavily glossed, with some scribes going to great lengths to argue with her, prove her wrong and counter her voice with their own, as we see here in this fifteenth-century manuscript. London, British Library, Egerton MS. 2864, fol. 82v.

For instance, the Wife of Bath describes how her husband lectured her with misogynistic proverbs, commenting that 'Ne I

Cach who so may / who renneth best lat see
But this word / is nat take of every wiht
But ther as god / wol yeve it of his myght
I wot wel that / thapostle was a mayde
But natheles / thouh that he wroot & sayde
He wolde that every / wiht / were such as he
Al nys but consayl / to virgynyte
And for to been a wyf / he yaf me leve
Of indulgence / so it is no repreve
To wedde me / yif that my make dye
Withouten / any excepcioun of bigamye
Al were it good no woman / for to touche
He mente as in his bed / or in his touche
ffor peryl is bothe / fyr and touh tassemble
Ye knowe wel / what this ensample may ressemble
This al and som / he heeld virgynyte
More pfit / than weddyng in frelte
ffrelte clepe I / but that he & she
Wolde leede al hir lyf in chastite
I graunte it wel / I have noon envye
Thouh maydenheed / preferre bygamye
It liketh hem be clene / in body & goost
Of myn estaat / ne wol I make no boost
ffor wel ye knowe / a lord in his houshoolde
Ne hath nat every vessel al of golde
Som been of tree / and doon her lord servise
God clepith folk / to hym in sondry wyse
And everich hath / of god a propir yift
Som this som that / as that hym lyketh shift
Virgynyte is greet perfeccion
And contynence eek / with devocion
But cryst / that of perfeccion is welle
Bad nat every whiht / he sholde go selle
Al that he hadde / and yeve it to the pore
And in such wise / folwe hym and his lore
He spak to hem / that wol lyven pfytly
And lordynges / by your leve that am nat I
I wil bestowe / the flour of myn age
In thactes / and the frut of mariage

Volo autem omnes homines esse sicut me ipm / Aplus ad corinthios / Hoc autem dico secundum indulgenciam non secundum imperium / Aplus ad corinthios /

Bonum est mulierem non tangere /

Nunquid potest homo abscondere ignem in sinu suo vt vestimenta illius non ardeant / aut ambulare super prunas & non comburentur plante eius / Sic qui ingreditur ad mulierem proximi sui non erit mundus cum tetigerit eam & c / parabole salamonis / & alibi / bonum est homini mulierem non tangere / Aplus ad corinthios /

In magna autem domo non solum sunt vasa aurea & argentea sed & lignea et fictilia & c / aplus ad titum

Divisiones graciarum sunt / aplus ad corinthios / Et vnusquisque proprium donum habet ex deo alius quidem sic alius vero sic / Aplus ad corinthios

Si vis perfectus esse vade & vende omnia que habes & da pauperibus / Mathei & alibi / vade quecunque habes vende & da pauperibus & c / Marci evangeliste & alibi / omnia quecunque habes vende & da pauperibus / Luce evangeliste /

wolde nat of hym corrected be. / I hate hym that my vices telleth me, / And so doo mo, God woot, of us than I' (661–663). In other words, she could not stand her husband's criticisms, and she, like many people, does not like to be told of her faults. The scribe responds to this with outrage, penning a long note alongside. The note includes nine separate biblical quotations, all from Proverbs, as he piles up examples of why Alison is wrong to reject reproof and correction. He sees his role not as literary but as *moral* – he himself is taking on the role of correcting Alison, and of making sure that readers see that they should not be admiring of her, or on her side. And he is so anxious about this that he feels he needs an extraordinary number of examples to shore up his own position and present a decisive counter-argument. Furthermore, his examples are telling. The first one reads: 'Disciplinam autem domini fili mi ne abicias', which comes directly from Proverbs 3:11 (with the addition of the 'autem', 'but'). The verse means 'My son, reject not the correction of the Lord.' It is clearly inappropriate to what Alison is saying: she is explicitly talking about her husband's criticisms of her, while this verse is about God correcting humans. The glossator is comparing Jankyn – by any standards a paranoid, aggressive domestic abuser – with God, suggesting that a husband automatically has a divine status. And the fact that the scribe is himself trying to correct Alison aligns him with Jankyn and, by his own logic, God. He has set up an asymmetrical power dynamic, in which he, Alison's husband and God are on one side, and her unruly, sinful voice is isolated on the other. His desire to correct her, indeed, seems to be a driving force of his programme of glossing. Reading this manuscript involves not only reading 'The Wife of Bath's Prologue', but reading a dialogue between the Wife of Bath and a hostile reader.[12]

A Changing Text

The text that a medieval reader experienced, then, was quite different in different manuscript contexts. If we take the example of the end of 'The Man of Law's Tale', we can see how varied the text could be. A reader of Hengwrt would have seen a blank page (now mainly covered in records of seventeenth-century births), followed by 'The Squire's Tale'. It is likely that the scribe expected to receive a link to insert here and left space for it, but either never received it or decided that it was not appropriate. A reader of MS. Arch. Selden. 14 would come to the end of the tale and read an Epilogue, in which the Shipman jokingly berates the Parson and then tells a tale. However, if one were reading Oxford, Bodleian Library, MS. Hatton donat. 1, or many other manuscripts, this link would feature the Squire, not the Shipman, teasing the Parson and then telling his tale. Oxford, Bodleian Library, MS. Rawl. poet. 223 has the Summoner as the Parson's interlocutor. In the Ellesmere, there is no link, and the 'The Wife of Bath's Prologue and Tale' follows on from the Man of Law.[13]

While we can't be certain about Chaucer's writing and revision processes, it is clear that he changed his mind about many aspects of his texts, as most authors do. 'The Shipman's Tale', indeed, is initially spoken by a female voice, and seems to have been originally intended for the Wife of Bath. The authoritative modern edition of Chaucer's complete works, *The Riverside Chaucer*, prints 'The Man of Law's Tale', followed by the endlink (with the Shipman speaking to the Parson), followed by 'The Wife of Bath's Prologue and Tale'. This doesn't make sense as a coherent text, but none of the manuscripts do quite make sense. Chaucer probably at one point planned to follow 'The Man of Law's Tale' with an endlink featuring the Wife of

Bath and the Parson. The speaker in this link refers to their 'joly body', and to having 'litel Latyn' (1185, 1190) – which sounds like the Wife of Bath's voice. The first version of a 'Wife of Bath's Tale' – in other words, the tale that became 'The Shipman's Tale' – then followed. Later in his compositional process, Chaucer changed his mind, giving the Wife of Bath a different Prologue and Tale. Perhaps he decided to keep the *tale* order the same and to change the speaker in the endlink to the Shipman. Or perhaps he wanted to keep the *speaker* order the same, but scribes confused the issue. Maybe he experimented with placing 'The Squire's Tale' here, but did not get around to adding a new endlink, and a scribe changed the speaker to the Squire, even though the voice really does not sound like the Squire. Although thirty-one manuscripts place 'The Squire's Tale' after the Man of Law's, the earliest, most authoritative manuscripts do not, so it is probable that this was not an authorial plan, but developed later in the fifteenth century. The key point is that readers did not get the same experience from reading different manuscripts – they were not reading 'The Canterbury Tales', but a particular material text.

This variation can also, at times, be seen at a more micro-level, in the very words of the poems. For instance, at lines 93–94 of 'The Merchant's Tale', the Ellesmere manuscript reads:

> *And if thou take a wyf unto thyn hoold,*
> *Ful lightly maystow been a cokewold.*
> (And if you take a wife into your possession / You may easily be a cuckold)

Other versions include:

And if thow take a wife of highe lynage
She shall be hauten and of grete costage
(And if you take a wife of high class
She shall be pretentious and expensive)
(Oxford, Christ Church, MS. 152; London, British Library, Egerton MS. 2726)

And if þat þou take a wif be war
Of oon peril which declare I ne dar
(And if you take a wife, beware
Of a danger which I do not dare to declare)
(London, British Library, Harley MS. 7334)

And if þou take a wif þat to þe is vntrewe
Ful ofte tyme it shal þe rwe
(And if you take a wife who betrays you
Very often you will regret it)
(Petworth House, MS. 7)

In Hengwrt, the main scribe wrote 'And if thow take a wyf', but then left the remainder of the line, and the next line, blank. Another scribe filled in the gaps with 'she wole destroye / Thy good substance and thy body annoye'. The range of different readings suggest there was a problem with these lines. Either Chaucer changed his mind or early exemplars were damaged or unclear.[14]

When we read a modern edition we are reading a cleaned-up text, and a text that is partly the invention of editors. The chaos of manuscript culture, and the collaborative role of multiple scribes and overseers, can become almost invisible to modern readers. In contrast, in the fifteenth century the Chaucer that you experienced would be very different depending on the manuscript that you happened to access. And, while some versions might not represent Chaucer's views at all, others might represent different stages in his thought. It is also likely that he never got to the point where he decided on a fixed or final order for the *Tales*, for instance, and perhaps he never would have – but a modern editor needs to make decisions about this.

Go Little Book

Chaucer himself was worried about scribal incompetence and intervention. In his short poem to Adam his scribe, 'Chaucers Wordes Unto Adam, His Owne Scriveyn' – perhaps addressed to Adam Pynkhurst – he jokingly criticizes and curses Adam for his negligence. Chaucer also expresses concerns in *Troilus and Criseyde* that scribes might corrupt the metre of his poems, praying to God that no one will 'myswrite' or 'mysmetre' his poem (Book V, 1795–1796). On the other hand, Chaucer also knew that it was inevitable that texts would change once they left their author's hands. In 'The Manciple's Tale', the line 'Thyng that is seyd is seyd and forth it goth' (355) encapsulates the fact that texts are released into the world and cannot be recalled. The context is a tale in which someone's words are appallingly misinterpreted, and the truth is seen as a lie. Even more dramatically, the end of the *House of Fame* features texts – a lie and a truth – actually coming to life and taking on their own autonomy away from the control of their speakers/authors. The lie and truth speak to each other, and ultimately resolve to join together, perhaps rather like Chaucer's *Parliament of Fowls* was to join with the Scottish ending in Selden, or his *Canterbury Tales* accepted the 'Tale of Gamelyn' in Christ Church 152.

Medieval scribes and readers respected authors. But they also saw texts as dynamic. It was normal to read texts with glosses and explanations, common for unfinished texts to be added to by someone else, usual to rewrite other people's texts or add sequels. (Robert Henryson, a fifteenth-century Scottish poet, wrote a sequel to *Troilus*, for instance.) We might see this literary culture as chaotic, but in many ways it was a glorious chaos that allowed diverse interpretations, and that valued readers as active and creative collaborators. In this way, the fifteenth century set the scene for more than six hundred years (so far) of readers making Chaucer's texts their own.

Whan that Apprill with his shouris sote
And the droughte of marche hath pc'd yͤ rote
And badid every veyne in suche licour
Of whiche vertu engendrid is the flour
Whanne zepherus eke with his sote breth
Enspirid hath in every holte and heth
The tendir croppis, and the yong sonne
Hath in the ram half his cours y ronne
And smale foulis make melodie
That slepyn al nyght with opyn ye
So prikith hem nature in her corage
Than longyng folk to gon on pilgremage
And palmers to seche straunge londis
To serue halowis couthe in sondry londis
And specially fro every shiris ende
Of yngelond to Cauntirbury thy wende
The holy blissful martir forto seke
That them hath holpyn when they were seke
And fil in that seson on a day
In Suthwerk atte tabard as I lay
Redy to wende on my pilgremage
To Cauntirbury with devout corage
That nyght was come in to that hosterye
Wel nyne & twenty in a companye
Of sondry folk be aventure y falle
In feleship as pilgrymys were they alle
That toward Cauntirbury wolden ryde
The chambris and the stablis were wyde
And wel were they esid atte beste

2

AUTHORIZING THE CANON: CHAUCER IN THE WORLD OF PRINT

Jeff Espie and Alexandra Gillespie

In 1476 William Caxton set to work in Westminster on the first printed edition of Chaucer's *The Canterbury Tales* (FIGURE 2.1). The books from his 1476/7 edition hold major significance in literary and cultural history – and an outsize value in the modern market, as the description from a late-twentieth-century auction at Christie's suggests. A copy of Caxton's 1476/7 *Tales*, the auction catalogue explains, represents 'the greatest work of Middle English literature, one of the earliest books printed in England, and the first substantial book of poetry [printed] in English'.[1]

The edition does not declare itself with such fanfare. Like the small editions of Lydgate's minor poems that he printed earlier the same year – and unlike the edition of the *Collection of the Histories of Troy* he printed previously in Bruges – Caxton's edition of the *Tales* has no title page or extravagant decoration; no dedication to a noble patron or celebratory preface; no explanatory notes or scholarly apparatus; no illustrations. The start and end of each tale come marked with inconspicuous titles; the author's name appears only sporadically, mentioned without comment in headers for 'The Tale of Melibee' and for 'The Parson's Tale' on penitence. The most extended discussions of Chaucer's reputation appear internally in the *Tales*' fiction, in 'The Man of Law's Prologue' and the *Retraction*. In the

2.1
The opening of the 'General Prologue' to *The Canterbury Tales*, from Caxton's iconic first edition (1476), one of the most famous early printed books. Interestingly, the page looks very like a manuscript page with its beautiful initial 'W' and decorated borders, added by hand by a later reader or owner. Oxford, Merton College, 111.C.9, 2r.

former, Chaucer's Man of Law names Chaucer himself as the unassuming poet of unrefined metres and love complaints, who does the best he can in English rhyme. In the latter, Chaucer catalogues his verse and prose and entreats heavenly forgiveness for its worldly vanities, including for his love poetry and those *Tales* that encourage sin. Caxton prints these self-reflective passages – and the entire self-conscious text – without editorial comment or celebration. The book that starts Chaucer's momentous tradition in print, and that sold for over £4.6 million at auction in 1998, doesn't make a show.

Skip forward 130 years or so, to London, 1602, when Thomas Speght published his second edition of Chaucer's complete works, printed by Adam Islip.[2] Framed by a grand title page, which praises our 'ancient and learned English poet', the edition surrounds Chaucer's *œuvre* with an apparatus that proclaims its author's importance. It spans a dedication to Sir Robert Cecil, Chancellor of Cambridge and Secretary to Queen Elizabeth I, which aligns Chaucer's poetry with English sources of learning and power; a genealogy of Chaucer's family, which implies the poet's connection to the Tudor dynasty; a glowing letter from Cambridge scholar Francis Beaumont, which champions Chaucer's eloquence alongside classical models; a hefty glossary, which restores Chaucer's linguistic vitality for Elizabethan readers; and a biography, which spans the erudition of Chaucer's education, the scope of his public service and the influence of his precedent on later poets.

Chaucer's reflections on the business of authorship now share space with the editor's. Every Canterbury tale, and almost all his other works, come framed with an editorial argument, which identifies Chaucer's sources, summarizes his content and vaunts his talent – as in the argument to the 'General Prologue', which

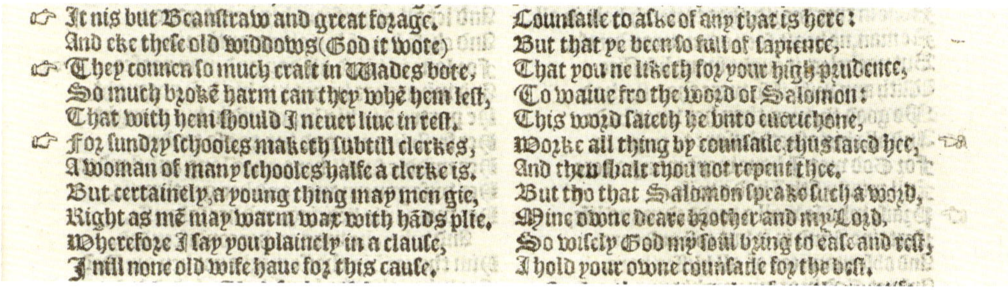
It nis but Beanstraw and great forage.
And eke these old widdows (God it wote)
They connen so much craft in Wades bote,
So much broke harm can they whē hem lest,
That with hem should I neuer liue in rest.
For sundry schooles maketh subtill clerkes,
A woman of many schooles halfe a clerke is.
But certainely, a young thing may men gie,
Right as mē may warm wax with hāds plie.
Wherefore I say you plainely in a clause,
I nill none old wife haue for this cause.
Counsaile to aske of any that is here:
But that ye been so full of sapience,
That you ne liketh for your high prudence,
To waiue fro the word of Salomon:
This word saieth he vnto euerichone,
Worke all thing by counsaile, thus said hee,
And then shalt thou not repent thee.
But tho that Salomon speake such a word,
Mine owne deare brother and my Lord,
So wisely God my soul bring to ease and rest,
I hold your owne counsaile for the best.

celebrates his classical decorum. Most pages contain manicules in the margins (FIGURE 2.2): illustrated hands that point out Chaucerian verses of special wisdom. Some imprints contain illustrations of Chaucer's pilgrims, which realize literally his unique ability to, as Beaumont says, write characters that appear as if before your eyes. Speght's expansiveness even encompasses material reproduced from prior editions. It includes the dedication from William Thynne's 1532 *Workes*, which addresses King Henry VIII as defender and protector of Chaucer's brilliance and aligns Chaucer's English with past linguistic triumphs of the Latins and Greeks (FIGURE 2.3). Here and elsewhere, Speght's book insists on Chaucer as England's answer to the classics as an authority at once poetic and political – an author as fit for the English canon as for an English monarch.

Caxton's *Tales* and Speght's *Workes* represent two poles in Chaucer's history in print, conceptually and temporally. The former, Chaucer's first printed edition, precipitates an outpouring of others in the decades and century to come. The latter is the last major printed edition of Chaucer's works for more than one hundred years, which shapes how a century of readers – including Shakespeare, Milton and Dryden – encountered Chaucer's poetry and prose. This chapter connects these poles as complementary parts of Chaucer's legacy, which

2.2

A page from Speght's 1602 edition of Chaucer. 'The Merchant's Tale' is framed by several manicules – pointing fingers at the side of the text that direct the reader's attention to particular lines that are deemed to be of especial moral or proverbial importance, for example 'Worke all thing by connsaile [advice], thus said hee'. *The Workes of our ancient and learned English poet, Geffrey Chaucer*, 1602. Oxford, Bodleian Library, A 2.5 Art.Seld., fol. 27.

come into focus to differing degrees in printed editions across the fifteenth and sixteenth centuries. Caxton has a prominent place in this story, not only because he comes first but because he anticipates what comes next. The difference between Caxton's first edition and Speght's second – and between other early editions – realizes a possibility that Caxton himself opened up, in his own bifurcated response to ideas about authorship he found in Chaucer's works.

Caxton projects two potential futures for Chaucer in print: miscellaneous and monumental. The first extends the heterogeneity of fifteenth-century vernacular manuscript culture, where books routinely combined multiple texts from various (frequently unnamed) sources, arranged in idiosyncratic and disaggregated form. The second gives this miscellaneousness a unifying order, anchored in the coherence of a standard design and the power of a recognized authority. Both futures have precedents in *The Canterbury Tales*, which Chaucer puts in play through the planned planlessness of the pilgrims' tale-telling contest. The monumental Chaucer dominates his sixteenth-century afterlife in print, symbolized by the six big folio editions of his works published between Thynne's in 1532 and Speght's in 1602. Organized around the poet's authority, these editions represent Chaucer as the origin of an English canon and tie his works to narratives of English cultural vitality and royal power. But the miscellaneous Chaucer persists in print, too: in early-sixteenth-century editions of his poems, in the accretive development of his folio's contents and in the substance of his poetry itself. These traces of miscellaneousness qualify a familiar story about the inevitable impact of print technology and suggest alternative trajectories that Chaucer's poetry took – and might still take.

2.3
The dedication to Henry VIII from William Thynne's 1532 edition of Chaucer's *Workes* was reprinted in many later editions. In it, Chaucer's triumphs in English are associated with classical linguistic triumphs in Latin and Greek. The association with the monarch further emphasizes that Chaucer is a national figure. *The workes of our ancient ... poet Geffrey Chaucer. [Followed by] The storie of Thebes*, by I. Lidgate, 1602. Oxford, Bodleian Library, A 2.5 Art.Seld., fol. 17.

To the Kings Highnesse, my most gracious soueraigne Lord, Henry the eight, by the grace of God, King of England, and of France, defensor of the faith, and Lord of Ireland, &c.

AMongs all other excellencies, most gracious soueraine lord, wherewith almighty God hath endowed mankind, aboue the residue of earthly creatures, as an outward declaration of reason or reasonablenesse, wherein consisteth the similitude of man vnto angels, and the difference betweene the same and brute beastes, I veraply suppose, that speech or language is nat to be reputed amonges the smallest or inferiours. For thereby is expressed the conceit of one to another, in open and plaine sentence, whych in the residue of liuely creatures, lacketh and is not shewed amongs them, but by certaine couert and derke signes, and that in fewe thyngs, hauing course and operation onely of nature. This speech or language, after the confusion of tongues, sent by Gods punishment for pride and arrogancie of people, hath been by a certaine instinct and disposition naturall, deuised and inuented in sundry parts of the world, as fellowships or companyings of folkes one with another chaunced, much to the outward expressing of the thing in word or sound, according to that whereof it had meaning or signification. But in processe of time, by diligence or pollicie of people, after diuers formes, figures, and impressions in mettall, barks of trees, and other matter vsed for memorie and knowledge of thyngs, then present or passed, sundry letters or carectes were first amongs the Phenices deuised and found, with such knittings and ioynings of one to another, by a maruellous subtiltie and craft, as counterueiled was and is equiualent to the same languages. So as the conceit of mans mind, which at the beginning was vsed to bee declared by mouth onely, came to such point, that it was as sensibly and viuely expressed in writing. Hereupon ensued a great occasion and courage vnto them that should write, to compone and adorne the rudenesse and barbarietie of speech, and to forme it to an eloquent and ordinate perfection: whereunto many, and many great Poets and Oratours haue highly employed their studies and courages, leauing thereby notable Renoume of themselues, and example perpetuell to their posteritie. Amongs other, the Greekes in all kinds of sciences seemed so to preuaile, and so to ornate their tongue, as yet by other of right noble languages, cannat be perfitely imitated or followed. The Latines by example of the Greekes, haue gotten or wonne to them no small glorie, in the forming, order, and vttering of that tongue. Out of the which two, if it be well searched, that is to say, Greeke and Latin (thogh by corruption of speech it should seeme much otherwise) haue been deriued the residue of the languages, that be written with the letters or carectes of either of them both: But of all speeches, those which most approch to the Latine, bee the Italian and Spanish tongues, of whome the one by corruption of the Gothes and Longobardes had her beginning, as Latine spoken by strangers of a barbare vnderstanding. The other being also Latine, was by Vandales, Gothes, Moores, Sarracenes and other so many times blemished, as marueile it is to see now vnto what perfection these two formed out of the Latine and Barbares speeches be reduced. Next vntothē in similitude to the Latin is the French tongue, which by diligence of people of the same, is in few yeares passed, so amended, as well in pronunciation as in writing, that an Englishman by a small time exercised in that tongue, hath not lacked ground to make a Grammere, or rule ordinarie thereof. Though of trouth (which some shall scarcely beleeue) the Germanes haue so formed the order of their lauguage, that in the same is both as much plentie and as nere concordaunce to the phrase of the Latin, as the French tong hath. And veraily, like as all these and the rest haue ben thus vigilant and studious, to meliorate or amend their languages: so hath there nat lacked amongs vs Englishmen, which haue right well & notably endeuored and emploied them-

Caxton's Chaucer: Miscellaneous and Monumental

The significance of the 1476/7 Chaucer comes into focus alongside other books Caxton printed in the year after he established his Westminster shop. They include a Sarum Use Ordinal, which contains liturgical rites developed at Salisbury Cathedral. It represents a safe investment as a popular local service book, thousands of which were used and needed at churches across fifteenth-century England. He made a similar investment shortly thereafter in printing fifteenth-century literary staples in small editions, including *Table Manners for Children*; *The Morality of Cato*; *The Debate of the Horse, Goose, and Sheep*; *The Churl and the Bird*; and *The Temple of Glass*, all written in English. Many are now attributed to John Lydgate, Chaucer's famous and ambitious disciple, but they project here a more quotidian aesthetic: unascribed and unadorned.

Their format contrasts with the first text that Caxton edited (and translated) in Bruges in 1473/4, the first book ever printed in English, based on a French model by Raoul Lefèvre: *The Collection of the Histories of Troy*. Here, framed by lavish illustrations, Caxton asserts his voice as the text's translator and evokes a named tradition, modelling his work on that of 'John lidgate, monke of Burye' in worrying he is 'not worthy to bere his penner and ynke [ink] horne'.[3] His modesty gives way to a higher purpose to please his patron, 'bounde', Caxton says, to the 'good grace [of] my sayd lady': Margaret, Duchess of Burgundy, sister of King Edward IV, who appears prominently in the book's presentation engraving. The appeal to his patron echoes Lydgate, too: Caxton aims for the same fame and preferment that Lydgate won with his poetry from English courts a generation earlier.

Caxton's books from 1476/7 make a different appeal, to the market rather than to a patron. In an advertisement published contemporaneously, Caxton signals his value, promising customers that they can purchase their printed Sarum Ordinal from him 'good chepe'. He engages an established market on new terms. The texts he printed in 1476/7 were already circulating in manuscripts in Westminster, copied by amateur and professional scribes, and available through neighbouring booksellers, courtiers and merchants. But they weren't available here in print. Caxton capitalizes on the advantage of selling familiar, in-demand material in a novel, ready-to-hand form. He also capitalizes on familiar methods of book compilation. All his small volumes of printed poetry from 1476/7 that now survive come from a single *Sammelbänd*, where a reader bound together miscellaneous works that the printer provided.[4] This method of assembling a book – from pieces, according to individual, context-specific preferences – carries on the established mode of medieval manuscripts in a new medium and frames Caxton's approach in first printing Chaucer: to tap in print existing market demands and expectations.

So, Chaucer enters a world of print that depends on precedents of a vernacular manuscript culture. That culture circulated books unpredictably and inconsistently: scribes and readers often copied, bound and recombined unattributed texts in idiosyncratic forms, in ways that reflect the material they happened to have at hand, as we saw in the previous chapter. But that culture also cared deeply about authorship and authority. Late-medieval English writers had become 'newly articulate about their work'. They 'name themselves playfully or cautiously, but they do so with far more frequency than the English writers of earlier generations'.[5] Caxton carries this tradition into print in his second edition of the *Tales* (1483), which becomes increasingly articulate about his poet's authority. The book now begins with an effusive introduction, in which Caxton celebrates our 'grete philosopher Gefferey chaucer', whose ornate writing and eloquence have raised the English language from obscurity and made him worthy of 'the name of laureate poete' (sig. A2r) (FIGURE 2.4).

The praise echoes Caxton's epilogue to his 1478 printed edition of *Boece*, Chaucer's fourteenth-century translation of Boethius' sixth-century *The Consolation of Philosophy*. There, Caxton lauds Chaucer as the 'first foundeur and enbelissher of ornate eloquence in our englissh', worthy 'eternelly to be remembrid', and describes his tomb in Westminster Abbey, including his epitaph from 'a poete laureat'. Like the tomb's physical monument, Chaucer's *Tales* represent what Caxton calls a monument of English culture, the integrity of which he works to protect. Caxton has, his 1483 preface explains, 'dylygently ouersen [overseen] and duly examyned' the *Tales*' text 'to thende that it be made acordyng vnto his [Chaucer's] owen makynge' (sig. A2r). Caxton's vigilance corrects mistakes from six years prior, in the *Tales*' first edition, when he printed a bad text, which set 'in some thynges that he [Chaucer] neuer sayde ne made', and left out 'many thynges … whyche ben requysite to be sette in' (sig. A2v). The errors came to his attention from a gentleman reader, whose father, he explains, owns a true, original copy of Chaucer's *Tales* and who offers to share it for Caxton to print. The new book, Caxton suggests, enables his second edition to replace editorial error with authorial originality: he corrects his first edition 'accordynge vnto hys [Chaucer's] owen first book by hym made' (sig. A2v). The result implies the power of print in fixing a poetic canon. In place of unattributed, miscellaneous verse, Caxton champions the stability of a single authorial text, which preserves Chaucer's reputation and words as a monument for cultural memory.

2.4
Caxton's second edition of *The Canterbury Tales* (1483) is framed by an introduction which eulogizes the 'grete philosopher Gefferey Chaucer'. Caxton claims that Chaucer's ornate writing and eloquence have raised the English language from obscurity and made him worthy of 'the name of laureate poete'. Oxford, St John's College, A.2.5.

GRete thankes lawde and honour / ought to be gy-
uen vnto the clerkes / poetes / and historiographs
that haue wreton many noble bokes of wysedom
of the lyues / passiōs / & myracles of holy sayntes
of hystoryes / of noble and famous Actes / and
faittes / And of the cronycles sith the begynnyng
of the creacion of the world / vnto thys present tyme / by whyche
we ben dayly enformed / and haue knowleche of many thynges /
of whom we shold not haue knowen / yf they had not left to vs
theyr monumentis wreton / Emong whom and inespecial to fore
alle other we ought to gyue a synguler laude vnto that noble &
grete philosopher Gefferey chaucer the whiche for his ornate wry-
tyng in our tongue maye wel haue the name of a laureate poe-
te / For to fore that he by hys labour enbelysshyd / ornatyd / and
made faire our englisshe / in thys Royame was had rude speche &
Incongrue / as yet it appiereth by olde bookes / whyche at thys day
ought not to haue place ne be compared emōg ne to hys beaute-
uous volumes / and aournate writynges / of whom he made ma-
ny bokes and treatyces of many a noble historye as wel in me-
tre as in ryme and prose / and them so craftyly made / that he cō-
prehended hys maters in short / quyck and hye sentences / es-
chewyng prolyxyte / castyng away the chaf of superfluyte / and
shewyng the pyked grayn of sentence / vtteryd by crafty and su-
gred eloquence / of whom emonge all other of hys bokes / I pur-
pose temprynte by the grace of god the book of the tales of caun
tyrburye / in whiche I fynde many a noble hystorye / of euery asta
te and degre / Fyrst descryuyng the condiciōs / and tharraye of eche
of them as proprely as possyble is to be sayd / And after theyr
tales whyche ben of noblesse / wysedom / gentylesse / Myrthe / and
also of veray holynesse and vertue / wherin he fynysshyth thys
sayd booke / whyche book I haue dylygently ouersen and duly
examyned to thende that it be made acordyng vnto his owen ma
kyng / For I fynde many of the sayd bookes / whyche wry-
ters haue abrydgyd it and many thynges left out / ¶ And in
some place haue sette certayn versys / that he neuer made ne sette
in hys booke / of whyche bookes so incorrecte was one brought to
me vj yere passyd / whyche I supposed had ben veray true & cor-
recte / And accordyng to the same I dyde do enprynte a certayn

The difference between Caxton's editions of the *Tales* replays in a new key a dynamic represented in the *Tales* itself, which emerges from Chaucer's engagement with medieval manuscript culture. Chaucer crafts his *Tales* as an 'elaborate artistic response to the conditions of medieval book production', playing on the traditions of single- and multi-text manuscripts that shaped his reception.[6] The diverse stories – of Theban knights and English carpenters – that might circulate independently and haphazardly in other books here come together in a single poem, arranged by an overarching authorial design and directed by an explicit plan: for each pilgrim to tell two stories on the way from Southwark to Canterbury and back. But that plan itself invites randomness and change, exemplified by the sudden intrusion of the Canon's Yeoman, the impertinent interruption by the Miller or several other moments of drunken disorder. The combination of authorial design and uncontrolled variation represents Chaucer's wager on his text's uncertain future. It anticipates the *Tales'* circulation in fifteenth-century manuscripts, where individual narratives in the pilgrimage frame appear in many different orders, depending on the exemplar a particular scribe happened to have at hand (as we have seen in Chapter 1).[7] It anticipates, too, Caxton's dual presentation of the *Tales* as both unadorned stories fit for an idiosyncratic *Sammelbänd* and as a canonical monument set by its author's design. The connection means that Caxton's two Chaucers realize in print what Chaucer had imagined in narrative: the possibility that the planned design of a canonical author will live on in the world in unplanned and varied forms – that Caxton's monumental preface to his second edition of the *Tales* introduces a text that imagines the miscellaneousness of his first.

Chaucer's Poems, Chaucer's *Workes*

The same pattern extends to Chaucerian books produced in subsequent decades, including the 1492 edition of *The Canterbury Tales*, coordinated by Richard Pynson (FIGURE 2.5). Pynson follows Caxton's lead in choosing the *Tales* as one of his first English books to print and a solid foundation on which to build a career – and he follows Caxton, too, in printing a revised version of his monumental preface to the 1483 edition, along with much of Caxton's revised 1483 text. Wynkyn De Worde takes a similar tack six years later, again carrying forward the 1483 preface for his 1498 edition of the *Tales*, which he produced as the new head of Caxton's old print shop. De Worde attributes the preface to Caxton in a heading that also signals Caxton's death: 'his soule in heuen won'. The language echoes the conclusion of the preface proper, where Caxton, in looking toward 'euerlastyng lyf in heuen', entreats God to 'remember the sowle of … Gefferey chaucer' (sig. A2v). It also echoes Caxton's memorializing gestures in his 1478 *Boece* and his 1483 *House of Fame*, both of which pray for readers to remember Chaucer's soul alongside the textual monuments of his poetic fame. De Worde extends the textual monument to include the dead Caxton himself, who, alongside his soul in heaven, has left behind an earthly legacy printed for memory.

De Worde's monument leaves room for miscellaneousness, too. In 1498, at almost the same time as he printed *The boke of Chaucer named Caunterbury tales*, De Worde published an anonymous edition of *The Assembly of Gods*, a fifteenth-century dream vision. The two poems, however disparate in subject, became linked as books in print. They share the same folio format and page layout, with their texts arranged in two long columns. They share the same prominent woodcut illustration of a large group seated together around a table. The group's members do double symbolic duty, representing the pilgrims feasting at the Tabard, in the first, and the gods assembled at a divine palace, in the second. De Worde – or a contemporary retailer – amplified these books' connection after production, binding some copies of the two editions together in one volume. The result continues the legacy of Caxton's engagements with manuscript culture, forming an idiosyncratic multi-text compilation – the canonical Chaucer alongside the anonymous *Assembly* – now repackaged in print.

De Worde went on to print more Chaucerian books, including an edition of *Troilus and Criseyde* in 1517, as did Pynson, who published another edition of the *Tales* in 1526, along with editions of *Troilus* and the *House of Fame* in the same year. Pynson's *House of Fame* contains, as the title page advertises, 'dyuers [diverse] other of [Chaucer's] workes', such as the *Parliament of Fowls*, here attributed explicitly to 'the famous clerke Geffray Chaucer' (sig. D2r). The book contains, too, other Middle English poems that Pynson doesn't ascribe to Chaucer directly, including the *Complaint of Mary Magdalene*, plus more texts that Pynson credits to other authors, such as the Proverbs of Lydgate. The result suggests, again, the continuity in print of aspects of manuscript culture, positioning the *House of Fame* alongside the sort of content with which it first circulated: that is, variously Chaucerian and non-Chaucerian verse, organized in a multi-text compilation. Pynson opens the possibility for further compilation still. He prints his 1526 *Tales* and *Troilus* in distinct volumes that readers might bind in new miscellaneous arrangements, including with non-Chaucerian works, as happened with De Worde's *Tales* and *Assembly* two decades earlier.[8]

2.5
Richard Pynson's 1492 edition of *The Canterbury Tales* includes this lovely woodcut image of the pilgrim company gathered around a table at the Tabard Inn in Southwark, talking over a meal. Four lines below the image, you can see the line beginning 'Strong was the wyne'. Oxford, Bodleian Library, Douce 218, fol. c2v.

Eke plato seyeth who can it rede
The worde must be cosyn to the dede
Also I praye you foryeue it me
Al though I set nat folk in theire degre
Here in these tales as they shulde stonde
My witte is shorte ye may wele vndrestonde

Rete chere made oure ost to vs euerechone
g And to the soupere sette he vs anone
He seruyd vs with vitaylle at the best
Stronge was the wyne and wele drinke vs lyst
A semely man oure ost was with alle
For to be a marshalle in a lordes halle
A large man he was with eyen stepe
A feyrer burgges is ther none in chepe
Belde of his speche and wele was y taught
And of manhode lacked he right naught
Eke therto was he right a mery man
And after souper to pleyen he began
And spake of mirth amonge other thinges

Pynson's 1526 editions also pull in a different direction. Their binding history suggests that, though printed independently, the three editions were often sold together as a single unit – a kind of Chaucerian greatest hits that Pynson planned for his readers to combine. The books' connection moves the miscellaneous Chaucer towards the monumental. Sold and later bound together, Pynson's *Tales*, *Troilus* and *House of Fame* give a new order to the multi-text compilation, one arranged not by chance or personal preference but by the named authority of one famous poet. Other aspects of the editions project the same Chaucerian authority. They contain monumental features familiar from Pynson's predecessors, including a prologue from the printer for the *Tales* and an epilogue to the *House of Fame* modelled on Caxton's 1483 editions and woodcuts that build on De Worde's *Tales* in 1498. They also comprise new editorial details that highlight Chaucer's controlling presence, including a new title for the *Tales'* pilgrimage frame as 'the prologue of the auctour'. They contain, too, a distinction specific to Pynson himself, which advertises his role as Henry VIII's official printer: 'printer to the kynges most noble grace', as he often brags. Pynson's role lends Chaucer's poetic authority a political weight, moving England's laureate toward an ambit of royal privilege and power.

This authority gains even more weight in 1532 from William Thynne, who realizes the possibility toward which Pynson's 1526 editions gestured: he prints for the first time in one grand volume the collected *Workes of Geffray Chaucer* (FIGURE 2.6). The volume asserts Chaucer's European fame, monumentalizing his poetry and prose in a format modelled on the collected *Opera* of classical and Continental authorities, such as Virgil, Petrarch and Chartier. It also asserts Chaucer's distinctly English power, aligning his works with the authority of the Tudor monarchy.

2.6
This title page of William Thynne's 1532 edition of Chaucer introduces his writings as 'The Workes of Geffray Chaucer'. This was the first time that a vernacular author's texts were gathered together as 'works', a term previously used only for classical authors. It marks the increasing authority of 'Father Chaucer'. Oxford, Bodleian Library, Ashm. 1095.

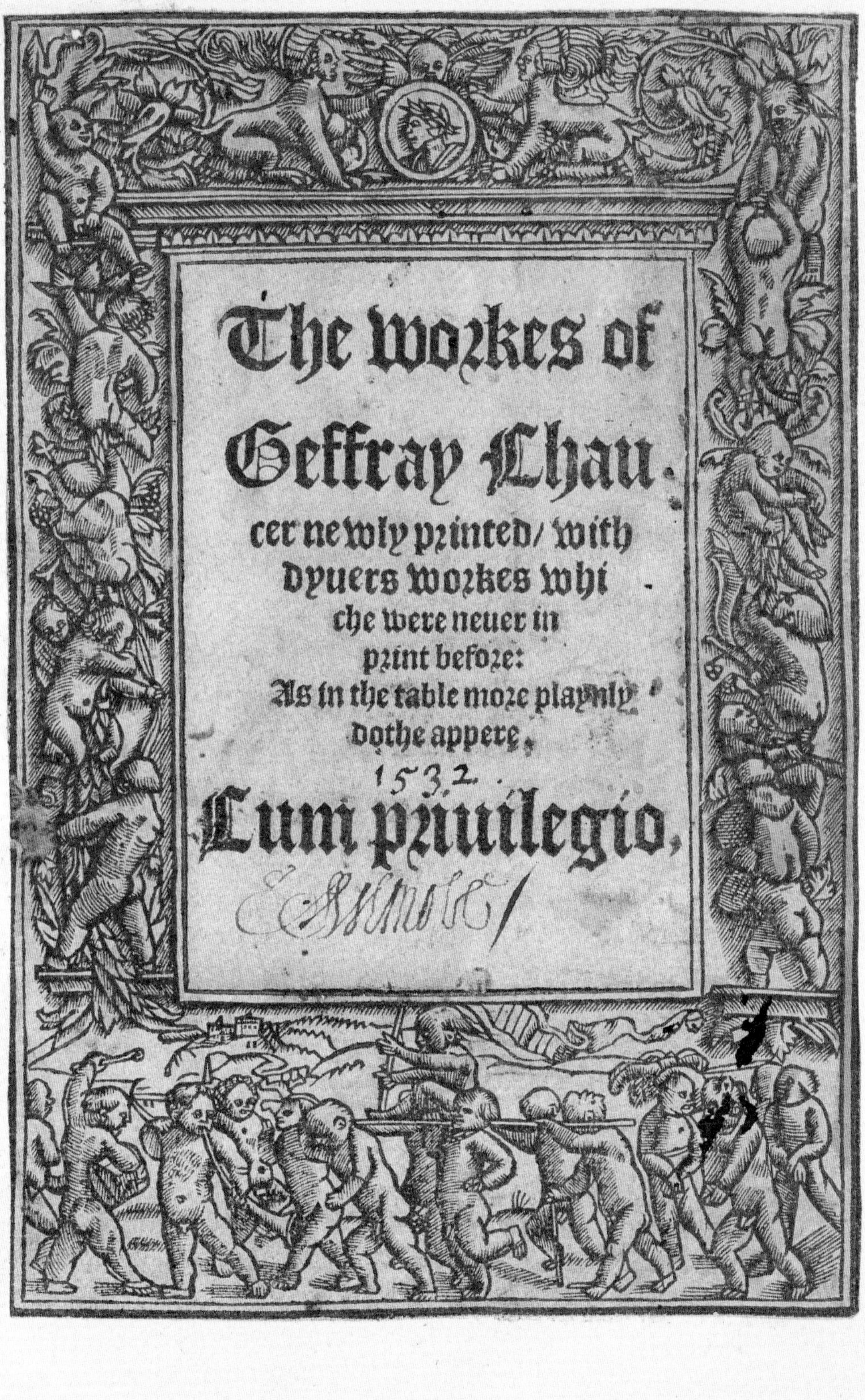
The workes of Geffray Chaucer newly printed/ with dyuers workes whiche were neuer in print before: As in the table more playnly dothe appere.

1532.

Cum priuilegio.

Thynne's book begins with a dedicatory letter to Henry VIII, written by Sir Brian Tuke, which describes Chaucer's centrality to early modern national identity. Chaucer, Tuke suggests, bettered and beautified the English tongue, refining a language now on a par with Continental vernaculars. He elevated English poetry in a rude age, preserving 'good letters' when they seemed 'in daunger to haue vtterly peryshed' (sig. A2v). He displayed English learning in 'all kyndes of doctrynes and sciences', sharing knowledge so precious that only the English king, 'as moost absolute in wysedome and all kyndes of doctryne', would 'adde or gyue any authorite her vnto' (sig. A2v–3r). This English authority amplifies the significance of the editorial project: assembling Chaucer's works in print now becomes a labour done, as Tuke writes, 'in loue to my country', one that complements politics on a national scale (sig. A3r). In collecting the *Workes*, Thynne's edition consolidates a usable English past around Chaucer's authority even as Henry consolidates a reformed English present around his.

The consolidated edition sets the shape of Chaucer's canon for the rest of the century. It unites texts previously printed separately by Caxton, De Worde, Pynson and others, such as *Troilus and Criseyde*, the *House of Fame* and *Boece*. It includes, too, as the title page promotes, diverse Chaucerian 'workes whiche were neuer in print before', such as *The Legend of Good Women*, *The Book of the Duchess* and *A Treatise on the Astrolabe*. And it encompasses, as well, what Kathleen Forni calls the Chaucerian apocrypha: both (a) texts consistent enough with Chaucer's presumed themes to be treated as his, such as Henryson's *The Testament of Cresseid*, Ros's *La Belle Dame sans Merci* and Clanvowe's *The Cuckoo and Nightingale*; and (b) texts ascribed to other medieval writers overtly, such as 'Scogan vnto the yonge lordes and gentylmen of the kynges house'.[9] The whole is framed by *The Canterbury Tales*, which begins the volume – as it still begins the modern *Riverside* – and anticipates some of the complexities of authorship that follow. Like his *Tales*, Chaucer's 1532 *Workes* construct a poetic authority from disparate, miscellaneous parts, not all of which belong to Chaucer himself. On a pilgrimage to Canterbury, as in the pages of a monumental volume, Chaucerian authorship encompasses the different voices – of English pilgrims and English poets – that can come together in one place.

Subsequent editions both reprint this canon and add more voices to the mix, beginning with the 1542 and 1550 *Workes*, printed respectively by Richard Grafton and Nicholas Hill. The first includes the apocryphal *Plowman's Tale* for the first time: the Protestant version, rather than Hoccleve's Catholic tale. It is inserted at the end of the Canterbury collection, after the point at which Caxton's, De Worde's and Pynson's *Tales* had stopped. The second incorporates *The Plowman's Tale* more fully into the Canterbury frame, moving its religious complaint to appear before the Parson's sermon. Its insertion, which complements Chaucer's sixteenth-century reputation as a religious reformer, also capitalizes on the fluidity of Chaucer's *Tales* as a monument of miscellaneousness. Added to a collection that admits the unexpected intrusion of a Canon's Yeoman; that leaves unrealized its promise of four stories per pilgrim; and that circulates in fifteenth- and sixteenth-century books in various inconsistent orders, 'The Plowman's Tale' becomes in the printed *Workes* just the latest revision to the Canterbury plan. The revision creates an enduring impact on Chaucer's reception, shaping engagements with his authority by Milton and Spenser.

Spenser – like many of his Elizabethan contemporaries – read Chaucer in the 1561 *Woorkes*, coordinated by John Stow, who amplifies the presence of non-Chaucerian voices and brings into focus the living legacy of his *Tales*. Informed by his extensive reading of medieval manuscripts, Stow adds to the canon occasional and lyric poems not previously in print, including 'Chaucers woordes vnto his owne Scrivener', which stresses the importance of preserving the exact letter of the poet's text. But Stow also highlights content in the *Woorkes of Geffrey Chaucer* not written by Chaucer himself, including 'The Floure of Curtesie, made by Iohn lidgate', 'Iohn Gower, vnto the noble King Henry the iiij', 'Three Sayings of dan Iohn Lydgate' and 'A balade of good counseile, by dan Iohn Iidgat cleped the monke of Buri'. Their inclusion implies the metonymic scope of Chaucer's authority, where his *Woorkes* comprise the contours of a larger English tradition – indeed of a familiar medieval English triumvirate: Chaucer, Lydgate, Gower. Stow expands this tradition by inserting another major poem at the volume's end, also by Lydgate: *The Siege of Thebes*. Like *The Plowman's Tale*, the *Siege* capitalizes on the planned planlessness of Chaucer's Canterbury collection, imagining itself as a new tale told among the pilgrims on the way back to Southwark. Its insertion here enacts, again, a broad definition of Chaucer's works, extending their scope to encompass part of the history of their reception.[10]

The same logic applies for Thomas Speght in his 1598 and 1602 editions, which again cap Chaucer's *Workes* with Lydgate's *Siege* and add to the existing canon four new items: *The Flower and the Leaf* and *The Isle of Ladies* in 1598 and *Jack Upland* and *An ABC* in 1602. The last is written by Chaucer himself; the others reinforce the tradition he encapsulated as a poet of courtly eloquence and religious reform. As discussed later in this volume, in his *Fables* Dryden chose *The Flower and the Leaf* as one of the four texts most representative of an authentic Chaucer. Speght's editions make their largest contribution in their editorial apparatus, which adorns Chaucer's authority in diverse trappings of scholarship and praise: dedications, letters, verse tributes, illustrations, glossary definitions. The apparatus registers a new pressure on Chaucer's reception, recognizing that changes to English language and culture over the past two hundred years have made his poetry hard to understand. Speght's editions turn this challenge into a narrative of national pride, explaining Chaucer's words and works with the scholarly care usually reserved for famous authors in classical, Italian and French traditions. As they had their interpreters, so Chaucer now finds his, whose labour, as Beaumont explains, proves that his English author is 'no lesse worthy than the best of them amongst all the Poets of the world' (sig. A6r). The act of publishing Chaucer remains, as for Thynne and Tuke, a service done for love of author and country, though it now involves not only consolidating and printing his works but illuminating their meaning.

His life invites explanation, too, offered in an imaginative biography that emphasizes the prominence of Chaucer's political connections and the depth of his knowledge. He attended Oxford, the biography notes – and Cambridge, as well, sharing an education that connects him to his editor. Speght attended Cambridge himself, falling in love with Chaucer there even as he acquired the knowledge to interpret Chaucer's difficult works. Some of his learning also stems from Chaucer's previous editor Stow, 'whose library', Speght indicates, 'helped me in many things', including a written copy of the *Complaint to His Purse*, 'wherein ten times more is adionied, than is in print' (sig. B6v), and a manuscript of 'The Plowman's Tale'. The tale is 'made no doubt by Chaucer', Speght asserts, 'for I haue seene it in written hand in Iohn Stowes Librarie in a booke of suche antiquite' (sig. N1v). The argument invokes a rich world of manuscripts that lies just beyond the printed page. Speght set most of his texts directly from Stow's 1561 printed edition, but he appeals here to the authenticity and copiousness of handwritten copies.

The edition similarly engages a manuscript culture in its full-page portrait of Chaucer, based, as its inscription indicates, on an illustration from the medieval poet Thomas Hoccleve in a fifteenth-century manuscript of his *The Regiment of Princes*. The portrait places Chaucer in the centre of a family tree that – thanks to some artistic creativity – implies visually Chaucer's genealogical connection to Edmund de la Pole, Duke of Suffolk, on the one hand, and Kings Henry IV and Henry VII, on the other (FIGURE 2.7). The genealogy builds on Tuke and Thynne's dedication to Henry VIII, amplifying Chaucer's authority as a national printed poet: he not only honours kings with his English works but belongs in their company. It also attests to the ongoing vitality of medieval manuscripts, which provide not only the portrait's source but one of its destinations. Shortly after purchasing Speght's 1598 edition, the antiquarian Joseph Holland picked out its portrait and inserted it into one of his fifteenth-century manuscripts, where it frames an assortment of Chaucer's poetry. There, alongside other material from Speght's edition that Holland copied into his book by hand, the portrait exemplifies a reciprocal relation between manuscript and print as complementary rather than successive technologies: a manuscript illustration of Chaucer inspires a printed image before it enters into another manuscript.

2.7
Thomas Speght featured this fascinating image of Chaucer in his 1598 and 1602 editions. On the right, Chaucer's own family tree is represented, down to his great-great-grandson. On the left is the family of Chaucer's sister-in-law, Katherine Swynford. Katherine was the mistress and then wife of John of Gaunt; their illegitimate children, the Beauforts, were retrospectively legitimated and were the ancestors of Henry VII. Both family trees are under the general title 'The progenie of Geffrey Chaucer'. Speght manages, rather spuriously, to connect Chaucer with the monarch and thus the nation. *The Workes of our ancient and learned English poet, Geffrey Chaucer*, 1602. Oxford, Bodleian Library, A 2.5 Art.Seld.

THE PROGENIE OF GEFFREY CHAUCER
Payne Roet Knight
Blanch daughter to Henry D of Lancast
Iohn of Gaunt D. of Lancaster
Cathren Swinford Duches of lancast
The Daughter of Payne Roet
Geffrey Chaucer
Sir Iohn Burwash Knight
Henry 4 Kinge of Englan
Mary Daughter to Humfry Bohun Earl of Herefor
Imania Daughter to Simon Hannap
Sir Iohn Burwash Knight
Iohn Duke of Bedford
Humfrey Duke of Gloscester
Iohn Beaufort Earl of Somerset
Thomas Chaucer esq Lord of Ewelme
Maude Daughter & coheir to S. I. B.
Margaret maried to Ioh Arundal of deuo
Margaret D. of Sr Ioh Beauchamp of bletso
Iohn the first Duk of Somerset
Alce Countes of Sal. & Duches of Suf
William De La Pole Duke of Suffolk
Margaret Countesse of Richmond
Iohn De La Pole Duke of Su
Henry 7 Kinge of England
Edmund De La Pole Duke of Suffolk
The true portraiture of GEFFREY CHAUCER the famous English poet, as by THOMAS OCCLEUE is described who liued in his time, and was his Scholar.
Hic iacent Thomas Chaucer armiger quondam dominus istius villæ, et patronus istius ecclesiæ qui obijt Decem. 13. Aº Dñi 1434. et Mathildis uxor eius Ap. 27. 1436

This interaction across media brings our story full circle, back to Caxton, whose ingenuity in print remains embedded in habits of manuscript circulation (FIGURE 2.8). Caxton, we argued, opens two futures for Chaucer's printed poetry, exemplified by the miscellaneous and monumental aspects of his 1476/7 and 1483 editions, which subsequent editors take up across the century ahead. So what? One of these futures retells a familiar, larger story about print as transformative technology with inexorable effects: the creation and standardization of literary canons; the consolidation of authority; the development of national identities and cultures. Chaucer's afterlife in print suggests this story's continued force. Fifteenth- and sixteenth-century editions confirm his authority as a national poet, reproducing at scale a canon tied to the strength of English language, English culture and English political power. But they also preserve a different story about print, one where manuscripts retain their vitality and multi-text compilation lives on: where Chaucer's authority admits other voices and grand plans remain open to change. This story suggests the limitations of a technological determinism, both in explaining the significance of print media and in understanding the trajectories of Chaucer's reception. Chaucer became a singular authority and national monument in print. But he also left a legacy of miscellaneousness – and he might still become something else, too.

2.8
A vivid image of the Wife of Bath from Caxton's second edition of *The Canterbury Tales*, placed above her description in the 'General Prologue'. Dressed in red, as she almost always is in depictions right across time, she also – perhaps less predictably – demonstrates her piety by carrying a rosary. Oxford, St John's College, A.2.5.

H Good wyf ther was of beside bathe
And she was somdeel deef & that was scathe
Of cloth makynge hadd she suche an haunt
She passyd them of ypre and of gaunt
In al the parisshe wyf was ther non
That to the offrynge before hyr sholde goon
And yf ther dyd certayn wroth was she
Than was she oute of al charyte
Her kercheuys ful fyn were of ground
I durste swere they weyed thre pound
That on a sonday were on hyr hed
Hyr hosyn were of fyne scarlet reed
Ful streyte I teyd and shoos ful moyst and newe
Bold was her face fayr and rede of hewe
She was a worthy womman al hyr lyue
Husbondys at the chyrche dore hadde she fyue
Wythoute other companye in youthe
But her of nedyth not to speke as nowthe

CONTENTS
OF THE
First VOLUME.

The

3

'HERE IS GOD'S PLENTY': TRANSLATING CHAUCER

Adam Rounce

The influence of Chaucer in the period from 1660 to 1800 is pervasive, but also latent: Chaucer was adapted, translated and modernized, in versions that often found a far larger readership than his original writings (which were themselves successively edited – sometimes haphazardly – and republished). The most significant poets and critics of the period were involved with Chaucer's work, often in terms of what can be called translation, or in works that are looser in their relation to the original texts, and can be described as adaptations, imitations or modernizations.

This chapter looks at some of the types of Chaucerian writing that emerged in the period, from near-translations to texts where the Chaucerian impulse is present, but the connections with his writing and its form are far looser. It concludes with a brief look at how Chaucer was edited. There are other types of Chaucerian writing that are not discussed here: composite collections of versions by various writers, such as George Ogle's *The Canterbury Tales of Chaucer, Modernis'd by Several Hands* (1741), were very popular, and telling in their mix of famous and obscure contributors, and in the ways that certain tales (not least the obvious, bawdy ones, such as 'The Miller's Tale') found a new readership in their modern forms (FIGURE 3.1).[1] There is also pseudo-Chaucerian writing, where an anthology of topical

3.1
In George Ogle's edited *Canterbury Tales* (1741), different writers translated different parts of the text, demonstrating the wide interest that Chaucer held for eighteenth-century writers. The contributors were John Urry, Thomas Betterton, John Dryden, Samuel Cobb, Samuel Boyse, Henry Brooke, Alexander Pope, Jeremiah Markland and Mr Grosvenor. Oxford, Bodleian Library, Vet. A4 e.489, table of contents.

satire will be given an imprimatur of Chaucer, while having next to nothing to do with it, beyond being a sort of tutelary spirit. We begin with the most important response to Chaucer in the period, in a volume of poems published in the first year of the eighteenth century.

Dryden's Rough Diamond

John Dryden's *Fables ancient and modern* (1700) remains a pre-eminent critical and creative response to Chaucer's work; translation is too blunt a term to reflect the complicated ways in which Dryden adapts and presents some of Chaucer's writings, and also makes significant critical comments. In *Fables*, Dryden collects original poems of his own, presented alongside translations from other writers (Ovid, Chaucer, Boccaccio) and in such a way that various ideas and concepts (love, fate, power, the mutability of all things) are reiterated. This comparative mingling of different writers shows a difference from the twenty-first century, with its perceived division between translation and 'original' writing (even if it is not pejorative); for Dryden, translation was no more or less a creative act than the writing of such poems in the volume as 'Alexander's Feast', or 'To My Honored Kinsman, John Driden', and the mixing of such works was meant to build, cumulatively, on their complementary aspects.

The connections between all the poems collected in *Fables* repay close attention, but here it is sufficient to note that Dryden found Chaucer a highly sympathetic poetic predecessor and cherry-picked from his writings accordingly. Dryden adapted 'The Knight's Tale' as 'Palamon and Arcite' (the first work in *Fables*) (FIGURE 3.2), turned 'The Nun's Priest's Tale' into 'The Cock and the Fox', and kept Chaucer's title for 'The Wife of

3.2
John Dryden translated several of Chaucer's texts for his *Fables* in 1700: 'The Knight's Tale', 'The Wife of Bath's Tale', 'The Nun's Priest's Tale' and the spurious *The Flower and the Leaf*, as well as developing the portrait of the Parson. Here is the opening of 'The Knight's Tale', translated as 'Palamon and Arcite'. *Fables ancient and modern translated into verse, from Homer, Ovid, Boccace, & Chaucer: with original poems*, 1700. Oxford, Bodleian Library, EFL YJ63.1[Fab], p. 1.

PALAMON AND ARCITE: OR, The Knight's Tale.

In Three Books.

BOOK I.

IN Days of old, there liv'd, of mighty Fame
A valiant Prince; and *Theseus* was his Name:
A Chief, who more in Feats of Arms excell'd
The Rising nor the Setting Sun beheld.
Of *Athens* he was Lord; much Land he won,
And added Foreign Countrys to his Crown:
In *Scythia* with the Warriour Queen he strove,
Whom first by Force he conquer'd, then by Love;
He brought in Triumph back the beauteous Dame,
With whom her Sister, fair *Emilia*, came.

Bath's Tale'. He also took the short portrait at the centre of the 'General Prologue' extending it as 'The Character of a Good Parson'; the misattributed *The Flower and the Leaf* rounds out the contributions.

Dryden reveres Chaucer: 'as he is the Father of English Poetry, so I hold him in the same Degree of Veneration as the Grecians held Homer, or the Romans Virgil.'[2] In both his theory and poetic practice, this reverence towards Chaucer is combined with a pragmatic sense, hence his adapting the original texts into modern English. The paradox presented is that the ideas of Chaucer are vital and timeless, but the linguistic barriers towards a full modern appreciation of him necessitate the element of translation; these are, for Dryden, practical problems, such as the apparent inconsistencies of scansion in Chaucer's texts. Rather than simply denouncing Chaucer's poetry as metrically flawed, Dryden's admiration for Chaucer's facility with language coexists with an awareness of the oddities of the verse to a modern reader; he enjoys the sound of it, even though it is not always harmonious to him. Moreover, the Chaucerian originals are included in the back of *Fables* (FIGURE 3.3), allowing for comparison, also suggesting that they were now distant enough in time and recognition to require such inclusion (it is telling that his appendix printings are the first appearance of Chaucer in English in roman type, rather than blackletter).

3.3
John Dryden included the originals of the texts that he translated in his *Fables* (1700). Here is his version of the original 'Knight's Tale'. Compare the opening, 'Whylom, as old Stories tellen us / There was a Duke that hyght Theseus', with the translation in figure 3.2, 'In Days of old, there liv'd, of mighty Fame / A valiant Prince; and Theseus was his Name'. *Fables ancient and modern translated into verse, from Homer, Ovid, Boccace, & Chaucer: with original poems*, 1700. Oxford, Bodleian Library, EFL YJ63.1[Fab], p. 567.

Dryden's genuine homage, combined with necessary adaptation, will become familiar in the century. Chaucer's ideas and types are universal: his wit, comic wisdom and irony, the models for his satire, and the tone of his narratives will still be conveyed via such adaptation, if done sensitively. For Dryden, Chaucer 'must have been a Man of a most wonderful comprehensive Nature', and his task is to convey that nature.

THE KNIGHT'S TALE,

BY

GEFFREY CHAUCER.

WHylom, as old Stories tellen us,
There was a Duke that hight *Theseus*;
Of *Athens* he was Lord and Governour,
And in his time such a Conquerour,
That greater was non vnder the Son;
Full many a rich countrie had he won
What with his Wisdome, and his Chiualrie
He conquered all the reigne of *Feminy*:
That whylom was icleped *Cithea*:
And wedded the Queen *Ipolita*:
And brought her home with him into his countrie
With mikell glorie and solemnitie,
And eke her young sister *Emely*.
And thus with victorie and melody
Let I this worthy duke to *Athens* ride,
And all his host in armes him beside.
And certes, if it nere to long to here,
I would have told fully the manere
How wonnen has the reigne of *Feminy*
By *Theseus*, and by his chiualrie:
And of the great Battaile for the nones
Between *Athenes* and *Amasones*:
And how besieged was *Ipolita*,
The yong hardie queene of *Cithea*.
And of the feast, that was at her wedding,
And of the tempest at her home comming:
But all that thing I mote as now forbere;
I have, God wot, a large field to ere;
And weked bene the oxen in the plowe:
The remnant of my tale is long ynow.
I will nat letten eke non of this rout,
Let every fellow tell his tale about,
And let se now who shall the supper win,
And there I left, I will again begin.
This duke, of whom I make mencioune,
When he was come almost to the town
In all his wele and his most pride,
He was ware, as he cast his eye aside,

To do so, he has to revise some aspects of Chaucer, who 'I confess, is a rough Diamond, and must first be polish'd, e'er he shines'.[3] Dryden adds and takes away, trying to convey the spirit of Chaucer. His remarks on his practice in the *Fables* make striking claims, whilst showing the wider questions raised by the act of translating:

> I have not ty'd myself to a Literal Translation; but have often omitted what I judg'd unnecessary, or not of Dignity enough to appear in the Company of better Thoughts. I have presum'd farther in some Places, and added somewhat of my own where I thought my Author was deficient, and had not given his Thoughts their true Lustre, for want of Words in the Beginning of our Language.[4]

Dryden is offering a version where he can feel free to omit, or to enlarge where he feels it could be improved, given the (to him) wider linguistic range of modern English. This is, in a sense, closer to the meaning of 'imitation', where a translation updates its source to its own world, but it largely resists precise definition. Dryden felt an intellectual and poetic bond with Chaucer, and a sense of lineage – Chaucer is a father figure, and Dryden sees himself as his descendant, not as a usurper. There are no claims to exclusivity – if they wish, later figures can rewrite Dryden too: 'Another Poet, in another Age, may take the same Liberty with my Writings; if at least they live long enough to deserve Correction.'[5] His own versions of Chaucer are only as permanent as readers make them; Dryden is not appropriating Chaucer, so much as re-presenting him in a modern form.

The practical forms taken by Dryden's versions differ, but some general patterns can be illustrated. Dryden follows

Chaucer closely at many points, sometimes adding inflections to define an idea. In other places, Dryden will enlarge a Chaucerian image or theme, until the general direction is still reflected, but the specifics are expanded greatly. Sometimes these additions have a topical slant: 'The Character of a Good Parson' is subtitled 'Imitated from Chaucer, and Enlarged'. The 51 lines of the original are extended to 140, in using the simple virtues and incorruptibility of Chaucer's Parson, in contrast with the other assorted pilgrims who are all too happy to serve God and Mammon both. The Catholic Dryden modernizes this type of abnegation, in an implicit tribute to the spiritual honesty of those clergy who refused to pledge allegiance to William and Mary after the 'Glorious Revolution' of 1688. Chaucer's Parson resists all worldly calls or possibilities of advancement: 'a povre PERSOUN OF A TOUN, / But riche he was of hooly thoght and werk'. He does not hire out his parish to another, and run to London for further advancement, but instead exemplifies the teachings of the New Testament: 'But Cristes loore and his apostles twelve / He taught; but first he folwed it hymselve' ('General Prologue', lines 529–530). Dryden's larger portrait adds allusions to recent British history and its troubles, including the idea that all Anglican clergy were obliged to obey the new monarch. Dryden's Parson cannot: 'He joined not in their choice, because he knew / Worse might, and often did, from change ensue'. Refusing to overrule his religious duty for civil ends, instead, 'his benefice forsook', and he preached 'through the land', 'like a primitive apostle'.[6] The outline of the Parson is the same in both versions, but Dryden's version embroils him in contemporary theological and political debate, developing his integrity and refusal to forsake his principles.

Dryden's own style is often defined through Chaucerian imitation, with clear modern intellectual influences. 'The Cock and the Fox', his version of 'The Nun's Priest's Tale', is a mock-epic that shows the effects of *Paradise Lost*: the resemblance between Reynard, 'the Artificer of lies',[7] and Milton's Satan is comically clear, in various traces of vocabulary. Likewise the warning to Chanticleer via his dreams that on this dangerous day he should avoid his usual public exhibitionism, as a foe will enter into his Eden. This leads to a debate on predestination and free will: 'But what that God forwoot moot nedes bee, / After the opinioun of certein clerkis' (lines 3234–3235). Dryden turns this into 'But here the Doctors eagerly dispute: / Some hold Predestination absolute', and continues:

> Some clerks maintain, that Heav'n at first foresees,
> And in the virtue of foresight decrees.
> If this be so, then prescience binds the will,
> And mortals are not free to good or ill...[8]

Does divine foreknowledge determine our actions? For Chaucer it is the debate without end, from St Augustine onwards: 'That in scole is greet altercacioun / In this mateere, and greet disputisoun' (lines 3237–3238). Dryden's version is also filtered through the Miltonic sensibility of his era, recalling the debates of Adam and Eve: 'But God left free the Will, for what obeys / Reason, is free, and reason he made right'.[9]

In this example and many others, Dryden's version of Chaucer is not merely 'translated' so much as transfigured, true to its larger sense and its generic qualities (comic or otherwise) but altered in terms of the range and nature of its details; the odd effect is of poetry that is both Chaucerian in character yet clearly by Dryden in essential qualities too. These poems are very far from translation in any simple way. Although Dryden's is the most influential and sophisticated, the same can be said of many examples of Chaucerian writings in the period, but there are also examples where the spirit of the original is far harder to locate in either language or form.

Alexander Pope and Fame

Whereas Dryden's homage to Chaucer came at the end of his career, it was in the 1710s, relatively early on in his, that Alexander Pope wrote his versions of Chaucer (FIGURE 3.4). As well as 'The Merchant's Tale' and 'The Wife of Bath's Prologue' (regularly reprinted in collections of Chaucerian works and adaptations), Pope's most significant dialogue with Chaucer is *The Temple of Fame* (1715), where Pope himself (in some ways the most deliberate of all English poets in his choices of subject), explains its origins:

> The Hint of the following Piece was taken from *Chaucer*'s *House of Fame*. The Design is in a manner entirely alter'd, the Descriptions and most of the particular Thoughts my own: Yet I could not suffer it to be printed without this Acknowledgment, or think a Concealment of this Nature the less unfair for being common.[10]

Pope here makes a typically personal point about literary property – he has rewritten and almost entirely altered the Chaucerian original (he is using pentameters, unlike Chaucer's octosyllabic couplets), but still feels obliged to acknowledge his source, not least because such general borrowings are often concealed and passed off without any comment (suggesting, through innuendo, how unfair this is, whilst making clear that his own work is both original and in Chaucer's tradition).

Pope takes his 'Hint' from Book III of *The House of Fame*, and builds his temple from similar materials, paying tribute to classical poetic divinities and other grand and sublime sources of creative inspiration, as well as the less positive sides of fame (its transitory and arbitrary nature; the way it attracts scurrilous gossip and rumour, the critics who 'deface' the reputations of authors to build their own). The result is Chaucerian, but with the original allegory filtered through an eighteenth-century sensibility very aware of his own place in the artistic world. Towards the end the poet is confronted by a figure who asks if he is looking for the eponymous allegorical quality, and the Chaucer surrogate tells them that, no, he is not after fame: 'Sufficeth me, as I were ded, / That no wight have my name in honde. / I wot myself best how y stonde', as he is 'Certeyn, for the more part, / As fer forth as I can myn art' (lines 1876–1882). He is as sure as he can be of the value of his work. Pope expands this modest statement:

> One came, methought, and whisper'd in my Ear;
> What cou'd thus high thy rash Ambition raise?
> Art thou, fond Youth, a Candidate for Praise?
> 'Tis true, said I, not void of Hopes I came,
> For who so fond as youthful Bards of Fame?
> But few, alas! the casual Blessing boast,
> So hard to gain, so easy to be lost:
> How vain that second Life in others Breath,
> Th' Estate which Wits inherit after Death![11]

3.4
Alexander Pope's *Temple of Fame* (1715), inspired by Chaucer's *House of Fame*. Pope also wrote versions of 'The Merchant's Tale' and the 'Wife of Bath's Prologue', which he radically censored. Oxford, Bodleian Library, Dunston B 1473.

Pope takes something implicit at best in the Chaucerian sentiment, and develops it into his own definition of the artist as striving almost always in vain. Chaucer is remade in terms that put most attention onto the modern poetic claims for fame:

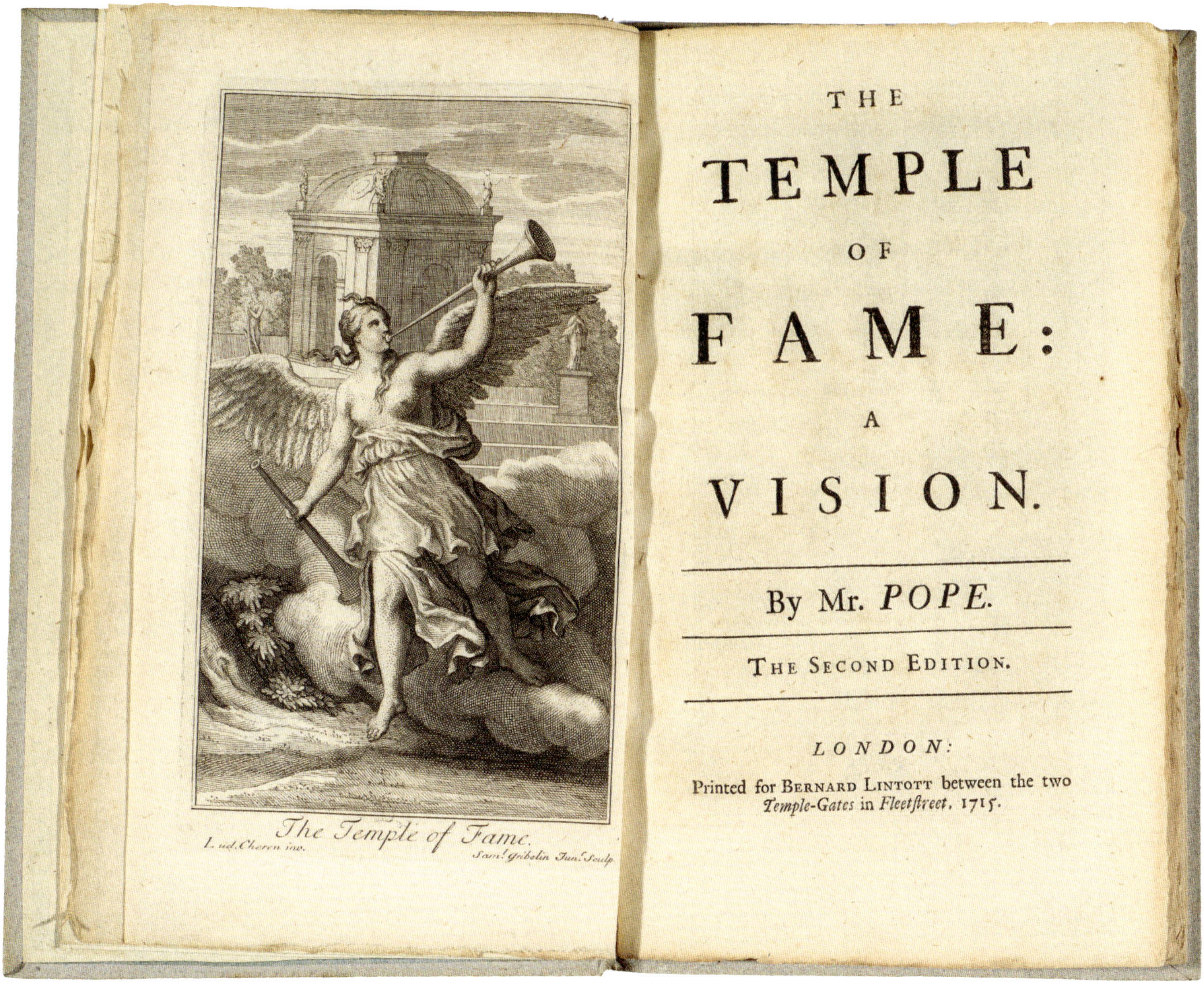

The Temple of Fame.

L. ud. Cheron inv. Saml. Gribelin Junr. Sculp.

THE

TEMPLE

OF

FAME:

A

VISION.

By Mr. *POPE*.

THE SECOND EDITION.

LONDON:

Printed for BERNARD LINTOTT between the two *Temple-Gates* in *Fleetstreet*, 1715.

Or if no Basis bear my rising Name,
But the fall'n Ruins of Another's Fame:
Then teach me, Heaven! to scorn the guilty Bays;
Drive from my Breast that wretched Lust of Praise;
Unblemish'd let me live, or die unknown,
Oh grant an honest Fame, or grant me none![12]

For Pope, creativity is in contest with an arbitrary and often unjust world, where the only consolations are the poet's honesty and integrity; Pope self-consciously constructs an ideal version of himself, nobly dealing with potential rejection and refusing to profit at the expense of others. He does this in part by standing in Chaucer's shoes to give his own modern representation of the inconstancies of fame further credibility. *The Temple of Fame* moves away from its source in a way that leaves the young Pope as the predominant subject, using the Chaucerian model as a basis for its own creative expression.

The Ubiquitous Wife of Bath

3.5
'The Wanton Wife of Bath', a ballad dating from sometime in the sixteenth century, was reprinted many times in the seventeenth century and beyond. It tells the story of the Wife of Bath at heaven's gate. A later, Scottish version removed the 'wanton' from the title, sometimes replacing it with 'worthy'. In 1600 and 1632 the ballad was censored and the printers punished for printing it. Oxford, Bodleian Library, Wood E 25 (93), p. 1.

Pope's other versions of Chaucer included the 'Prologue' to the tale of the Wife of Bath, the most memorable of Chaucer's characters by the seventeenth century. The Wife regularly pops up as a character type – the witty, outspoken, lascivious widow – which is repeatedly revisited as a comic idea, to the point of leaving her formal poetic relation with Chaucer; instead she is a familiar comic character with catchphrases, using completely different linguistic and poetic means to meet her original ends. Her staying power as a universal comic figure shows the versatility of some foundational parts of Chaucer's reputation, but also its oddities: at times the appeal of the Wife of Bath is as a satiric representative possessing emotional and sexual honesty,

The wanton Wife of BATH.

To the Tune of, Flying Fame.

In Bath a wanton wife did dwell
 as Caucer she doth write,
Who did in pleasure spend her days
 in many a fond delight.

Upon a time sore sick she was,
 and at the length did dye:
Her soul at last at Heavens gate,
 did knock most mightily.

Then Adam came unto the gate,
 who knocketh there, quoth he,
I am the wife of Bath she said,
 and fain would come to thee.

Thou art a sinner Adam said,
 and here no place shall have:
Alas for you, good sir she said,
 now gip you doting Knave.

I will come in, in spight, she said,
 of all such churles as thee:
Thou wast the causer of our woe,
 our pain and misery.

And first broke Gods Commandements,
 in pleasure of thy wife:
When Adam heard her tell this tale,
 he ran away for life.

Then down came Iacob to the gate,
 and bids her pack to Hell:
Thou false deceiver, why? said she,
 thou maist be there full well.

For thou deceivest thy Father dear,
 and thine own brother too:
Away went Iacob presently
 and made no more ado.

She knocks again with might and main
 and Lot he chides her straight:
Why then, quoth she, thou drunken ass,
 who bids thee here to wait.

With thy two Daughters thou didst lye
 on them two Bastards got:
And thus most tauntingly she chaft
 against poor silly Lot.

Who knock there, quoth Iudith then,
 with such shrill sounding notes?
Alas fine Minks, you cannot hear,
 quoth she, for cutting throats.

Good Lord how Iudith blusht for shame,
 when she heard her say so:
King David hearing of the same,
 he to the gate did go.

Quoth David who knocks there so loud,
 and maketh all this strife?
You were more kind, good sir, she said,
 unto Vriahs Wife.

And when thou caused thy Servants
 in battel to be slain;
Thou caused then more strife then I,
 who would come here so fain.

speaking truth to power; at other points, her appeal is more in the simple comic farce of innuendo and bawdry.

These two sides of the Wife of Bath are not mutually exclusive, of course. A striking example that manages to challenge religious hypocrisy, and exploit the Wife's notorious passions, is the anonymous ballad 'The Wanton Wife of Bath' (printed versions of which date from *c.* 1665, but its reception history suggests that it certainly circulated for decades before) (FIGURE 3.5). In variant versions, it seems to have been the cause of no little controversy, perhaps unsurprisingly, given its central premiss: upon dying, the Wife tries to gain access to heaven, only to be rebuffed as a sinner by various figures from biblical history, whereupon she points out that they have not perhaps remembered the beam in their own eye.

The poem was well known: Byron read it, in some form, and Joseph Addison in *The Spectator* mentions the 'excellent old Ballad of The Wanton Wife of Bath', in reference to the loquacity of women.[13] It is Chaucerian, and wears its lineage on its sleeve, but it also departs from Chaucer in significant ways: it is in the loose ballad metre so common to anonymous works, and it points half its moral in the title – the 'Wanton Wife' is a reduction of (and apparent judgement upon) Chaucer's figure. The narrative, though, refutes this, as the morally lax Wife triumphs over the complacent scriptural figures who chide her. The Wife embarrasses her august interlocutors by speaking plainly. The first man tells her 'Thou art a sinner':

> I will come in, in spight she said,
>   Of all such Churles as thee;
> Thou wert the Causer of our Woe,
>   Our Pain and Misery.

And first broke God's Commandments,
  In pleasure of thy Wife:
When Adam heard her tell this Tale,
  He run away for Life.

(lines 17–24)

The Wife manages to fulfil the desire of multitudes of people over the centuries, in telling Adam that it's all his fault. Her irreverent version of original sin might not be Miltonic, but it is effective, as Adam flees for the hills. It can also be seen that the nature of the form (simple diction, call-and-response syntax, measured rhyme) militates against the density of linguistic meaning and satiric effect found in Chaucer's couplets. This is poetry with a simple task to perform, that deviates from Chaucer's depth of satiric approach, even if it adopts the spirit of his attacks on religious cant and self-righteousness.

The success of the poem is based on its unveiling of hypocrisy, especially in matters of sex: the Wife undermines Solomon's authority through reference to his unusual domestic arrangements. She also identifies a similar lack of self-awareness in other characters:

No Sinner enters in this Place,
  Quoth *Mary Magdalen* then.
'Twere ill for you, fair Mistress mild,
  She answer'd her again.

(lines 85–88)

Saint Peter is told that, unlike him, 'I never did deny my Christ' (line 111). By the end she tells Christ that he has preached of mercy for repentant sinners, like the Good Thief, and 'yet the loving Father did / His prodigal Son forgive' (lines 133–134). She wins her case, and in so doing seems to stumble upon the essence of true Christianity (as opposed to its many self-serving adherents), in seeing the real impulse behind morals and parables. The poem's appeal and longevity are also based on outrage and shock – Chaucer's Wife of Bath is a character who can be adapted to say the apparently unspeakable, which no one else would dare utter.[14]

Not all the posthumous appearances of the Wife of Bath were so effective. John Gay remains famous for the blackly comic genius of *The Beggar's Opera*, but his earlier comedy *The Wife of Bath* (1713) has not travelled down the centuries quite so memorably. It is an odd attempt to represent the Chaucerian milieu, with an appearance by the poet himself, the Franklin (attempting to marry off his unwilling daughter), an Astrologer, various other medieval mummers, and Alison, the titular Wife of Bath, who appears frequently, rarely failing to mention the joys of marriage, and her own passions being undimmed by age. A modern reading of the play makes it hard to concur with the Franklin's description that 'The wife of *Bath* is enough to make any mortal split his sides.'[15] The play relies on those comic mainstays: innuendo and the Wife as 'merry widow'. By the end, even the equally aged Franklin is not safe from her charms:

> Look again, Man, —— view me all over, old Boy —— Slidikins, my face is like an ancient Medal —— Antiquity does but add to its Value; —— what say you, my lad, are you for another bout of Matrimony, t'other trip to the Temple of *Hymen?*[16]

The problem is that the drama (such as it is) is predicated on these appearances. It indicates the cultural centrality that Chaucer's figure had attained by this time, but to little other end, as Alison repeatedly falls back into the groove of her worn-out husbands.

In the Epilogue (apparently by Pope) the Wife continues in the expected strain of double entendre: 'Was I to single Combat ever slow / Did I e'er turn my Back upon the Foe?' The play ran for only two nights. Gay revived it in 1730, with extensive changes: the Franklin was renamed, Chaucer removed and the Wife reduced. It still closed after three nights and has never been revived.

Such ersatz works suggest that the appeal of certain Chaucerian aspects was connected to a wider atmosphere or tone, rather than their specific characteristics; in this sense, the way the Wife is recreated in ballads and plays is testament to a level of popularity that has a much looser relation to the text than, say, Dryden's versions. It is a paradox of all literary reception that works may be misread or rewritten, and then become more popular than the original. In this sense, the Wife of Bath contains multitudes.

Editing Chaucer

The portrait of the Wife of Bath in the 'General Prologue' ends with a couplet that acknowledges, slyly, her ruling passion, with a nod to Ovid's *Remedia Amoris*: 'Of remedies of love she knew per chaunce / For she koude of that art the old daunce' (lines 475–476). This can be paraphrased as the Wife knows everything about that old game (and can perhaps supply love potions and the like, maybe even contraception). A look at the way these lines appeared in the eighteenth century illuminates some of the problems of Chaucerian editing and reception. Thomas Betterton, in George Ogle's 1741 collection of modern versions of *The Canterbury Tales*, renders it as 'Her Talk did notably Love's Art advance; / For she had practis'd long that old, new Dance.'[17] This seems to extend but also confute the original, with the added 'Talk', and her practising rather than knowing about love and sex. Betterton shows the difficulty of rendering a concept in language sympathetic to a poetic source that was not textually straightforward. Given the absence of an authoritative manuscript, and instead a plethora of manuscript collections containing different versions of certain tales and poems, plus related non-Chaucerian material, the idea of a precise, fixed text of Chaucer is impossible. Instead, editors had to find their way through conflicting versions.[18]

The reader, in 1722, of John Urry's edition of Chaucer (completed after the editor's death) will there find the Wife described thus: 'Of remedies of love she knew perchaunce, / For she couth of that art the oldè daunce.' Urry seems to want an extra stress on the end of 'oldè', and 'koude' (understood) becomes 'couth'. Even Thomas Tyrwhitt, regularly seen as the first authoritative modern editor of Chaucer in his *Canterbury Tales* of 1775, has 'For of that arte she coude the old dance', with 'coude' ('koude' in most modern editions) meaning 'knowed', and the word order changed.[19]

3.6
A page from John Urry's 1722 edition of Chaucer. Urry worked hard to 'tidy up' and regularize Chaucer's metre according to eighteenth-century norms. Here, for instance, the line 'He taught; but first he folwed it hymselve' (the last line of the description of the Parson) is instead 'He taught, but first he followed himselve ', which makes little sense. Oxford, Bodleian Library, Douce C subt. 252, p. 5.

Urry's edition is unusual, in that he seems to regularize the lines of Chaucer in order to make them sound like his contemporary idea of a pentameter (i.e. with five stresses and, usually, ten syllables). This led him into some odd areas. A few lines on, with Chaucer's Parson, 'He taught; but first he folwed it hymselve'[20] is instead 'He taught, but first he followed himselve', which makes little sense, as the 'it' is dropped to make the

The Wife of Bath.

A gode wife there was alſo beſide Bathe,
But ſhe was ſomdele deſe, and that was ſcathe.
Of Clothmaking ſhe haddè ſuch a haunt,
She paſſid them of Ipre, and of Gaunt.
In all the Pariſh wife ne was there none,
That to the offryng ſhould before her gone,
And if there did, certaine ſo wroth was ſhe,
That ſhe was outin of all charite.
Her coverchеifes were large and fine of ground,
I durſt to ſwere that thei weyid thre pound,
That on a Sonday were upon her hedde;
Her hoſin werin of fine Scarlet redde,
Full ſtrait yſtrainid, and her ſhoos full new;
Bold was her face, and fayr and red her hew:
She was a worthy woman all her live,
Husbandes at the Chirche dore had ſhe had five,
Withoutin other companie in youth,
But thereof nedith not to ſpeke as nouth.
Thries haddè ſhe ben at Jeruſalem,
She had paſſid many a ſtraungè ſtreme,
At Rome had ſhe ben, and als at Boloine,
In Gallice, at Seint Jame, and at Coloine;
She couth much talk of wandring by the way;
Gap-tothid was ſhe, ſoothly for to ſay:
Upon an Ambler eſily ſhe ſatte,
All wimplid well, and on her hed an hatte
As brode as is a bokeler or a Targe;
A foot-mantill about her hippis large,
And on her feet a paire of Spurris ſharpe.
In felawſhip wele couth ſhe laugh and carpe,
Of remedies of love ſhe knew perchaunce,
For ſhe couth of that art the oldè daunce.

The Parſone.

A gode Man there was of Religioun,
And he was a pore Parſone of a Toune:
But riche he was of holy thought and werke,
He was als a lernid Man, and a Clerk,
That Chriſt'is goſpell trewly woldè preche,
His Pariſh'ners devoutly wolde he teche.
Benigne he was, and wonder diligent,
And in Adverſitè full pacient:
And ſoch one he was provid oftè ſithes.
Full loth were him to curſin for his tithes,
But rather wolde he gevin out of dout,
Unto his pore Pariſh'ners all about,
Both of his offryng and of his ſubſtaunce;
He couth in lityl thing have ſuffiſaunce.
Wide was his pariſh, and houſis aſonder,
But he ne left, neither for raine, ne thonder,
In Sikeneſs, ne in miſchief to viſite
The ferthiſt in his pariſh, much or lite,
Upon his fete, and in his hand a ſtaffe;
This gode enſample to his ſhepe he yaffe,
That firſt he wrought, and afterward he taught;
Out of the Goſpell he the wordis caught,
And this figure he addid eke therto,
That if gold ruſtid, what ſhould iron do?
For yef a Prieſt be foule, on whome we truſt,
No wonder is it a lewde man to ruſt:
And ſhame it is (but that a Prieſt take kepe)
To ſee a ſhittin Shepherd and clene Shepe.
Well ought a Prieſt enſample for to yeve,
By his own clenеſſe how his Shepe ſhould live.
He ſettè not his Benefice to hire,
And let his Shepe acomber in the mire;
And ren to London, unto Seintè Powles,
To ſekin him a chauntèrie for Soules;
Or with a broðerhede to ben withhold:
But dwell'd at home, and keptè well his fold,
So that the wolf ne made 'hem not miſcary,
He was a ſhepherd, not a mercenary.
And though he holy were and vertuous,
He was not to ſinfull men diſpitous.
Ne of his ſpechè daungerous, ne digne,
But in his teching diſcrete and benigne,
To drawin folk to hevin bi faireneſſe,
Bi gode enſample, this was his beſneſſe.
But if were any perſon obſtinate,
Whether he were of high or low eſtate,
Him woulden he ſnibb ſharpely for the nonis:
A better Prieſt I trowe no where none is.
He waitid after no pomp ne reve'rence,
Ne makid him no ſpicid Conſcience,
But Chriſt'is lore and his Apoſtles twelve
He taught, but firſt he followed himſelve.

The Ploughman.

With him there was a Ploughman his broðer,
That had lad of dong many a fother;
And a trewe Swinker, and a gode was he,
Living in pece and perfite charite.
God lov'd he beſt with all his wholè herte,
At allè timis, though him gained or ſmerte;
And then his neighbouris right as himſelve;
And he would threſh, and thereto dike and delve,
For Chriſt'is ſake, for every porè wight,
Withoutin hire, if it lay in his might.
His tithis payid he full faire and well,
Both of his proper ſwink, and his cattell:
In a Tabbarde he rode upon a Mare.
There was alſo a Reve, and a Millare,
A Sompnour, and a Pardoner alſo,
A Manciple', and my ſelf, ther was no mo.

The Millare.

The Millare was a ſtout Carle for the nones,
Full bigge he was of braune and eke of bones,
That prov'd he wele, for o're all there he cam
At wraſtling he would have away the Ram.
He was ſhort ſhulder'd, and a thickè gnarr,
There n'as no dore but he would have the barr,
Or breke it at a renning with his hedde;
His berde as anie Sow or Fox was redde,
And thereto brode as though it were a Spade:
Upon the Coppe right of his noſe he hade
A wert, and thereon ſtode a tuffte of heeres,
Red as the briſtelles of a Sow'is eres;
His noſtrilles alſo black werin and wide,
A Swerde and bokeler bare he by his ſide;
His mouth as wide was as a grete forneis,
He was a jangler and a Golierdeis,
And that was moſt of Sinne and harlotreis;
Wele couth he ſtelè corne, and tollè thrys,
And yet he had a thombe of gold pardè.
A white Cote, and a blew hode werid he;
A Baggè pipe well couth he blow and ſowne,
And therewithall brought he us out of towne.

The Manciple.

A Manciple there was of the Temple,
Of which all Catours might take enſample,
For to ben wiſe in buying of Vitaile;
For whether he payid or toke by taile,
Algate he waitid ſo in his aſhate,
That he was ay before in gode eſtate.
Now is not that of God a full faire grace,
That ſuch a lewdè Mann'is wit ſhall pace
The wiſdome of a hepe of lernid Men?
Of Maiſters had he mo than thryis ten,

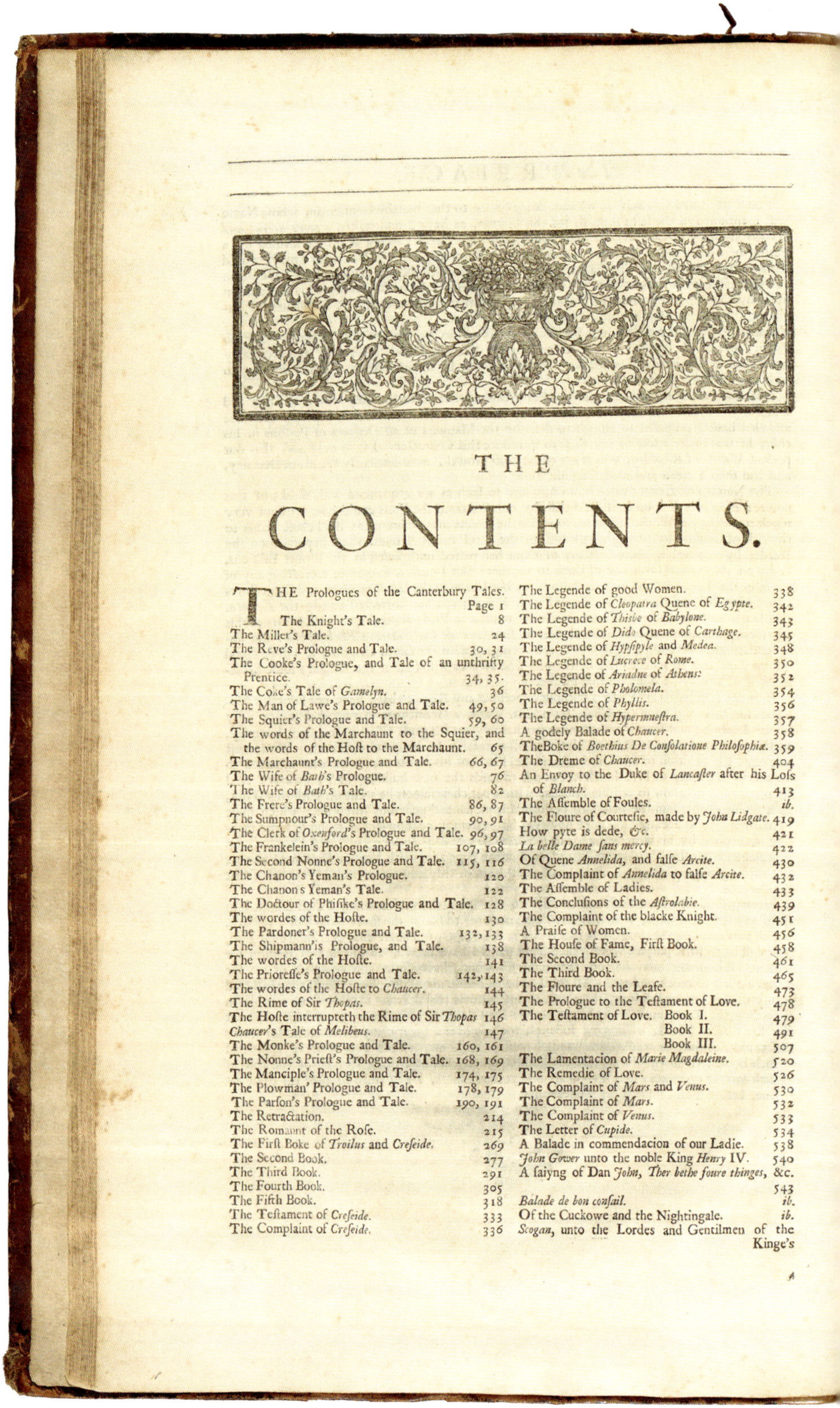

THE

CONTENTS.

A

3.7
The 'Contents' of Urry's Chaucer reveals how many non-Chaucerian items he packed into his text, including texts such as *Jack Upland* and the later version of 'The Plowman's Tale' (both texts that appealed to a Protestant version of Chaucer), as well as Thomas Usk's long, three-volume prose *Testament of Love*, and the fifteenth-century *Canterbury Interlude*. The title page also includes an image that should have been placed elsewhere in the text. Oxford, Bodleian Library, Douce C subt. 252.

N. B. The follownig Cut ſhould have been placed before the Rhime of Sir *Thopaz*.

line read like a pentameter (FIGURE 3.6). Half a century later, Tyrwhitt described how 'The strange licence, in which Mr. Urry appears to have indulged himself, of lengthening and shortening Chaucer's words according to his own fancy, and of even adding words of his own, without giving his readers the least notice, has made the text of Chaucer in his Edition by far the worst that was ever published.' This reflects a larger inconsistency in the editing of Chaucer, which has been done so haphazardly by his predecessors that Tyrwhitt 'has proceeded as if his author had never been published before'.[21]

Other problems facing the Chaucer editor can be seen in the contents of Urry's edition: a definitive set of works was not agreed upon; instead, various poems were connected to *The Canterbury Tales* in some way or were from (roughly) the same era. Urry includes all such pieces, including 'La Belle Dame Sans Mercy' (a translation by Richard Roos) and 'The Complaint of the Black Knight' (by John Lydgate) (FIGURE 3.7). Half of his contents are of doubtful authenticity, or known to be by someone else, and later editors would strip them away, or consign them to apocrypha: Tyrwhitt does not include Urry's additional *Tales* found in some manuscripts, 'The Cook's Tale of Gamelyn', 'The Merchant's Second Tale' and 'The Adventure of the Pardoner and Tapster at the Inn at Canterbury'; 'Three Tales are added which were never before Printed', as Urry's subtitle has it (though it does not say who wrote them, of course).

Tyrwhitt's significance is in trying to establish textual and linguistic principles for understanding Chaucer, and an ordered canon, as well as reducing the misinformation that had entered into biographical accounts. He 'was not disposed, either to repeat the comments and inventions, by which former biographers have endeavoured to supply the deficiency of facts'.[22] The academic seriousness of Tyrwhitt's edition reflects the post-mid-century enthusiasm for the rediscovery of older 'Gothic' and medieval literature, seen in works such as Thomas Warton's groundbreaking *History of English Poetry* (1774–81), and the contemporary controversy over the authenticity of Thomas Chatterton's medieval forgeries (in which Tyrwhitt was also a major participant).[23] By the end of the eighteenth century, there are different ideas of Chaucer, from the scholarly to the more mainstream: far more people in this period read the versions and adaptations by Dryden, Pope and others than the original poems. The general and specific influence of Chaucer abided, but it was more complicated than any simple narrative of Chaucer being 'modernized' or 'translated' can allow. To adapt Dryden's famous phrase, here was God's plenty, but it came in many different forms, and people did not always know quite what to do with it.

HERE BEGINNETH THE TALES OF CANTERBURY AND FIRST THE PROLOGUE THEREOF

WHAN THAT Aprille with his shoures soote
The droghte of March hath perced to the roote,
And bathed every veyne in swich licour,
Of which vertu engendred is the flour;
Whan Zephirus eek with his swete breeth
Inspired hath in every holt and heeth
The tendre croppes, and the yonge sonne
Hath in the Ram his halfe cours yronne,
And smale foweles maken melodye,
That slepen al the nyght with open eye,
So priketh hem nature in hir corages;
Thanne longen folk to goon on pilgrimages,
And palmeres for to seken straunge strondes,
To ferne halwes, kowthe in sondry londes;
And specially, from every shires ende
Of Engelond, to Caunterbury they wende,
The hooly blisful martir for to seke,
That hem hath holpen whan that they were seeke.

BIFIL that in that seson on a day,
In Southwerk at the Tabard as I lay,
Redy to wenden on my pilgrymage
To Caunterbury with ful devout corage,
At nyght were come into that hostelrye
Wel nyne and twenty in a compaignye,
Of sondry folk, by aventure yfalle
In felaweshipe, and pilgrimes were they alle,
That toward Caunterbury wolden ryde.

4

EMPIRE, EDUCATION AND ENGLISHNESS: DOMESTICATING CHAUCER

David Matthews

I want to begin this chapter by imagining a well-off, bookish household in a smart suburb of London in the year 1896. In a book-lined study the man of the house is reverently examining a large volume in which the title, *The Works of Geoffrey Chaucer now newly imprinted*, is surrounded by an elaborate border (FIGURE 4.1). On the facing page there is an elegant depiction of a tall man in a gown standing in an enclosed garden. This is the Kelmscott Chaucer, just out from the press of the designer and artist William Morris with illustrations by Edward Burne-Jones.[1] Morris and Burne-Jones are old friends, both devoted to the Middle Ages and especially keen on Chaucer; when Morris married in 1859 he was given a cabinet painted by Burne-Jones with illustrations of Chaucer's 'Prioress's Tale' (FIGURE 4.2). (The cabinet stood in the bedroom of the Morrises' first home; what Jane Morris made of Chaucer's somewhat grim antisemitic tale is unrecorded.)

The man is obviously a collector, as on the shelves in this study there are other Chaucer editions: *The Complete Works of Geoffrey Chaucer* in six volumes edited by Walter W. Skeat (1894), for example, along with the uniform volumes of the Chaucer Society. These have been appearing since 1868 and among them are the serial volumes of another Chaucer edition. Loosely known as the 'Six-Text Edition', this work is by the Society's

4.1
This stunningly decorated page, the opening of William Morris's Kelmscott Chaucer (1896), exemplifies Morris's Arts and Crafts aesthetic. The decorated page and elaborate 'W' at the beginning of *The Canterbury Tales* are reminiscent of medieval manuscripts. The text is illustrated with an image of the isolated poet, in a rural landscape, holding a book. Oxford, Bodleian Library, Kelmscott Press b.1, fol. 10r.

founder, Frederick Furnivall himself, and it prints six different manuscript texts of the *Tales* in parallel columns.[2] In it, Furnivall brought to prominence the two earliest manuscripts of the *Tales*, the Hengwrt and Ellesmere manuscripts, which were then largely unknown but have formed the basis of every Chaucer edition since.

The man has a son in whom he has instilled his love of Chaucer; we will come to him in due course. Elsewhere in the same house his adolescent daughter (we might imagine) is contemplating a book entitled *The Riches of Chaucer*, the full title of which claims that 'impurities have been expunged' and 'obsolete terms explained'.[3] In 1896 the fourth edition of this work had just appeared. Its editor, a man named Charles Cowden Clarke, explains that he has left out anything of what he calls 'ill-favoured complexion' because this book is aimed at 'those ornaments of this civilised age … the ingenuous, intelligent, well-informed, and artless young women of England'[4] (FIGURE 4.3). If this particular young woman decides she is not insulted by this, and persists with her reading, she will find a text that is halfway between Chaucer's Middle English and modern spelling, with accents added to help her pronounce it. The 'General Prologue' of *The Canterbury Tales*, for example, begins: 'WHENNÉ that April, with his showrés sote, / The drouth of March hath piercéd to the rote…' At the bottom of the page both 'sote' (sweet) and 'rote' (root) are explained in footnotes, though not 'drouth' (drought).

The feminine emphasis Clarke highlights is explicit throughout the text in various ways. Illustrations of female figures are quite striking, as for example an image of Griselda, the submissive wife of 'The Clerk's Tale'. While both the marquis Walter, her future husband, and her father, look like

4.2
Detail from 'The Prioress's Tale' cabinet, gifted by Edward Burne-Jones to William and Jane Morris for their wedding in 1859. The shield encloses the dedication, from 'EBJ to WM' against a background of beautiful flowers, arguably at odds with the violent and antisemitic topic of the illustrations on the front of the cabinet. Ashmolean Museum, University of Oxford, WA1939.2.

EBJ
to
WM

stereotypes of medieval figures, Griselda herself could have stepped from the pages of a novel by Dickens. There are other things that Clarke intends his female reader *not* to notice. At the beginning of 'The Wife of Bath's Tale' in Chaucer's original, a knight rapes a maiden, stealing, as the Middle English has it, her 'maidenheed'. But in Clarke's version the reader will find only that the young woman has been 'misuséd'.[5]

Finally we can imagine a nursery where the mother in the household sits with the youngest child, a small boy, leafing through a copy of *Chaucer for Children: A Golden Key*, by Mrs H.R. Haweis. The boy's mother quickly sees that Mrs Haweis thinks it is natural that children should know something of Chaucer, who was the founder of the English language. She is reassured to read that Haweis also believes that Chaucer is 'a thoroughly religious poet' and that 'all his merriest stories hav[e] a fair moral'. His works, Haweis concludes, 'breathe a genuine faith in God, and a passionate sense of the beauty and harmony of the divine work.'[6]

And so she turns to the text of Chaucer, and reads:

Whan that Aprilla with his shōōres sohta
The drŏŏkht of March hath pairsed to the rohta,
And bahthed ev'ry vīn in sweech licōōr,
Of which vairtú enjendrèd is the flōōr...[7]

(When April with its sweet showers has pierced the drought of March to the root, and bathed every [plant's] vein with such liquor, by the power of which flowers are engendered...)

This is a little daunting and perhaps she thinks about whether she ought to go back to a battered copy of a much older book she

4.3
Title pages from Charles Cowden Clarke's *The Riches of Chaucer*, a popular nineteenth-century version of Chaucer, aimed especially at young women, and promising a version of the text in which, 'his impurities have been expunged'. Oxford, Bodleian Library, (OC) 280 j.263.

Engraved by W. H. Mote.

GEOFFREY CHAUCER.

Published by Lockwood & Co. 7, Stationers' Hall Court.

THE

RICHES OF CHAUCER:

IN WHICH

HIS IMPURITIES HAVE BEEN EXPUNGED;
HIS SPELLING MODERNISED; HIS RHYTHM ACCENTUATED;
AND HIS OBSOLETE TERMS EXPLAINED:

ALSO HAVE BEEN ADDED

A FEW EXPLANATORY NOTES

AND A

New Memoir of the Poet.

BY

CHARLES COWDEN CLARKE,

AUTHOR OF
'TALES IN PROSE FROM CHAUCER,' 'SHAKESPEARE-CHARACTERS,'
'MOLIÈRE-CHARACTERS,' &c.

SECOND EDITION, CAREFULLY REVISED.

LONDON:
C. LOCKWOOD & CO., 7 STATIONERS'-HALL COURT.
1870.

has noticed on the shelf, entitled *Tales from Chaucer*. Another of Charles Cowden Clarke's modernizations, this one was first published back in 1833.[8] Perhaps this copy is left over from the childhood of the man of the house; if she has looked at it, the woman will have seen that rather than attempting to render Chaucer's verse directly, in this version Clarke offered prose retellings of *The Canterbury Tales*, no doubt influenced by the model of the very successful *Tales from Shakespeare* (1807) by Charles and Mary Lamb. But in 1833, *Tales from Chaucer* was probably ahead of its time. Chaucer, as we will shortly see, did not have anything like the status of Shakespeare then, and there was little else like this book until the 1870s, when there seems to have been more demand and several writers, including Clarke and, after his death in 1877, his widow Mary Clarke, helped put into circulation a whole new genre: retellings of Chaucer as children's literature.[9]

Reading Chaucer in the Nineteenth Century

The household I have imagined here, in which every conceivable Chaucer edition was being read from the infantile to the scholarly, is perhaps an improbable one. The Kelmscott Chaucer was an expensive luxury item which very few individuals would have owned. Conversely, while copies of the Chaucer Society's books (such as the *Six-Text Print*) were relatively inexpensive, they were specialist works that went only to the Society's subscribers. In 1896, around 200 subscriptions were taken out, about a quarter of them by libraries.

But such a household was not impossible. At the end of the Victorian period it was easier to read Chaucer than ever before. There were more editions, translations and modernizations of the poet's work than had ever existed. Although there was relatively little academic study of Chaucer at the time, the poet's work was promoted by a group of enthusiasts, some of them professional, many of them decidedly amateur. The kind of work being done on Chaucer was very wide-ranging, from highly specialized studies of phonology (how Chaucer's language was supposed to have sounded) to manuscript studies (which tried to discover the manuscript texts closest to what Chaucer actually wrote), to very general appreciations of such things as Chaucer's humour or his creation of character. And in fact organized academic study of Chaucer was about to begin: 1896 was also the year in which Oxford University appointed its first university lecturer in English Literature. Israel Gollancz would go on to become perhaps the most important man in English studies for the next two decades, and was among other things a tireless promoter of the works of Chaucer.

As we see in my imaginary household, Chaucer's texts existed in academic editions (such as those of Skeat and Furnivall), which were based on philological learning and were addressed to coteries of learned people, mostly (though not exclusively) male. But those texts also existed in much more domestically focused and often explicitly feminized versions, aimed at women and children. These expurgated versions of Chaucer for children and adolescents were in fact very common and must have been a typical feature of the libraries of the late Victorian and Edwardian middle classes. Hence, Chaucer occupied very different positions at the same time. On the one hand, he was regarded as a canonical English poet, the founding figure of English verse, who, as we shall see, was thought to be close to the heart of power. But on the other hand, Chaucer was seen as being an ideal domestic poet, one whose work was perfect for the intimacy between mothers and young sons (FIGURE 4.4).

PREFACE.

To the Mother.

A CHAUCER for Children may seem to some an impossible story-book, but it is one which I have been encouraged to put together by noticing how quickly my own little boy learned and understood fragments of early English poetry. I believe that if they had the chance, many other children would do the same.

I think that much of the construction and pronunciation of old English which seems stiff and obscure to grown up people, appears easy to children, whose crude language is in many ways its counterpart.

The narrative in early English poetry is almost always very simply and clearly expressed, with the same kind of repetition of facts and names which, as every mother knows, is what children most require in story-telling. The emphasis * which the final E gives to many words is another thing which helps to impress the sentences on the memory, the sense being often shorter than the sound.

It seems but natural that every English child should know something of one who left so deep an impression on his age, and on the English tongue, that he has been called by Occleve "the finder of our fair language." For in his day there was actually no *national* language, no *national* literature, English consisting of so many dialects, each having its own literature intelligible to comparatively few; and the Court and educated classes still adhering greatly to Norman-French for both speaking and writing. Chaucer, who wrote for the people, chose the best form of English, which was that spoken at

* I use the word 'emphasis' in the same sense as one might speak of a *crotchet* in music, to which you count two, being more emphatic than a *quaver*, to which you count one.

CHIEFLY FOR THE USE AND PLEASURE OF

MY LITTLE LIONEL,

FOR WHOM I FELT THE NEED OF SOME BOOK OF THE KIND,

I HAVE ARRANGED AND ILLUSTRATED THIS

CHAUCER STORY-BOOK.

This was a relatively new state of affairs at the end of the nineteenth century. At the beginning of the century things had been very different. Although an interest in medieval writing – especially medieval romance – had been steadily building since the 1760s and a new scholarly edition of *The Canterbury Tales* had appeared in 1775 (as discussed in the previous chapter), it is probably the case that Chaucer was more known *about* than actually known.[10] Few people could really read Middle English with any facility and, despite the new edition of 1775, many people believed that Chaucer's language was not only too difficult for the modern reader, but actually had something wrong with it by reason of age. When the minor poet William Lipscomb published a collection of translations of *The Canterbury Tales* in 1795, his rationale for translating was that 'the Father of English poetry' deserved his fame, but 'the language, in which he wrote, hath decayed from under him'.[11]

But as interest in the medieval past grew, there were others who promoted the reverse idea that Chaucer's language was not in fact so difficult. The political radical William Godwin published his *Life of Geoffrey Chaucer* in 1803 (FIGURE 4.5), saying there that Chaucer's language is *not* obscure and is hardly more difficult than that of Shakespeare. 'All that repels us in the language of Chaucer is merely superficial appearance and first impression', Godwin wrote, before suggesting (somewhat ambitiously) that a mere 'fortnight's application would be sufficient to make us feel ourselves perfectly at home with this patriarch of our poetry'.[12] The actual biographical detail in Godwin's book was frequently, as we now know, completely wrong. But his picture of a man who was not only the greatest poet of the day but also the intimate friend of the great men of the time (including the monarch) was influential for most of the nineteenth century.

4.4
The Preface in Mrs Haweis's *Chaucer For Children* is explicitly addressed 'to the mother', encouraging mothers to help to educate their young children about medieval literature and culture. Mrs Haweis adds that she made this book primarily for her own son, Lionel, whose image is included here. Such children's versions were an important part of Victorian medievalism. Oxford, Bodleian Library, Opie P 8, pp ix and v.

LIFE

OF

GEOFFREY CHAUCER,

THE EARLY ENGLISH POET:

INCLUDING

MEMOIRS OF HIS NEAR FRIEND AND KINSMAN,

JOHN OF GAUNT, DUKE OF LANCASTER:

WITH SKETCHES OF THE

MANNERS, OPINIONS, ARTS AND LITERATURE

OF ENGLAND

IN

THE FOURTEENTH CENTURY.

BY WILLIAM GODWIN.

Come like shadows; so depart!

SHAKESPEAR.

IN TWO VOLUMES.

VOL. I.

LONDON:

PRINTED BY T. DAVISON, WHITE-FRIARS;

FOR RICHARD PHILLIPS, No. 71, ST. PAUL's CHURCH-YARD.

1803.

In the early nineteenth century, it is important to note, the reach of such Chaucerian works as Lipscomb's and Godwin's would have been limited, extending chiefly to a small circle of scholarly men. There is no sign that a wider public was prepared to give the 'fortnight's application' that Godwin called for and certainly no question that Chaucer's tales might appear in the middle-class nursery. As I have suggested, Charles Cowden Clarke's first attempt at an expurgated version of Chaucer for children, his *Tales from Chaucer* in 1833, was not an obvious success. When another minor poet, R.H. Horne, presented his collection of Chaucer translations in 1841, he praised Clarke's work but noted that it had not gone down well with the public. Horne was probably not greatly exaggerating when he claimed that 'although he is one of the great poets for all time, [Chaucer's] works are comparatively unknown to the world. Even in his own country, only a very small class of his countrymen ever read his poems.' Like his eighteenth-century predecessors but unlike Godwin, Horne felt that the 'grand obstacle' to reading Chaucer was 'his obsolete dialect'.[13] The choice of the word 'dialect' here is interesting, suggesting as it does that Chaucer wrote in an untypical and non-standard provincial language. In fact his language was the direct ancestor of standard London English. But Horne's answer to the problem, as in the eighteenth century, was translation or modernization rather than the learning of that language.

Yet even as Horne offered his collection, attitudes to medieval writing were changing and shifting more towards Godwin's position. The 1840s saw an acceleration of interest in the medieval period in all its facets – an interest observable among a relatively large public – which would ultimately impel the far wider interest we see by 1896. The 1840s was the decade of major works by John Ruskin and Augustus Pugin, both influential figures in the great

4.5
At the beginning of the nineteenth century, the famous radical William Godwin – author of *An Enquiry Concerning Political Justice*, husband of Mary Wollstonecraft, and father of Mary Shelley – wrote an influential and imaginative biography of Chaucer. *Life of Geoffrey Chaucer, including memoirs of John of Gaunt, duke of Lancaster*, 1803. Oxford, Bodleian Library, Godw. 4° 12 (v.1).

spread of neo-Gothic building. It was when the Pre-Raphaelite Brotherhood was founded, which had a broad and medievalizing influence on art. Alfred Tennyson published his poem *Morte d'Arthur* in 1842 (FIGURE 4.6) and Lady Charlotte Guest completed her translation of the Welsh *Mabinogion* in 1849, accelerating the intense interest in King Arthur that flourished for the rest of the century. Scholarly study of Middle English – though still a minority pursuit – also expanded in the 1840s.

Among the many consequences was the gradual rise of interest in Chaucer in the second half of the nineteenth century and the beginning of modern scholarly publication. The founding of the Chaucer Society in 1868 and the appearance of the *Six-Text Print* were key moments. This was the basis on which Skeat was able to edit his 1894 complete works, which stood as the authoritative edition of Chaucer for several decades.

Such are the broad outlines of the progress by which Chaucer became better known, better understood and more commonly read in the language in which he wrote rather than translation. In what follows I will consider the ways in which Chaucer's standing altered. In what ways did he change from being essentially a poet's poet as he was at the end of the eighteenth century – read by and translated by poets, for other poets – to being a treasured national icon, as he was at the end of the nineteenth? How, in the course of the nineteenth century, did the appreciation of Chaucer grow alongside new understandings of empire, Englishness and education so that he became a more fully national poet? Why, conversely, was he also adopted in the domestic sphere? Why was it thought essential that he should be placed at the heart of literary education?

Part of the answer lies precisely in the increasing sense of the medieval past which, as I have suggested, developed

4.6
An image from Alfred Tennyson's *Morte D'Arthur* (1842). Tennyson was influenced by the medieval writer Sir Thomas Malory in writing this and a number of other poems. The striking Pre-Raphaelite image is by Albert Sangorski (1912). Oxford, Bodleian Library, Johnson d.1163, p. 24.

after the 1840s. Another part of the answer lies in Britain's consolidation as a global power in the same period, one which sought to bolster that position through the promotion of a specific cultural identity. Since the sixteenth-century Reformation, the Middle Ages had been under suspicion in Britain because of the period's Catholic character. But as fears of Catholicism gradually subsided (at least at an official level, as the 1829 Act which allowed Catholics to sit in Parliament suggests), the value of the Middle Ages was increasingly recognized by the left, right and centre of politics. For socialists and their predecessors in the working-class Chartist movement of the 1830s and 1840s, the Middle Ages could offer a time of social justice: the ninth-century King Alfred was seen by many as an inspiring instance of what monarchy should be; alternatively, the leader of the 1381 revolt, Wat Tyler, was taken as a model for rebellion in a just cause. Conversely for conservatives, the later Middle Ages was a time when everyone knew their place and a nobility of blood ruled wisely over the peasantry. In a liberal vision, the signing of Magna Carta and the establishment of Parliament in the thirteenth century not only guaranteed essential English liberties but made England into an example to the parts of the world over which it ruled.

Thomas Babington Macaulay wrote in his influential *History of England* (which first appeared in 1848) that the English constitution created in the late Middle Ages 'deserves to be regarded as the best under which any great society has ever yet existed during many ages'.[14] Improbable as it now seems, it was the fourteenth century even more than the thirteenth to which Victorians frequently had recourse as a glowing example. Although it was a century of famine, pandemic, endless and generally fruitless warfare and increasing peasant unrest,

Victorians could focus on the literary efflorescence of the last third of the century and the emergence of English as the chief literary language. They admired the values of chivalry (without necessarily looking too closely at some of the consequences of chivalry in the Hundred Years War). For Macaulay, it was in the fourteenth century that 'Every yeoman from Kent to Northumberland valued himself as one of a race born for victory and dominion.' And, although he would concede the injustice of the pursuit of the Hundred Years War, Macaulay stated that 'The greatest victories recorded in the history of the middle ages were gained at this time', saying that they were victories 'of which a nation may justly be proud; for they are to be attributed to the moral superiority of the victors'.[15]

In such a view the fourteenth century staged a version of English domination which offered a precursor to the nineteenth-century rise of Britain to imperial status. The reputation of Edward III and his fifty-year reign was high in the Victorian period, as he was thought to have been a strong and just king. He was also a good model for any ruler with imperial ambitions: he inherited Wales; he brought Scotland to heel; he enforced what he believed were England's rights over large parts of France. At a time when industrialism was transforming the face of England in a way not seen in centuries, and when a rapidly expanding working class was transforming the cities, the England over which Edward had ruled formed an immensely attractive image: green and pastoral at home, warlike and imperial abroad.

Chaucer clearly formed part of this picture of English domination and superiority. He was acclaimed as having initiated the long eminence of the English language and its literature. While Edward was extending England's dominion over other lands, Chaucer was beginning to provide appropriate

4.7
Ford Madox Brown's detailed and fascinating painting, first exhibited in 1851, shows 'Chaucer at the Court of Edward III', in which Chaucer reads from 'The Man of Law's Tale' to the ageing king and his courtiers. This kind of art promoted the (incorrect) belief that Chaucer was a prominent court poet. Ashmolean Museum, University of Oxford, WA1920.3.

COLORAVIT
IN
1853

literary monuments; he could be for English literature what Dante was to Italian. Victorians tended to put king and poet side by side, accepting, as had been said since the sixteenth century, that Chaucer was a *court* poet who was the intimate of the kings and nobles for whom he was supposed to have written. William Godwin might have been politically a radical, but he perpetuated a very conservative vision of Chaucer when he suggested that King Edward III was Chaucer's 'patron and personal friend'. This king, Godwin postulated on very little evidence, kept Chaucer close, 'desiring to relieve the cares of empire by his conversation' and 'to have his hours of relaxation enlivened by the sallies of the poet, and probably to be the first hearer of his productions'.[16] We now know all of this to be incorrect (apart from anything else, Chaucer had written relatively little by the time of Edward's death in 1377). But in the nineteenth century the idea of Chaucer as the essential court poet was simply accepted. We see this powerfully (but almost certainly erroneously) illustrated in a major painting by Ford Madox Brown, first exhibited in 1851, *Chaucer at the Court of Edward III*, in which Chaucer reads from 'The Man of Law's Tale' to the ageing king and his courtiers (FIGURE 4.7).

This vision created a large-scale, sweeping reason for the reading of Chaucer. He was in a way a poet of empire. Illustrating this, we can imagine for a moment the older son in the fictional household with which I began, unseen in my earlier sketch because he was away at school. In a future life, such a person might go out into the world, taking a role in the colonial service or perhaps in education. As he comes to maturity in the early twentieth century (and steeped in his father's Chaucerian obsession) he will find a number of useful modernized versions of Chaucer such as Arthur Burrell's *Chaucer's Canterbury Tales for the Modern Reader*, produced for the Everyman's Library series in 1908.[17] The Everyman series, established in 1906, exploited a market for cheap popular classics; it became 'the basis of the colonial library', as Michelle Warren notes in her account of Jean Rhys's knowledge of Chaucer, probably gained through Burrell's book.[18] Through such works, exported to colonies and former colonies and used in education, colonial subjects learned about Chaucer. And even as they threw off their imperial ties, emergent postcolonial nations could still enthusiastically espouse the imperial power's medieval culture. In the fourth decade of Australia's independent existence, for example, one influential journalist argued that the Australian writer in the 1930s was in a similar position to Chaucer or John Wyclif in the late fourteenth century: like them, the Australian writer was trying to forge a new vernacular. As the journalist put it, 'we are in our Chaucerian phase'.[19] While post-imperial independence usually involved the repudiation of many aspects of the imperial presence, it often, as in this example, made a special exception for the English Middle Ages.

Didactic Chaucer

The older son in the Chaucer-reading household would have been enabled by both the scholarly and the more popularly oriented work on Chaucer in the 1890s to see Chaucer as an English national treasure whose work ought to form the basis of literary education while also being particularly well suited for export. The assumption of Chaucer's utility in this role was underpinned by the humanist reasoning that reading the author would be morally improving. In his 1833 *Tales from Chaucer*, Charles Cowden Clarke expressed this eloquently when he said that his 'object' in offering *The Canterbury Tales* in simple prose versions for children was so that they 'might become wise and good, by the example of the sweet and kind creatures you will find described in them…'[20] Like Godwin, whose *Life of Chaucer* he admired and drew on, Clarke was a political radical. But, as with Godwin, this did not produce a radical Chaucer. Rather, the point of reading Chaucer was that it would help form young minds, prompting them not to radical thoughts, but to conventionally moral ones.

As my imaginary Chaucer-reading household suggests, there were certainly different Chaucers for different people. My notional head of the household would have wanted to have kept them separate. He might have been happy for his daughter to read the expurgated *Riches of Chaucer* but he probably would not have wanted her to read his new Kelmscott Chaucer. Edward Burne-Jones never needed much encouragement to depict attractive young female bodies, and they appear in abundance, clothed and unclothed, in the Kelmscott Chaucer's pages. Perhaps more to the point, this and the scholarly editions in his study would allow anyone who could penetrate the Middle English language to read the explicit sexuality of Chaucer's fabliaux and such things as the rape of a virgin, already mentioned, in 'The Wife of Bath's Tale' by a Chaucer character who was clearly not 'sweet and kind'. At the time, even some of the most dedicated Chaucer scholars found Chaucer's treatment of sexuality unacceptable. Walter Skeat, the greatest Chaucer scholar of the age (but also originally a clergyman), thought such fabliau tales as those of the Miller, Reeve, Shipman and Merchant 'can hardly be defended'. He believed (probably correctly) they had all been written after the death of Chaucer's wife and he assumed that their 'coarseness' could be attributed to the loss of her supposedly softening influence.[21]

But despite the different versions of Chaucer, there were many shared assumptions among them, linking them quite closely. The people I have mentioned – Clarke, Morris, Skeat, Furnivall, Haweis – were very different from one another. But, apart from Clarke (who had left England years before his death in 1877), they all knew each other, in some cases very well. They all agreed that Chaucer was the Father of English Poetry. They all thought that every English man, woman and child should be reading his works. They regarded him as having lived in a cleaner, simpler and purer time: Mary Haweis notes that London was smaller and 'oh, so much prettier!'[22] (She forgets, or does not think it wise to tell her child readers, that when Chaucer was a young boy that same London had been ravaged by the worst pandemic in history.) They believed (quite reasonably) that Chaucer was devoutly religious. And if he was, regrettably, Catholic (unlike most of his British readers in 1896), that is only because at the time everyone was. In another of her works Haweis (herself married to a Church of England clergyman) states her belief that in 'The Parson's Tale' Chaucer expresses his 'true Protestant feeling' and this has only been obscured by the tampering of 'some orthodox Catholic scribe'. Chaucer, she says, promoted 'the new religious views' though 'long before Luther sounded the note of victory'.[23] Haweis also thought Chaucer was 'instinctively what we should now call an advanced Radical' and in the same work said he 'was a Liberal in religion as (at heart) in politics'.[24] Extending Chaucer's appeal to the modern Englishman, Frederick Furnivall meanwhile said (on very little evidence) that Chaucer was 'plucky' at football, hockey and other games.[25]

This, then, was a Chaucer who was both *different* and the same. He lived in a very different world, a simpler and in some ways a better one (untainted by a century and more of industrialism and class unrest, for example). Yet he was the same as any enlightened gentleman or -woman of the late nineteenth century, at a time when the era of Gladstonian Liberalism had only just come to an end. Like the Liberal of the 1890s, he had sensible, moderate views on a range of things. He was regarded as being central to English literature and consequently English literary study. Chaucer was seen as having kickstarted English poetry and as having done a great deal to extend the English language as well. He was the kind of author you would want to give to your children (after certain adjustments). Chaucer might have been medieval, but he would have been a Protestant if that had been possible, and a Liberal as well. Chaucer was wise; he was a man of the world. He was the kind of poet the English man or woman could be proud of.

There was an older English literature than that of Chaucer, the Old English literature of which *Beowulf* is the best-known example. But this was often treated as a quite separate thing from late medieval writing such as Chaucer's, and as needing a different linguistic training. Hence Chaucer's works took a central place in English literary education in universities, as this was formalized in the early years of the twentieth century.[26]

The End of Victorian Medievalism

When he produced the Kelmscott Chaucer, William Morris was already in poor health, and died within a few months of its appearance in October 1896. Burne-Jones, who had illustrated it, was dead two years later. The kind of medievalism they represented – romantic, Gothic in the most positive sense, elaborately ornamented, prone to focus on chivalry more than violence – had reached, and passed, its zenith. Mary Haweis also died in 1898. Frederick Furnivall died in 1910 and Walter Skeat two years after that. While Skeat was somewhat less given to the romanticism of Morris, Burne-Jones and Furnivall, he too shared a vision of Chaucer's centrality and a passion for promoting Chaucer among all kinds of readers.

These men, and one woman, were all of a generation who understood Chaucer through Godwin's ideas of the poet's political centrality (though Skeat was very cautious about Chaucerian biography). Their ideas about the Middle Ages were coloured by romanticism and their nearness to Tennyson's vision of a fantasy medieval past in his Arthurian poetry. We now know vastly more than they did about Chaucer and his context; we know that there were other poets around him and we are less likely to romanticize that context. It is easy to obtain Chaucer's works today, whether in printed form or on the Internet. And yet it could be said that the reading of Chaucer has contracted since the days of Morris, Furnivall and the rest. Given the very limited way in which Chaucer is taught in schools, it is today chiefly university students of English and those who teach them who read Chaucer. We are in fact much further away from a household, real or imagined, in which Chaucer is being read, to different purposes, by different people in different rooms.

simũ recolam᷒ q̃ i geitricis digtate
obtinuit i uirgialé pudicitiam n

amu
An
lis
is c
con
ne
lesi
gra
mu
ipt
ut

5

WOMEN READING CHAUCER

Marion Turner

Medieval manuscripts depict women reading (FIGURE 5.1). In particular, the idea of St Anne teaching the Virgin to read was a popular image (FIGURE 5.2), and Mary was often portrayed as reading a book at the Annunciation. Religious women such as Julian of Norwich or the nuns of Syon Abbey often had easier access to libraries, but wealthy secular medieval women also read books, gave them to each other and talked about them. Chaucer explicitly wrote about women reading his texts. In the *Prologue to The Legend of Good Women*, for instance, the author's avatar is told to give the poem to the queen, at Eltham or at Sheen (F version, lines 496–497) (FIGURE 5.3). The queen here is Anne of Bohemia, wife of Richard II, and when Chaucer rewrote this *Prologue* after her death he removed this reference. The queen may not have actually read the poem, but Chaucer had aspirations for his poems to be read in mixed-gender courtly circles. In *Troilus and Criseyde* the narrator addresses a group of female readers, warning them against unfaithful men (Book V, lines 1779–1785). He also, earlier in the poem, depicts a scene of women reading together which reflects medieval reading experiences (Book II, lines 81–84). These are privileged women, who sit together in a 'paved parlour' (line 82), reading a romance in a book decorated with red ink (lines 100, 103, 104), and discussing it. Chaucer was very familiar with sophisticated

5.1
In a fifteenth-century Italian manuscript, now held in the Bodleian, St Anne reads avidly in bed after giving birth, while another woman, probably a serving maid, bathes her baby – the Virgin Mary – in the foreground. Oxford, Bodleian Library, MS. Canon. Liturg. 388, fol. 371v.

households such as the royal court, or the households of John of Gaunt (where his wife worked) or of Elizabeth de Burgh (his own first employer, wife of Lionel of Antwerp), places where literate, educated, multilingual women led cultured circles. Female patrons sponsored poets and owned books in Chaucer's world.

Gendered Reading

Influential readings of Chaucer's texts, however, have been overwhelmingly male from Chaucer's own time until well into the twentieth century (as has been obvious in the previous chapters of this book). And many such readings were not merely by men but were clearly *gendered* – motivated by particular attitudes towards men and women.

Chaucer imagines such readers in *The Canterbury Tales*, especially in the figure of Harry Bailly, the Host of the Tabard Inn. Harry sees tale-telling, and reading, as gendered, even sexualized, experiences. After he hears a story about Griselda, a woman who swears to obey her husband in everything, even in thought, and keeps this promise even though it means agreeing to the murder of her children, he says that he wishes his own wife had heard this 'gentil' tale ('The Clerk's Tale', lines 1212c–1212e). Similarly, after 'The Tale of Melibee' – a tale in which a woman, Prudence, recommends reconciliation and peacemaking to her husband – Harry again says that he wishes his wife had heard the tale, and then bemoans the power balance and violence of his own marriage in some detail ('The Prologue of the Monk's Tale', lines 1893–1894). In this same section he then turns to the Monk and, bizarrely, eulogizes his sexual power, saying that he should not have gone into religion because he could have been a 'tredefowel' (line 1945) – a professional rooster – fathering many

5.2
St Anne teaching the Virgin Mary (her daughter) to read was a popular and much-depicted scene in medieval art and literature, modelling a domestic ideal of female education and nurturing, and promoting devout female reading. Oxford, Bodleian Library, MS. Liturg. 401, fol. 30v.

children. He emphasizes that the Monk is a 'myghty man' (line 1951) and that he 'sholde have a wyf' (line 1953), and seems to link his purported ability to impregnate many women with an ability to tell stories. Indeed, instead of fathering 'ful many a creature' line (1948), as Harry says he could have, the Monk promises to tell many tales, selecting them from a hundred that he has in his cell (line 1972). Telling stories seems to be a replacement for having sex – but the Monk turns out to be impotent as he tells a series of sterile examples and has to be stopped.

Harry then turns to a more promising cleric – the Nun's Priest – and after his very successful tale Harry blesses his buttocks and testicles, tells him that he too should have been a 'trede-foul' ('The Epilogue to the Nun's Priest's Tale', lines 3448, 3451), and adds that seven times seventeen hens would not have been enough for him (lines 3453–3454). It is an odd way of saying that he liked the story, but very much in keeping with Harry's view of tale-telling as a masculine activity, best performed by alpha males.

Across time, many male readers have also treated Chaucer's text in gendered ways, from scribes who attacked the Wife of Bath, as discussed earlier in this book, to critics of the 1960s and 1970s who fell 'in love' with Criseyde.

Indeed, in the twentieth century scholarly work and editing were also often viewed as gendered activity. As well as being in love with Criseyde (and saying that 'almost every male reader' will also fall in love with her), the renowned academic E. Talbot Donaldson wrote at length about editing a text as akin to choosing a wife, comparing line forms in different manuscripts to different girls, and lamenting the horror when you realize you 'married the wrong girl' – that is, chose the wrong text for your edition.[1]

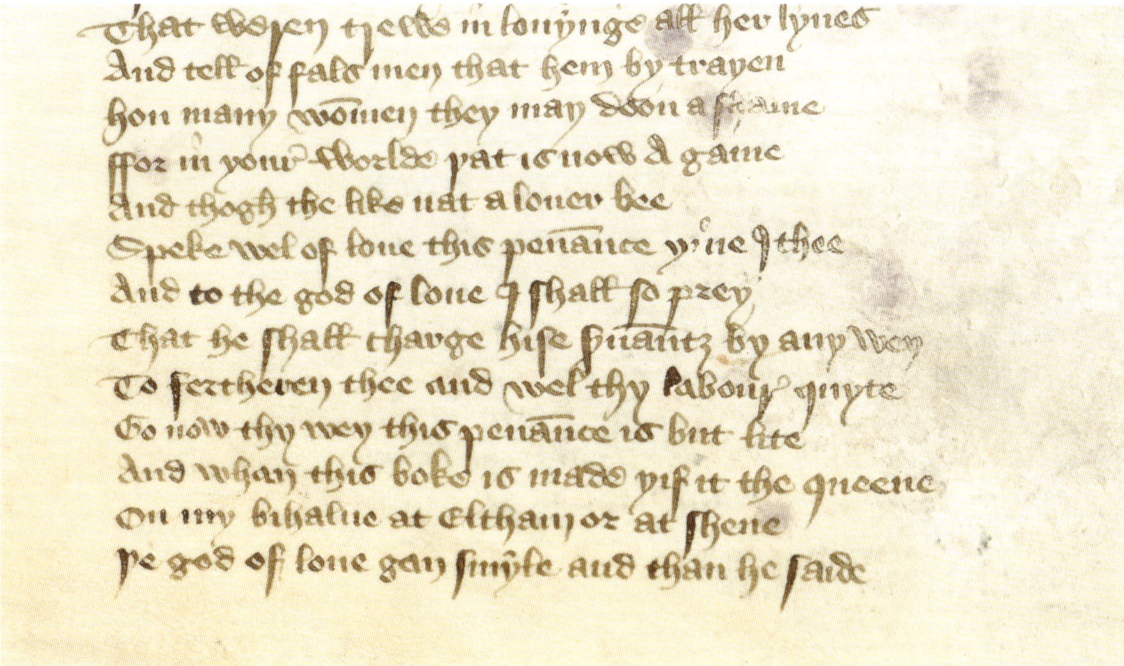

That weren trewe in lovynge all her lyves
And tell of false men that hem bytrayen
How many women they may doon a shame
For in your worlde that is now a game
And though the like nat a lover bee
Speke wel of love this penance yive I thee
And to the god of love I shall so prey
That he shall charge his servantz by any wey
To fortheren thee and wel thy labour quyte
Go now thy wey this penance is but lite
And whan this boke is made yif it the queene
On my bihalue at Eltham or at Shene
The god of love gan smyle and than he saide

5.3
In the early version of the *Prologue to the Legend of Good Women*, the Chaucer figure is exhorted by Alceste to give the book to 'the queen … at Eltham or at Shene'. These lines were removed in the later version, after Queen Anne of Bohemia's death in 1394. Whether or not Anne read the text, these lines demonstrate that Chaucer aspired to appeal to elite female readers. Oxford, Bodleian Library, MS. Tanner 346, 8r (detail).

One multi-volume scholarly edition of Chaucer was the joint work of a male and a female editor – John Manly and Edith Rickert. While Manly was emphatic in crediting Rickert as a full partner in the work, he also wrote in the 'Preface' that Rickert had 'the intuition of a woman with a woman's capacity for enormous drudgery'.[2] Much worse was to come, when the Medieval Academy awarded the prestigious Haskins Medal to Manly alone for his work on the edition. In the report of the committee, Manly is praised at length, with reference to his 'numerous skilled helpers'. The committee members add that Manly, with 'customary generosity', gave 'large credit' to his helpers, adding that Rickert was really even more than a helper; she was a 'collaborator'.[3] The committee refused to recognize her as an equal partner in the endeavour, however. Their award of the medal to Manly alone is somewhat reminiscent of, for instance, the Nobel Committee's attempt to award a prize to Pierre Curie alone – he refused, unless Marie was equally credited. Female scholars in all fields have struggled for recognition, very often being seen as helpers, supporters or secretaries when in fact they were playing a full intellectual part in the work.

Across time, the idea of 'Father Chaucer' encouraged a patriarchal sense of what it meant to read his poetry. Many creative responses to Chaucer's texts actually promoted a far more obviously misogynist agenda than Chaucer's texts do. In the fifteenth century, for example, Robert Henryson wrote a sequel to *Troilus and Criseyde* in which Cresseid is thoroughly punished for her infidelity by catching leprosy (often a metaphor for a sexually transmitted disease) and becoming a prostitute (*The Testament of Cresseid*). Indeed, this text was incorporated into print editions of Chaucer's works as if it were part of *Troilus and Criseyde* itself (FIGURE 5.4). In the eighteenth century, John Gay's revised play, *The Wife of Bath* (1730), pointedly excludes the Wife from a happy ending – all the other characters pair off but she remains alone – while the twentieth-century play *The Canterbury Pilgrims*, by Percy MacKaye, presents the Wife as scheming to marry Chaucer himself, but being forced to marry the vulgar, low-class Miller through the machinations of an alliance of king, lawyers, aristocrats and the poet.

5.4
Robert Henryson's fifteenth-century *Testament of Cresseid* – a sequel to *Troilus and Criseyde* in which a diseased Criseyde becomes a prostitute – often immediately followed *Troilus* in printed editions, implying that it was part of Chaucer's poem. *The workes of our ancient … poet Geffrey Chaucer. [Followed by] The storie of Thebes*, by I. Lidgate, 1602. Oxford, Bodleian Library, A 2.5 Art.Seld., fol. 182r.

However, despite the weight of overtly gendered readings of Chaucer, women have always read and responded to his texts in diverse ways, and not always in ways that we might expect. For the rest of this chapter, I'm going to take a case study – 'The Clerk's Tale' in the nineteenth century – in order to explore three different women's responses to that Tale.[4] Their responses

Thou one, two, and three, eterne on liue,
That raignest aie in thre, two, and one,
Uncircumscript, and all maist circumscriue,
Us from visible and inuisible fone
Defend, and to thy mercy euerichone,
So make vs Jesus to thy mercy digne,
For loue of maide, and mother thine benigne.

¶ Thus endeth the fifth booke, and laste of Troilus: and here foloweth the pitifull and dolorous Testament of faire Creseide.

The Testament of Creseide.

A Doly season till a carefull
dite,
Should corespond, and be
equiuolent,
Right so it was when I
began to write
This tragedy, the weder
right feruent,
When Aries in middes of the Lent,
Showres of haile can fro the North discend,
That scantly fro the cold I might me defend.

Yet neuerthelesse within mine orature
I stode, when Titan had his beames bright
Withdrawen doun, and syled vnder cure,
And faire Uenus the beaute of the night,
Upraise, and sette vnto the West ful right,
Her golden face in oppositioun,
Of God Phebus directe discending doun.

Throughout y glasse her beams brast so faire,
That I might see on euery side me by,
The northren winde had purified the aire,
And shedde his misty cloudes fro the skie:
The froste fresed, the blastes bitterly,
Fro pole Artike come whisking loud & shrill,
And caused me remoue ayenst my will.

For I trusted that Uenus, loues Quene,
To whom somtime I hight obedience,
My faded hart, of loue she would make grene,
And therupon with humble reuerence,
I thought to pray her high magnificence,
But for great colde as then I letted was,
And in my chambre to the fire can pas.

Though loue be hote, yet in a man of age,
It kindleth nat so soone as in youtheed,
Of whom the blood is flowing in a rage,
And in the old, the corage dull and deed,
Of which the fire outward is best remeed,
To help by Phisike where that nature failed,
I am expert, for both I haue assailed.

I made the fire, and beaked me aboute,
Then tooke I drinke my spirites to comfort,
And armed me wel fro the colde theroute,
To cutte the winter night & make it short:
I toke a queare, and left all other sport,
Writen by worthy Chaucer glorious,
Of faire Creseide, and lusty Troilus.

And there I found, after that Diomede
Receiued had that lady bright of hewe,
How Troilus nere out of his witte abrede,
And wept sore, with visage pale of hewe:
For which wanhope his teares gan renewe,
While Esperus reioysed him againe:
Thus while in ioy he liued, & while in paine.

Of her behest he had great comforting,
Trusting to Troy that she wold make retour
Which he desired most of al earthly thing,
For why she was his onely paramour:
But when he saw passed both day and houre
Of her gainecome, in sorow can oppresse
His wofull hart, in care and heuinesse.

Of his distresse me needeth nat reherse,
For worthy Chaucer in that same booke,
In goodly termes, and in ioly verse,
Compiled hath his cares, who wil looke:
To breke my sleepe another queare I tooke,
In which I founde the fatal desteny
Of faire Creseide, which ended wretchedly.

Who wote if al y Chaucer wrate, was trew?
Nor I wote nat if this narracion
Be authorised, or forged of the newe,
Of some Poete by his inuencion,
Made to report the lamentacion,
And wofull end of this lusty Creseide,
And what distresse she was in or she deide.

When Diomede had al his appetite,
And more fulfilled of this faire lady,
Upon another sette was al his delite,
And send to her a libel repudy,
And her excluded fro his company:
The desolate she walked vp and doune,
As some men saine, in the court as commune.

O faire Creseide, the floure and a per se,
Of Troy & Grece, how were thou fortunate,
To chaunge in filth al thy feminite,
And be with fleshly lust so maculate,
And go among the Grekes erly and late,
So giglotlike, taking thy foule pleasaunce?
I haue pite the should fall such mischaunce.

are formally different: a novel, a poem in two versions, and an illustrated adaptation for children. All of the responses are overtly interested in gender, but in varying ways, and in ways that are specific to the authors' own social moments and publishing contexts.

Adapting 'The Clerk's Tale' in the Nineteenth Century

Chaucer's 'Clerk's Tale', with its troubling heroine, patient Griselda, has always attracted extensive commentary and adaptation, especially about its gender politics. I focus here on three fascinating nineteenth-century adaptations, by Maria Edgeworth, Eleanora Hervey and Mary Haweis.

'The Clerk's Tale' tells the story of a tyrannical marquis, Walter, who marries a peasant girl on the understanding that he will receive total obedience from her. He proceeds to test her excessively, challenging her to acquiesce to the murder of first her daughter and then her son, which she does. He spirits them away, keeping them safe, and then tells Griselda that he is going to cast her off and marry a young aristocratic wife, sending her back to her father's hovel. She is required to prepare the palace for his new wife on his wedding day, which she does without complaint. However, it has all been a test and the 'new wife' is in fact their daughter. At the end, Walter returns Griselda's children to her and takes her back as his wife. This is a story that had been told by Italian poets such as Boccaccio (critically) and Petrarch (as an allegory), among others, and Chaucer's Clerk puts his own spin on it, piling high the possible morals, criticizing Walter throughout, and invoking the Wife of Bath at the end.

Edgeworth, Hervey and Haweis use radically different forms in their adaptations. While Edgeworth transposes the rhyme-royal tale into a novel, greatly expanding it, Hervey cuts it down into a short poem, and then cuts it again into a second version. Both use the tale as a jumping-off point to create texts that are very different from Chaucer's, and from each other's – but both are clearly focused on the issue of what is expected of women in society and in relationships. Haweis's version is much closer to Chaucer's, including some verbatim parts of his text, some modern poetic translations, and some prose summaries, as well as illustrations and notes at the end.

Edgeworth's *The Modern Griselda*, published three years after her very successful *Belinda*, tells the story of a contemporary woman who seems to be the very opposite of Chaucer's Griselda (FIGURE 5.5).[5] Rather than being obedient or submissive, she is demanding, manipulative, and indeed tyrannical, obsessed with having power over her husband. At one point she pretends that her husband is a despot, and performs the role of cowed, submissive wife. This 'modern Griselda' is a completely unreasonable figure. In the end she tells her husband that she wants to leave him as a final 'test' for him – but by this point he has been driven to his wits' end, and does not oppose her. She self-destructively drives away the man that she does, in fact, love.

Chaucer's text plays an important role in the novel. The characters discuss it, and Griselda arranges a reading of the tale. She mocks another woman, Emma Granby, saying that she is the new Griselda. After the reading, they all give their views on the medieval Griselda's behaviour: almost all the married women object, while the unmarried ones are equivocal, or say that perhaps love might justify it. The admirable Emma says that she would never have promised such submission and that she could never esteem a man who required it. She also says that in Chaucer's time women were 'slaves' while 'now they are free'.[6]

THE

MODERN GRISELDA.

A TALE.

BY

MISS EDGEWORTH,

AUTHOR OF PRACTICAL EDUCATION, BELINDA, CASTLE RACKRENT, HISTORY OF IRISH BULLS, LETTERS FOR LITERARY LADIES, POPULAR TALES, &C.

" And since in man right reason bears the sway,
" Let that frail thing, weak woman, have her way."

POPE.

LONDON:

PRINTED FOR J. JOHNSON, N° 72, ST. PAUL'S CHURCHYARD;

By Bye and Law, St. John's Square.

1805.

Is that really what the novel shows? The awful behaviour of the modern Griselda reflects some contemporary ideas about femininity, particularly ideas about women's capacity for reason, which demonstrates how far from 'free' women were in this era before emancipation. They were still battling all kinds of retrograde attitudes, some of which seem to have been internalized by Edgeworth herself. In *An Enquiry into the Duties of the Female Sex* (1799), Thomas Gisborne wrote that

> The gay vivacity and the quickness of the imagination, so conspicuous among the qualities in which the superiority of women is acknowledged, have a tendency to lead to unsteadiness of mind; to fondness of novelty; to habits of frivolousness.... Of the errors and failings which have been already specified, several are occasionally aggravated by the acute sensibility peculiar to women.[7]

The faults that the modern Griselda demonstrates are faults that at least some contemporary writers saw as quintessential female faults – although Edgeworth does not suggest that *all* women have these faults. But her suggestion that women have a propensity to specific character flaws was even highlighted disapprovingly by an early reviewer, in the *Annual Review* (1804). He says of Edgeworth that, in this book, 'her own sex are treated with harshness, and we think with injustice'. The reviewer goes on to note that 'ladies' will feel themselves 'aggrieved', and that it is 'ungraceful in a woman to take arms against the liberties of the sisterhood'. The reviewer specifically mentions that Edgeworth suggests that some faults (such as envy and jealousy) are particular to women and that she implies that women should not be allowed to dominate in

5.5
Maria Edgeworth, a very successful female author in the early nineteenth century, wrote a novel inspired by 'The Clerk's Tale', *The Modern Griselda*. The 'modern Griselda' is a deeply problematic figure – with more in common with tyrannical Walter than patient Griselda. Oxford, Bodleian Library, (OC) 249 r.51.

relationships.[8] Edgeworth's reworking of Chaucer's tale was itself seen as a misogynist text.

A later nineteenth-century female-authored response to the Griselda story does something very different. Eleanora Louisa Hervey wrote a poem from Griselda's point of view, 'Griseldis, with her Children', which was published in *The Athanaeum* in 1850.[9] It is divided into two parts: 'Griseldis, The Childless' and 'Griseldis, With Her Children'. The first part comprises eight quatrains (four-line verses); the second part six quatrains. The whole poem is in Griselda's lamenting voice, first of all from her perspective when she believes that her children are dead, and then when they have been returned to her. Motherhood is the preoccupation of the poem:

> O motherhood is strong as life, – and strongest in the least,
> It findeth out sweet channels in the poor four-footed beast;
> She giveth suck to the strange kid if it waileth for its dam, –
> But I, my bird to the kite I gave and to the wolf my lamb
>
> (lines 9–12)

Griselda is consumed with sorrow and guilt, blaming herself for allowing the atrocities that were perpetrated on her children, and seeking only death and oblivion for herself.

The second half – when the children are restored to her – does not offer redemption. We might expect a sharp change in tone, a joyous reversal, but Hervey does something different. The children are 'shadowy forms', whose eyes are 'cold and passionless'; when they embrace her their arms are loose like 'tendrils long since riven from a crushed and trampled vine' (lines 33, 34, 39–40). She thinks they blame her, but they are also more generally depicted as victims of abuse who cannot suddenly or easily move on from their trauma. Griselda laments that both the past and the future are 'as blotted scrolls in Nature's broken bond' (line 52). The forcible and inexplicable separation of the infants from their mother cannot be made good; no magical happy ending or restitution can wipe out what has happened.

There are many intriguing things about this poem. On the one hand, its focus on a natural, animal-like instinctual motherhood reinforces stereotypes about women, although the poem is also forceful in its critique of patriarchy (the marriage is presented as an economic transaction between men – 'my father clutched his gold' [line 15]). The exclusive focus on Griselda's point of view, unmediated by the voices of male characters or a male narrator or commentator, is a radical way of approaching the story that actually prioritizes the female voice and female experience. Griselda – so often either an object or an allegorical symbol – is made the subjective centre of the story. And the stark horror of the second half, with its suggestion that domestic abuse destroys lives, is extremely unusual and innovative.

It is all the more significant, then, that in a revised version, published in 1869, Hervey completely removes the second half of the poem.[10] This second version was published in a kind of 'gift book', called *Our Legends and Lives: A Gift for All Seasons*. Such books tended to be socially conservative and were aimed at an audience that included children. While the first version had appeared in the highbrow magazine/periodical *The Athenaeum*, framed by reviews of books including a new translation of Virgil's *Georgics* and by obituaries and letters about a new dissenting college at St John's Wood, this second version was being marketed in a cosier form, to a market that might expect texts to be safe, didactic and uncontroversial. The spectacle of irredeemably damaged children would not easily fit into this gift-book context. It is also possible that Hervey cut and altered her poem partly because of her own changed situation: when she published the first version, she was protected by the fact that her husband was the editor of *The Athenaeum*; by 1869 she was not only a widow but also under pressure to earn money. It may be, as Renee Ward has argued, that she now needed to 'adhere to certain social conventions in order to be acceptable and therefore profitable'.[11]

The pressure to write in certain ways often extended to genre. Indeed, the area of Chaucer adaptation that tended to be seen as particularly 'female' in the nineteenth century was children's adaptations. One of the more influential children's versions was Mary Haweis's *Chaucer For Children: A Golden Key* (1877), also discussed in the previous chapter.[12] Mary Haweis both wrote and illustrated her books, and was a prolific Chaucerian – also publishing *Chaucer for Schools: With the Story of His Times and Work* (1881), *Chaucer's Beads: A Birthday Book, Diary, and Concordance of Chaucer's Proverbs* (1884) and *Tales from Chaucer* (1877). Her other books included *The Art of Beauty* (1878), *The Art of Dress* (1879), *Beautiful Houses: Being a Description of Certain Well-Known Artistic Houses* (1882) and *The Art of Housekeeping: A Bridal Garland* (1889).

Haweis's brief 'Notes' on 'The Clerk's Tale' give us a sense of the mixed views she had of the tale. She explains, for instance, that in the medieval era ('a ruder time') 'almost everybody gave way habitually to violent emotions of all sorts',[13] so that Griselda's self-command is both impressive and impossible for Walter to believe. Like Maria Edgeworth, she also emphasizes that women were in a very different position in the Middle Ages compared to the nineteenth century. There is also a curious explanation of the omission of the last stanzas of Chaucer's tale: Haweis devotes about a quarter of her brief notes to a discussion of the last few stanzas, praising the 'real artistic power' of these 'beautiful verses'. However, she adds that she has not included these lines, as she feels that the 'ironical directions to wives to be bad wives would be probably not understood by a child'. It is intriguing that she takes such pains to tell her readers about this alternative ending, while also making it clear that there is a risk that such ironies be misunderstood – perhaps children might think that female dominance and rebellion were, in fact, acceptable.[14]

Haweis makes clear the abhorrence that she, and other readers, feel about Griselda's behaviour, and warns against ahistorical readings, when she tells her readers that

> If a modern wife cheerfully consented to the murder of her children by her spouse, she would probably be consigned to a *maison de santé*, while her husband expiated his sins on the scaffold; and if she endured other persecutions, such as Griselda did, it is to be hoped some benevolent outsider would step in, if only to prevent cruelty to animals.[15]

There is a lot going on in this sentence: Griselda does not consent cheerfully; it is significant that a woman consenting to such atrocities can only be seen as mad, rather than wicked; and the reference to animals makes a disturbing suggestion about women's moral status. What does she mean by this? Presumably that in allowing herself to be treated so badly, a woman becomes like a vulnerable animal who cannot defend herself – practically or legally.

Light is also thrown on this odd comment if we look at Haweis's illustrations. Griselda is, in fact, particularly associated with animals. The image of her marriage features a cow lurking

GRISELDA'S MARRIAGE.

'This is ynough, Grisilde myn, quod he.

5.6

Mrs Haweis's version of 'The Clerk's Tale' included a number of illustrations, including this one of Walter and Griselda's marriage. They are depicted in her humble home, surrounded by animals and her anxious father, with Walter's luxurious garb contrasting with Griselda's rags. *Chaucer for Children: A Golden Key*, 1877. Oxford, Bodleian Library, Opie P 8, after p. 68.

behind her, horses outside the doorway and a chicken at her feet (FIGURE 5.6). A later image, 'Griselda's Sorrow' (FIGURE 5.7), includes a dog (and a toy horse), and is glossed with the lines:

> And as a lamb sche sitteth meeke and stille,
> And let this cruel sergeant doon his wille.

5.7
In another illustration of Mrs Haweis's version of 'The Clerk's Tale', Griselda is still and passive as the sergeant, brandishing his knife, takes her baby son away to his death (as she believes). Her son desperately reaches for his mother, who remains statue-like. *Chaucer for Children: A Golden Key*, 1877. Oxford, Bodleian Library, Opie P 8, after p. 72.

Haweis thus chooses to emphasize Griselda's lamb-like quality, a comparison that makes her Christ-like, but that also illustrates her extreme passivity and inability to act. The image does focus on her stillness: her arms hang by her sides while her desperate son stretches out both his arms to her as his kidnapper takes him away. Indeed, his youth, and the fact that the sergeant is already unsheathing a knife, makes the boy, not Griselda, appear to be a lamb to the slaughter.[16] Griselda's lamb-like quality seems to inhere in the fact that she too is incapable of resisting the will of others – although that incapacity seems psychological or moral, rather than physical.

Haweis's connection of Griselda to animals also maps onto her understanding of the Middle Ages as foreign, and her view of societies that she perceives as primitive, such as the Irish, as medieval. At the end of the book, Haweis appends some 'Notes on the Pictures'. She comments on the picture of 'Griselda's Marriage' that, in Griselda's house, 'The draught beasts dwelt with their owners, much as the Hibernian pig resides with Pat and his family.'[17] It seems that, in her view, there is something basic and animalistic about the past, Catholics and women.[18] In terms of gender politics too, Haweis's 'cruelty to animals' comment is deeply disturbing, and it connects interestingly with Hervey's focus on comparing Griselda to animals. In 'Griseldis With Her Children', Griselda's shepherdess background, the affinity she feels with animals, and the unflattering contrast between her attitude to maternity and that of numerous animals are emphasized. While Griselda knows that she has a 'holier sense and higher gifts' than the animal kingdom, she also suggests that even an ant is a better parent than she.

The idea of women as creatures of instinct and nature seems, to a greater or lesser extent, to haunt all of these female-authored versions of 'The Clerk's Tale'. In other words, women writers are not inevitably able to write against the social norms in which they live. However, the very proliferation of women reading and writing (under their own names) about Chaucer, and in a wide variety of genres, including novel, poem and children's version, does bespeak a changing literary world, a world in which women were increasingly able to engage seriously and publicly with medieval texts.

Who Painted the Lion?

The simple fact of more women's participation in reading, translating, editing, responding to, adapting and being inspired by Chaucer's texts is in itself a crucially important trend in reception. The Wife of Bath famously asks in her Prologue: 'who painted the lion?' Her point is that if men write all the texts, we will have a very skewed view of the world and, particularly, of gender. Hervey restates this, in a way, with her retelling of Griselda's story in Griselda's voice. Another interesting example is Lady Diana Beauclerk's illustrations of Dryden's *Fables* in 1797. Beauclerk was the first person, to my knowledge, to include an image of the rape victim of the 'Wife of Bath's Tale' (FIGURE 5.8). This girl is passed over very briefly in the Tale itself. Subsequent retellings often sought to make her seem somehow culpable for what happened to her, or to imply that she consented: Voltaire, for example, emphasizes her physical appearance, presenting her as a temptress, and emphasizing her desire for money.[19] Beauclerk, in stark contrast, depicts her as a child, completely innocent, utterly vulnerable. Through her illustration she writes against interpretations that sought to exculpate the male rapist and blame the female victim. Moreover, by bothering to depict her at all, she reminds readers that her terrible experience lies at the heart of the story; that it should not be passed over and forgotten.[20]

Over the last century, women have played a very full part both in scholarly writing about Chaucer (e.g. Jill Mann, Carolyn Dinshaw, Helen Cooper) and in creative responses to Chaucer's texts. Indeed, as we shall see in the final chapter of this book, twenty-first-century poetic responses to Chaucer have been dominated by female voices – such as Zadie Smith, Caroline Bergvall, Patience Agbabi, Lavinia Greenlaw and

Marilyn Nelson. While some female-authored writings are focused on gender, others are not – and it is a regressive move if women are always supposed to be representing their sex, rather than themselves. But it is fascinating to note that, after centuries of being mainly seen as a manly man – either an important national patriarch or a bawdy, genial man-at-the-pub – Chaucer's complexity is now more fully appreciated.[21] It is no longer the case that most of the voices that we hear interpreting or adapting his works are from the same demographic. Indeed, Chaucer emphasized the importance of hearing multiple interpretations and voices: 'Diverse folk, diversely they seyde' ('The Reeve's Prologue', line 3857).

5.8
Dryden's version of 'The Wife of Bath's Tale' was illustrated by Lady Diana Beauclerk in 1797. For the first time, the rape victim was depicted – and is portrayed as a young child, entirely innocent, unlike in some other versions of the tale. *The fables of John Dryden*, 1797. Oxford, Bodleian Library, Vet. A5 b.72.

THE WIFE OF BATH'S TALE.

In days of old, when Arthur fill'd the throne,
Whose acts and fame to foreign lands were blown,
The king of elfs and little fairy queen
Gamboll'd on heaths, and danc'd on ev'ry green;
And, where the jolly troop had led the round,
The grass unbidden rose, and mark'd the ground:
Nor darkling did they dance, the silver light
Of Phœbe serv'd to guide their steps aright,
And, with their tripping pleas'd, prolong'd the night.

Cooke

Oure host answered y graunt it þe
Now telle on Roger loke þat it be gode
ffor many a pastey hastow latyn blode
And many a Iak of Dover hastow solde
þat hath byn twyes hote and twyes colde
Of many a pilgrym hastow cristes curs
ffor of þi p[er]sly yet þey fare þe wors
þat þey han eten in þy stopped goos
ffor in þi shoppe is many a flye loos
Now telle on gentil Roger by þy name
But yet y prey þe be not wroth for game
A man may sey ful sooth in game and pley
þou seyst ful sooth q[uo]d Roger by my fey
But sooth pley quade pley as þe flemmyng seith
And therfore harry Baily by þy feith
Be þou not wroth er we departe heere
þough þat my tale be of an hostelere
But natheles y wil nought telle it yet
But er we part ywis þou shalt be queyt
And therwith al he lough and made cheere
And seyd his tale as ye shal after heere

Here begynneth the Cookes tale

A prentys whilom dwelled in oure citee
And of a crafte of vitellers was he
Gaylerd he was as goldfynch in þe shawe
Brown as a bery a propre short felawe
With lokkys blake y kembed ful fetisly
Dauncen he kowde so wel and jolyly
þat he was cleped perkyn revelours

6

CHAUCERIAN MULTILINGUALISM PAST AND PRESENT

Jonathan Hsy

Geoffrey Chaucer lived in a multilingual world, and his works engaged three major literary languages of his time and place: Latin, the domain of the church and learning; French, the lingua franca of courtly culture and international affairs; and English, the vernacular shared by people in his London milieu. Born and raised in London to a merchant-class family, Chaucer was familiar with Latin and French as working languages of business and law throughout his career as a diplomat and customs official – in addition to vernacular languages he would have used during Continental travels.[1] French was not a 'foreign' language to Chaucer but a local medium of business, and the fictional Canterbury pilgrims convey divergent language capacities of individuals in this environment. The courtly Prioress 'Madame Eglantyne' speaks 'Frenssh [a]fter the scole of Stratford atte Bowe' (French in the manner of Stratford-at-Bow) even though she has never visited Paris ('General Prologue', lines 121–126). Clerical pilgrims, such as the Summoner, Parson and Pardoner (who has returned from Italy and whose tale is set in Flanders), show varied fluencies in Latin.

Throughout *The Canterbury Tales*, Chaucer explores linguistic diversity at home and abroad. In 'The Reeve's Tale' two clerks speak in a stereotypically northern Middle English. The Cook cites a Middle Dutch proverb: 'sooth pley, quad pley' (a true

6.1
'The Cook's Prologue' features a Flemish proverb, 'Sooth pley, quad pley'. This is typical of the multilingualism of *The Canterbury Tales*, which is sprinkled with quotations from other languages, especially Latin and French. Oxford, Bodleian Library, MS. Bodl. 686, fol. 54v (detail).

jest is a bad jest ['The Cook's Prologue', line 4357]) (FIGURE 6.1). 'The Shipman's Tale', set in France, adds local flavour to its dialogue: 'Quy la?' (Who's there? [line 214]). The Squire's chivalric romance set in 'Sarray [in] Tartarye' (Sarai, in the Turkic-Mongol kingdom of Tartary) describes an emissary from the 'kyng of Arabe and of Inde' who delivers a speech '[a] fter the forme used in his langage' (lines 9, 110, 100). Chaucer's experience with many languages – whether as a diplomat (in France, Flanders, Italy, Spain), prisoner of war (in France) or customs official for the Port of London – find expression in his poetic craft.

Language and Power

Chaucer's embrace of multilingualism suggests an openness to human variety and cultural difference, but his writing explores a sinister side to language as well: its potential to divide and harm. Alisoun (the Wife of Bath) describes her pain and rage upon hearing her Oxford-trained husband read aloud from misogynist texts compiled into his Latin 'book of wikked wyves' ('The Wife of Bath's Prologue', line 645). The Prioress narrates violent conflict in a multiethnic city in Asia where language simultaneously demarcates religious and ethnic difference: Latin is ascribed to a Christian schoolboy who sings the Marian hymn 'Alma redemptoris mater' (Loving Mother of the Saviour), whereas vilified people of the 'Jewerye' (enclave inhabited by Jewish residents) are ethnolinguistically characterized as 'Hebrayk peple' (Hebrew people) (lines 497, 560). The Roman Christian noblewoman Custance in 'The Man of Law's Tale', set adrift after a massacre in the 'Barbre nacioun' (foreign country) of Muslim Syria, washes ashore in Northumberland and uses '[a] maner Latyn corrupt' to be understood in this second precarious environment (lines 281, 519). Chaucer reveals how language can build bridges between social groups – yet it can also become a system of social control, a source of vulnerability or a tool to enforce unequal social conditions.

The capacity of language to connect people, but also to cause harm, is a pervasive concern of those who adapt Chaucer's works today. Some use Chaucerian language and allusions to explore power differentials between elite language and everyday speech. Composed in Jamaican Patois, Louise Bennett's poem 'Bans O'Killing' (1966), roughly translating to 'lots of killing', features a Black Caribbean speaker who demonstrates that one particular form of Standard British English is not inherently superior to other varieties of English around the world. The speaker asks: 'Yuh gwine kill all English dialect / Or jus Jamaica one?' (Are you going to kill all English dialects, or just the Jamaican one?). Prestigious literary traditions that trace their origins to Chaucer 'spring from dialect [f]rom the fourteen century' (spring from a dialect from the fourteenth century), and efforts to suppress nonstandard forms of English worldwide would also mean 'killing' established varieties of English within Britain.[2]

The speaker jokes that 'killing' nonstandard English would require removing Chaucer from *The Oxford Book of English Verse*: 'Yuh wi haffee get the Oxford book / O' English verse, and tear / Out Chaucer, Burns … An plenty o' Shakespeare!' (You would have to get the *Oxford Book of English Verse* and tear out Chaucer, Burns and plenty of Shakespeare!). Bennett's imagery recalls Chaucer's Wife of Bath tearing pages from the book of her Oxford-trained husband, and Bennett uses her distinct Jamaican Patois to counter everything the modern 'Oxford book' represents. *The Oxford Book of English Verse* (1900) in this context is not just a globally influential anthology published by Oxford University Press, but is also an apt symbol for longstanding systems of elitism, patriarchy, imperialism and racial discrimination.[3]

High and Low

The interplay between elite language and everyday speech, and its questions of power and privilege, are features of Chaucer's work when it enters languages beyond English. Throughout much of East Asia, including Japan, Korea and Chinese-speaking areas of China, Hong Kong, Macau, Singapore and Taiwan, literary traditions have long been shaped by the use of Chinese characters (FIGURES 6.2, 6.3). Within this cultural sphere, Classical aka Literary Chinese (古文 *guwen* 'ancient writing' or 文言 *wenyan* 'literary speech') can provide an analogue to medieval Latin as a prestigious international language of learning that marks a contrast to local vernaculars. Sun Yuxiu (孙毓修) and Lin Shu (林紓), two of the earliest Chinese translators of Chaucer's works (from 1913 to 1925), adapted simple fables such as the story of the rooster and the fox in 'The Nun's Priest's Tale', but they chose to compose such works in *wenyan* out of appreciation for the didactic tone of such stories and their potential alignment with Confucian ethical values such as righteousness, loyalty and respect for correct social relations. Later translators in the 1930s, who urged engagement with Western literature and more modern ideas, used contemporary Chinese vernacular (白話 *baihua* 'colloquial language') instead, incorporating proverbial expressions into their prose.[4]

Kenji Kaneko (金子健二), one of the earliest philologists in Japan and in 1917 the first Japanese translator of *The Canterbury Tales*, imported religious vocabulary from Buddhism or Shinto practices rather than transliterating Latin or Middle English

6.2
The front cover of a Japanese edition of selected *Canterbury Tales* (2021), strikingly juxtaposing a famous image of Chaucer pointing to his Middle English text (from a medieval manuscript, the Ellesmere Chaucer) with kanji characters. This is a collaborative volume, with translation and commentary by several different scholars, overseen by Tadahiro Ikegami.

カンタベリ物語
The Canterbury Tales
ジェフリー・チョーサー 著
Geoffrey Chaucer
池上忠弘 監訳
共同新訳版
いかめしげな宗教談義
みやびな宮廷風ロマンス
猥雑な笑話（ファブリオー）
〈人間喜劇（コメディア・フマナ）〉の一大絵巻（ページェント）！

terms. For instance, his translation of the Wife of Bath's utterance 'God give his soule reste! … God lat his soule never come in helle!' ('The Wife of Bath's Prologue', lines 501–504) employs the Japanese verbs 往生 (*ōjō* 'to die') and 成仏 (*jōbutsu* 'rest in peace'), which are familiar Buddhist terms. In Kaneko's translation, *knight* is 武士 (*bushi*), and 武士道 (*buishidō*, the so-called 'way of the warrior' and ethical-martial code for Edo-era *samurai*) offers an imperfect equivalent to medieval European *chivalry* and related terms.[5]

Throughout the Middle East and predominantly Muslim countries, Classical Arabic (الفصحى *al-fuṣḥā*), a standardized literary form of Arabic derived from language used in the Qur'an, can serve in place of Chaucer's medieval Latin to express learned or religious discourse. In his 2009 Persian verse translation of selected *Canterbury Tales*, Alireza Mahdipour uses the rhythm and metre (*vazn-e-aruzi*) of rhyming classic Persian poetry to render Chaucer's Middle English iambic-pentameter couplets, and the living practice of pilgrimage among Shia Muslims to numerous holy shrines of martyrs, saints and imams today allows the modern-day poet to use the Classical Arabic word *Mashhad* (مشهِد the place of martyrdom) to describe Canterbury – that is, the place of Thomas Becket's martyrdom and shrine. In his Turkish translation of *The Canterbury Tales*, Nazmi Ağıl's *Canterbury Hikâyeleri* (1994) synthesizes high and low registers of language, incorporating Turkish folk tales and oral proverbs into the poetry.[6]

In areas of the world that use European languages today, the interplay of elite and vernacular varieties of languages takes on complex resonance in geographies beyond Europe. In Mexico, for instance, Chaucerians have long used Spanish-language translations produced in Europe rather than producing

6.3
The title page from a Korean edition of Chaucer (2007). The traditional image of Chaucer features, and the words 'The Canterbury Tales', and 'Middle English' are interspersed with Korean hangul script. *The Canterbury Tales* translated by Dong-ill Lee and Dongchoon Lee, 2007.

The Canterbury Tales

초서 시대 중세영어(Middle English)의 원의미를 문헌학에 입각하여 우리말로 되살린 고증번역판

캔터베리 이야기

제프리 초서 지음 | 이동일 · 이동춘 옮김

한국외국어대학교 출판부

translations in local forms of Spanish. In his verse Brazilian Portuguese *Contos da Cantuária* (2013), by contrast, José Francisco Botelho incorporates poetic stylings from medieval Europe into contemporary local vernaculars (FIGURE 6.4).[7]

In Botelho's Chaucerian Brazil, medieval Galician-Portuguese *cantigas de amigo* (genre of courtly lyrics) and idioms derived from the globetrotting early modern Portuguese epic *Os Lusíadas* (*The Lusiads*) by Luís de Camões convey the speech of high-status characters such as Chaucer's Knight, who has fought in crusades across Europe, Africa and Asia. To convey Chaucer's educated and rustic voices, Botelho juxtaposes urbane speech patterns of São Paulo with popular music and regional forms of poetry throughout Brazil such as *repentismo* from the north-east and *pajada* from the south, genres that are familiar and recognizable to a contemporary Brazilian audience.[8]

In each iteration of Chaucer, authors find culturally appropriate analogues to medieval Latin or other historical languages around the world traditionally associated with power and prestige. At the same time, each writer creatively transports the everyday social dynamics of Chaucer's medieval European vernaculars into a new time and place.

Invention and Reinvention

The theme of language invention and creative world-building is not just evident in works that are written in local vernaculars but also in translations into languages that consider themselves international or even universal. The earliest endeavours to translate Chaucer's works out of Middle English into another language were not into any living vernacular languages, but into the international classical language of Latin. In *Amorum Troili et Creseidae Libri Quinque* (1639; The Loves of Troilus and

6.4
A poster from the Brazilian production of *A Mulher de Bath*, based on the Portuguese translation of *The Canterbury Tales*, *Contos da Cantuária*, by the Brazilian poet José Francisco Botelho (2013). The play, starring Maitê Proença, premiered in 2017.

MAITÊ PROENÇA em
A MULHER DE
BATH
16
obra de
GEOFFREY CHAUCER
tradução
JOSÉ FRANCISCO BOTELHO
direção
AMIR HADDAD
produção
MAITÊ PROENÇA
participação especial
ALESSANDRO PERSAN

Creseid in Five Books), Francis Kynaston translated Chaucer's major Middle English poem *Troilus and Criseyde* into rhyming Latin stanzas[9] (FIGURE 6.5). Chaucer derived his *Troilus* from Continental sources (primarily Giovanni Boccaccio's fourteenth-century Italian *Il Filostrato*, in turn derived from Benoît de Sainte-Maure's twelfth-century French *Roman de Troie*), but Chaucer's narrator ascribes his story to a non-existent Latin 'auctor [author] called Lollius' (Book I, line 394).

By converting Chaucer's Middle English into Latin, Kynaston not only reinvents what the hypothetical 'Lollius' might have composed, but also monumentalizes Chaucer through a standardized and prestigious language. Chaucer's Middle English reflections about the mutability of living vernaculars changing over time and how 'forme of speech is chaunge / Withinne a thousand yeer' (Book II, lines 22–23) accrue additional significance in a Latin tongue that is simultaneously living and dead, new and old.

The prospect of remaking Chaucer in a universal language repeats itself centuries later with the invention of Esperanto by L.L. Zamenhof. Born into a family of Litvak Jewish descent in a region of present-day Poland, which was at the time part of the Russian Empire, Zamenhof constructed the language of Esperanto in the 1880s by drawing its vocabulary from multiple European languages (including German, French, Polish, Russian and Yiddish), with the aim of creating an international auxiliary language that could bridge cultural differences and promote world peace.[10] In the first volume of English literature translated into Esperanto, entitled *Angla Antologio 1000–1800* (English Anthology 1000–1800), the poetry editor William Auld claims Chaucer as *unika poeto* (a unique poet) who is *esence angla* (essentially English) yet also *universale homa* (universally human), simultaneously

6.5
In 1635, *Troilus and Criseyde* was translated from Middle English into Latin, as *Amorum Troili et Creseidae*, by Francis Kynaston. For many writers, Latin was seen as a more stable language, in contrast with ever-changing English. Oxford, Bodleian Library, Lawn e.222.

AMORVM TROILVS ET CRESEIDÆ

Libri duo priores
Anglico-Latini.

OXONIÆ,
Excudebat *Iohannes Lichfield*,
Anno Domini
1635.

GEOFFREY CHAUCER

el LA ANTAŬPAROLO DE LA VIRINO EL BADO

'La saĝa reĝo Salomon' senpune
edzinon havis pli ol unu, ĉu ne;
ho dio! estu al mi permesate,
eĉ duontiom refreŝiĝi sate!
Pro dia ben' li edzinspecialis!
Neniu en la mondo lin rivalis.
Tre certe tiu nobla reĝ' multfoje
en la unua nokt' per viglo ĝoje
regalis ĉiun, ĉar li tre voluptis!
Dankon al dio, ke mi kvinon nuptis!
Bonvenon siatempe al la sesa:
ĉar nepre mi ne restos senkaresa;
Kiam la mondon lasas edzo mia,
tuj edzinigas min kristan' alia;
ĉar, dia nom'! la apostolo diras:
mi rajtas nupti, kie mi deziras.
Laŭ li senpeka estas edza amo —
Pli bone nupto ol infera flamo!

'Ĉu tuŝas min popola malaprobo
pri damna Lameĥ pro edziĝduopo?
Mi scias, ke Abraham estis pia,
kaj ankaŭ Jakob, laŭ konstato mia,
kaj ili havis pli ol po edzino:
sanktulojn ofte trafis ĉi destino.
Ĉu iam ajn, laŭ via tuta scio,
la nuptostaton malpermesis Dio
per vort' preciza? Diru, mi vin petas:
kie al ni virgecon li dekretas?
Dirojn de l' apostol' mi bone regas,
kiam pri virgulinoj li prelegas —
laŭ propra dir', ne volis li instrui.
Oni konsilu al virin' unui,
sed ja konsili estas ne ordoni.

'Pri la afer' ni rajtas mem disponi,
ĉar se laŭ Dio la virgec' necesus,
li krom la ago nupton malpermesus.
Cetere, se la semon ni ne semus,
de kie poste virgulinoj venus?
Nu, kompreneble Paŭlo ne altrudis
ion, pri kio lia mastro mutis.

mezepoka kaj por ciuj epokoj (medieval and also for all times)[11] (FIGURE 6.6).

The Esperanto excerpt from 'The Wife of Bath's Prologue' maintains Chaucer's rhyming couplets and produces cross-linguistic wordplay: 'Cetere, se la semon ni ne semus, / de kie poste virgulinoj venus?' (Moreover, if we did not sow the seed, / Where would virgins come from?).[12] Appropriate for the Wife of Bath's celebration of sexual preproduction, 'venus' is the conditional form of the Esperanto verb 'to come'. This rhyme word additionally produces a Latinate double entendre that anticipates the speaker's reference to her own 'chambre of Venus' ('The Wife of Bath's Prologue', line 618). *Angla Antologio* pursues a mission to promote Esperanto and demonstrate the language's literary potential, and this Esperanto 'Wife of Bath's Prologue' reconfigures the speaker's relationship to the medieval 'universal' language of Latin.

The impulse to use Chaucer's verse to generate new forms of language continues today. David J. Peterson, the American linguist hired to craft an internally consistent language of Dothraki for the pseudo-medieval *Game of Thrones* HBO franchise, translated the first two lines of Chaucer's 'General Prologue' into rhyming Dothraki couplets and published the verses on Twitter.[13]

Contemporary poets increasingly use the flexible hybridity of Chaucer's Middle English to test the boundaries of national, racial and gendered identities. Chinese-born Australian poet Ouyang Yu (歐陽昱) integrates English, Chinese and Singlish (Singaporean English) in his verse novel *The Kingsbury Tales* (2008). French-Norwegian Londoner Caroline Bergvall hybridizes language and media in *Meddle English* (2011). Julian Talamantez Brolaski, a poet of European, Apache and Latinx

6.6
A page from the Esperanto version of the 'Wife of Bath's Prologue'. This is taken from an Esperanto collection of a range of classic English poetry, published in 1957. The Wife of Bath has become 'la virino el bado'. *Angla Antologio, 1000–1800*, 1957. Oxford, Bodleian Library, 2705 e.1715, p. 30.

ancestry, crafts nonbinary gender and queer language in *Of Mongrelitude* (2017). Jos Charles' *feeld* (2018) reinvents Middle English to create a new poetic space for trans experience.[14] The unfixed potential of Chaucer's Middle English allows linguists, translators and poets to experiment with the past and future of language: to reanimate old tongues, to build alternate worlds, or to imagine future worlds that have yet to arrive.

Repression and Resistance

While modern reworkings of Chaucerian texts have much creative potential, the project of translation or adapting the poet's work is not without its perils. In social environments (past or present) where government censorship sets limits to freedom of expression, translators and educators must resourcefully work within constraints. In Soviet Russia, for instance, the USSR's censorship bureau restricted exposure to foreign literatures, yet Chaucer's works sustained scholarly interest due to the author's perceived focus on stories of workers and peasants. An authoritative Soviet translation of Chaucer directly from Middle English into modern Russian poetry by Ivan Kashkin and Osip Borisovich Rumer contains seventeen of the *Canterbury Tales*, each illustrated by autolithographs by the artist Sergey Barkhin (FIGURE 6.7).[15]

6.7
An illustration from the tiny and beautiful Russian version of *The Canterbury Tales* published in 1980, translated by Ivan Kashkin and Osip Rumer with lithographs by Sergey Barkhin. Many elements of 'The Franklin's Tale' are alluded to here: the boat, the rocks, the idyllic garden in which men and women play games and dance. *Kenterberiĭskie rasskazy*, 1980. Oxford, Bodleian Library, 27976 g.2.

In the years after the founding of the People's Republic of China in 1949, educators and scholars followed Soviet modes of interpretation that valued Chaucer's interests in class conflict, social oppression and everyday people. The geopolitical implications of reclaiming Chaucer proliferate today, where authors and activists alike transform Chaucerian literary traditions to address historical and ongoing forces of colonialism, imperialism, sexism, xenophobia and racial injustice around the globe.[16]

In some cases, modern-day reworkings of Chaucer's works make strategic choices about what to omit or elide from his work, not due to any external system of censorship but out of sensitivity to current audiences and historical circumstances. R.M. Lumiansky, a Jewish American who witnessed the antisemitism of the interwar USA and Nazi Germany, chose not to include the antisemitic 'Prioress's Tale' in his famous 1948 modern English children's version of *The Canterbury Tales of Geoffrey Chaucer*. Such a decision may signal the desire to spare young readers the experience of reading a story about the horrific killing of a young Christian boy by Jewish villains, yet in the post-Holocaust context in which the edition appeared Lumiansky made a principled decision not to translate nor transmit antisemitic propaganda.[17] Arthur Szyk, renowned Jewish American artist born in Poland, did not include a portrait of the antisemitic Prioress among his exuberant illustrations in *Tales From Chaucer Told For Young People* (1947) – because the text followed Charles Cowden Clarke, who omitted the story from his English prose translations.[18]

Mediation, Media, Moving Image

Charles Cowden Clarke's *Tales from Chaucer in Prose*, written in simple prose, provided a venue for Szyk's illustrations published soon after World War II; an earlier edition of Clarke's work was the basis of Chinese translations by Lin Shu (mentioned above) printed between 1916 and 1925 during the early years of China's Republic. Since Lin did not know English, he relied upon a collaborative process of working with an oral interpreter who translated Clarke's text into vernacular Chinese, which Lin then rendered into his own Classical (Literary) Chinese prose.[19] Reprintings of Clarke's edition of Chaucer were often illustrated, and it's unknown whether the moralizing illustrations in one of Clarke's many editions influenced Lin's translation choices.[20] The fact that one oft-republished children's edition of Chaucer could circulate across languages, with or without new illustrations in each iteration, suggests how easily the poet's work moves into new contexts.

The recombination of Chaucerian texts and images as they circulate across languages today can generate a seemingly endless array of meanings and emphases. In one iteration of a complete modern Japanese translation of *The Canterbury Tales*, the text is accompanied by woodcut illustrations from the Kelmscott Chaucer (1896), the collaborative project of the English social reformer and writer William Morris and the Pre-Raphaelite artist Edward Burne-Jones (discussed in Chapter 4).[21] The predominantly slender and proper Victorian characters featured in Kelmscott illustrations may have the effect of visually emphasizing for modern Japanese readers the more dignified and pious elements of Chaucer's work over his more lewd or rustic materials. A picture book version of 'The Nun's Priest's Tale' by American writer-illustrator Barbara Cooney, *Chanticleer and the Fox* (1958), has yielded translations in Afrikaans, Arabic, Chinese, Danish, German, Japanese, Korean and Swedish, offering to young readers a lightly humorous story with a moral ending.[22]

Visual artists continue to explore the possibilities of Chaucerian storytelling. A comic book adaptation of selected *Canterbury Tales* by Belgian artist Lük Bey (pen name of Luk De Ryck), first published in Flemish in 2009 and republished in English in 2010, addresses adult themes, including Chaucer's scatological humour and physical comedy. Malaysian American artist and graphic novelist Shing Yin Khor's *The Canterbury*

Ghosts (2018) is an oracle deck of 'divination cards' based on Chaucer's pilgrims and tales, and Khor's simultaneously comedic and haunting imagery combines 'child-like glee' with horror, death and complicity with violence (FIGURE 6.8).[23]

Chaucerian storytelling can also inform languages that do not rely upon writing or the medium of sound. American Sign Language (ASL), a fully expressive language that uses hand gestures, facial expressions and spatial-kinetic movement to structure its grammar, allows Deaf Americans to reinvent medieval narratives, including analogues to 'The Wife of Bath's Tale' performed in Visual Vernacular: a physical theatre tradition that can incorporate ionic gestures, sign-language poetry, and mime. Deaf and hearing scholars alike continue to offer important reassessments of the 'somdeel deef' (somewhat deaf) Wife of Bath as a complex character whose gender and deafness shape her life story.[24]

Return to Sender

One of the most intriguing aspects of Chaucerian adaptations is when his works 'return' to their linguistic source or geographical point of origin. For instance, much of Chaucer's Middle English poetry was derived from French (such as courtly love poetry or dream visions), and when his work is translated into modern French the Middle English undergoes 'retraduction' (retranslation) of meaning and form.[25] Chaucer's *œuvre*, which was informed by Italian writers Dante Alighieri, Giovanni Boccaccio and Francis Petrarch, in turn shapes Chaucerian works in modern Italian. Pier Paolo Pasolini's Italian film *I Racconti di Canterbury* (1972), the middle instalment of the film-maker's 'Trilogy of Life', beginning with Boccaccio's *Decameron* and ending with *The Arabian Nights*, emphasizes Chaucerian

6.8
Malaysian American artist and graphic novelist Shing Yin Khor's *The Canterbury Ghosts* (2018) is an oracle deck of 'divination cards' based on Chaucer's pilgrims. The characters are animalized, and moments and themes from their tales inform the images, which are strikingly surreal.

the shipman
the yeoman
the physician
the squire
the knight
the franklin
the wife of bath
the parson
the friar
the summoner
the pardoner
the cook
the merchant
the miller
the monk
the manciple
the priest
the reeve

themes of sex and physical comedy. Dialect variance is conspicuous in the Italian version of the film, where Neapolitan dialect is used for its rustic and earthy associations, and the dubbed English version features non-professional actors speaking in cockney, West Country, Scottish, Welsh and Irish accents.[24] These two iterations of this film, as a pair, reflect Chaucer's debts to Italian writers while also reminding modern audiences of the heterogeneity of Chaucer's English.

One idiosyncratic instance of 'returning' Chaucerian material to its source is Lük Bey's *Verhaleen voor Canterbury* (2009) and its subsequent iPad app reiteration in English, *The Canterbury Tales* (2010). This comic book adopts a style with quintessentially Flemish roots – that is, the *klare lijn* (clear line) style distinguished by bold blocks of colour and figures with cartoonish faces against lifelike backgrounds. The book showcases Chaucer's Flemish materials: 'The Pardoner's Tale' (which Chaucer sets in Flanders), 'The Tale of Sir Thopas' (whose Flemish knight-protagonist is from Poperinge), 'The Nun's Priest's Tale' (reassigned to the Prioress) with its reference to Flemish stories of Reynard the Fox, and 'The Miller's Tale' (which has analogues in Middle Dutch). Not only does Lük Bey play up Chaucer's broad social satire and self-deprecating humour – rendering the Chaucer-pilgrim as the cartoonist's self-portrait, along with ample fart jokes – but the artist also pokes fun at the 'lower status' that Flemish holds compared to 'world classics' in more prestigious languages.[25]

Chaucer's travels in France, Italy and Flanders shaped his writings, so it is fitting that his works might eventually 'return' into French, Italian and Flemish. Perhaps less predicably, Chaucer's works have also 'returned' to cultural spaces far beyond Europe. Chaucer's 'Squire's Tale', set in the

Turkic-Mongol realm of Cambyuskan (Chinggis Khaan or Genghis Khan) in the Volga region of what is now south-eastern Russia, recalled a thirteenth-century cosmopolitan network linking locales as far-flung as East Asia and Byzantium.[26] In present-day Mongolia, Chinggis Khaan looms large as a leader of a vast Eurasian multicultural empire that laid groundwork for later eras of globalization, and on the grand staircase of the National Historical Museum are Chaucer's words praising the 'noble kyng … Cambyuskan, / Which in his tyme was of so greet renoun / That ther was no nowher [s]o excellent a lord in alle thyng' ('The Squire's Tale', lines 12–16).[27] A modern Mongolian translation of 'The Squire's Tale', in Cyrillic script (an indication of Mongolia's Soviet past) and in English, is a testament to the medieval ruler's impact upon an interconnected world.[28] Whether cultural receptions of Chaucer around the globe take shape as poetry, prose, visual art or performance, the poet's medieval multilingual past acts in dialogue with our heterogenous polyglot present.

7

CHAUCER ON FILM AND TELEVISION

Marion Turner

In the twentieth century, Chaucer entered the world of film and television. The author's recognizability as a character – the jovial, slightly rude patriarch, the knowing narrator and pilgrim – along with the fact that *The Canterbury Tales* is an inherently performative and rich text, has made adapting Chaucer for screen a popular pastime, testament to the extraordinary cultural capital still enjoyed by the author. Directors including Pier Paolo Pasolini, Julian Jarrold and Brian Helgeland have found inspiration in *The Canterbury Tales*. Actors who have starred in Chaucerian adaptations over the last couple of decades include Julie Walters (FIGURE 7.1), Bill Nighy, Keeley Hawes, Jonny Lee Miller, Sean Bean, Imelda Staunton and Robert Lindsay – many of the best-known and most respected British actors of recent years. Jonathan Myerson's animated version was nominated for an Oscar and won a BAFTA and four Emmy awards.[1] Many of these adaptations built on the success of the West End musical *The Canterbury Tales*, written by Neville Coghill and Richard Hill, which played from 1968 to 1973, with Elizabeth Taylor and Richard Burton attending the premiere. More generally, Coghill's very successful translation of the *Tales* has played a major part in popularizing Chaucer in the twentieth century and is the form in which many readers first encountered Chaucer's works.

7.1
Julie Walters stars as the Wife of Bath, now an ageing soap-opera actor with a toyboy, in the BBC adaptations of *The Canterbury Tales* in 2003. The iconic red dress – similar to that worn in Pasolini's earlier film or Zadie Smith's later play – makes her immediately recognizable.

There have been no notable film or television adaptations of Chaucer's non-*Canterbury Tales* texts, and so the adaptations have continued and extended the dominance of the *Tales* in the reception of Chaucer's work. While some adaptations are set in a medieval world (e.g. Pasolini's), others completely update the tales (e.g. the BBC six-episode series). Some films merely nod towards the *Tales* (*A Knight's Tale*) or have a tangential, if passionate, relationship to Chaucer (*A Canterbury Tale*), while others adapt a selection of *Tales* (the BBC adaptations, Pasolini, Myerson), with varying attention paid to the tellers and the frame. Although Pasolini has very little interest in the frame, he himself played the Chaucer figure, writing down the stories (FIGURE 7.2). Each director had to make difficult decisions about language. Myerson's animated tales were made in Middle English, Modern English and Welsh; Pasolini's film in English and in the Neapolitan dialect.[2] Most directors emphasize a wide range of accents from different regions. No one has attempted anything like the entire text – the BBC adaptations covered six tales; Pasolini eight; Myerson ten.

The BBC adaptations and Myerson's animated tales both paid attention to the principle of variety that underpins the conception of *The Canterbury Tales*. While the BBC episodes used different directors and casts, the animated tales were made by different animation studios utilizing diverse techniques of animation. In terms of content too, both collections include fabliaux (sexually explicit tales such as the Miller's), but also pay attention to other genres such as romance, folk tale and beast fable.[3]

In stark contrast, Pasolini, in his 1972 *I Racconti di Canterbury*, is only interested in one kind of Chaucer: an earthy, masculine, sex-obsessed figure. Gone is the principle of aesthetic variety, of

interest in the full range of human experience and perspectives. Pasolini recounts several fabliaux: 'The Merchant's Tale', 'The Cook's Tale', 'The Miller's Tale' and 'The Reeve's Tale'; he tells only 'The Wife of Bath's Prologue' (not Tale), focusing on the horror of older female sexuality by showing that sex with an older woman literally kills men; and although the three other tales that he tells are not about sex in Chaucer's text, he transforms them. 'The Friar's Tale' now opens with a scene of sodomy followed by torture; 'The Pardoner's Tale' starts in a brothel and depicts explicit and grotesque acts; 'The Summoner's Tale' expands a line from the Prologue into a horrifying visual

7.2
Pier Paolo Pasolini directed his film of *The Canterbury Tales* in 1972. He himself played Chaucer, the writer/director controlling the work of art. As a whole, his film eschewed Chaucerian variety, concentrating on sex and the body.

image of Satan's rectum. The whole film is punctuated with images of clothed erections and flaccid penises; bodies are easy to access; sex is exclusively physical, and ranges from the ecstatically pleasurable to the violent and disturbing. Overall, this is an astonishingly reductive response to *The Canterbury Tales*, a response that gives an entirely misleading idea of Chaucer's preoccupations, and of his range, in terms of both subject matter and style.[4]

In what follows I focus on three adaptations: the 1944 film *A Canterbury Tale* (FIGURE 7.3), one of the BBC adaptations (of 'The Man of Law's Tale'), and Myerson's animated *Tales*, exploring first how some writers and directors have thought about Chaucer's texts as a way to meditate on nationhood, and secondly how Chaucer's interest in experiment, variety and heterogeneity can be translated into a very different medium.

Nation

A Canterbury Tale (1944), directed by Michael Powell and Emeric Pressburger, is a wartime film that eulogizes a certain idea of Englishness. It is, on one level, a love letter to the English landscape, to English history and to Chaucer as an embodiment of a beautiful, spiritual image of the nation. It opens with bell-ringing and a glimpse of Canterbury Cathedral through the countryside, before cutting to the opening page of the 'General Prologue'. The first lines of *The Canterbury Tales* are then read aloud (with modern pronunciation and some changes), before we see a map of England with the Pilgrims' Way (an ancient track leading to Canterbury), and a picture of Chaucer's pilgrims. The pilgrims then become real people as Chaucer's characters are brought to life, riding through the countryside. Many are easily identifiable, such as the Miller and the Wife of Bath. The Squire

7.3
A poster advertising Powell and Pressburger's wartime film *A Canterbury Tale*. This fascinating 1944 film centres on a heroine called Alison (with a fiancé called Geoffrey). The English countryside, the Pilgrims' Way and Canterbury feature heavily, alongside a bizarre plot involving the sinister Glueman.

"Ranks with 'RED SHOES' and 'STAIRWAY TO HEAVEN' Powell and Pressburger score again!"
–New York Daily Mirror
J. ARTHUR RANK
presents
ERIC PORTMAN
IN
A Canterbury Tale
WITH
SHEILA SIM
DENNIS PRICE
KIM HUNTER
Sgt. JOHN SWEET, U.S.A.
A Production of the Archers
An Eagle Lion Films Release
Written, Produced and Directed by
Michael Powell and Emeric Pressburger

sends a falcon into the air, which changes into a Spitfire. Now we are in the world of the 1940s and the Second World War, with soldiers and tanks in the Kentish landscape, and a modern poem is read, telling us that, 'though little's changed since Chaucer's day / Another kind of pilgrim walks the way', and we enter into the extremely strange world of the film.

The basic plot is that three people arrive at a small village near Canterbury: they are a land girl (Alison, of course, like the Wife of Bath), a British soldier (Peter Gibbs, who will soon embark on the D-Day landings), and an American soldier (Bob Johnson, on a brief furlough).[5] Soon after they disembark from the train, late at night, Alison is attacked in the dark by a mysterious stranger who pours glue on her hair and runs off. The three all need to get to Canterbury for different reasons, but they also want to solve the mystery of the Glueman, who has now attacked eleven girls in the same way. Soon, their attention turns to Thomas Colpepper, a man at the heart of the local community: a highly respected and rich man, who lives in a manor house, owns a farm, is a magistrate and Justice of the Peace, and gives lectures about Chaucer, English history and the Pilgrims' Way. His central obsession is with the long history of the Kentish landscape.

All three of the new arrivals, particularly Alison, are drawn to Colpepper, and to his understanding of the past and of place, but they realize that he is, in fact, the Glueman. On the train to Canterbury he explains himself. Colpepper knows with absolute certainty that everyone should be educated about the medieval past and Englishness, but over the years he has found that no one is interested. He has lectured to empty halls, tried to speak to people in Hyde Park, done everything to make people listen to him. When the soldiers arrived to camp near the village, he was sure that this would be his moment, that this was a miracle, that he was a missionary who could convert them – but no. To his horror, all they were interested in was girls – going out with girls, dancing with girls, watching movies with girls in them. Colpepper felt that local girls shouldn't be going out with soldiers, and that soldiers should be listening to his lectures, so he came up with a plan. He would dress as a soldier and pour glue on girls' heads, so that they would be frightened of going out, and particularly frightened of going out with soldiers. Then, finally, the soldiers would come to his lectures and he could tell them all about the Pilgrims' Way. The three pilgrim characters agree that 'he meant well' and do not go to the police in the end – although Alison does suggest that he should simply have asked the girls to the lectures. In Canterbury, miracles happen for all of them: Alison finds out that her fiancé – Geoffrey! – is not dead, as she had thought; the American soldier discovers that his girlfriend has not betrayed him; the British soldier, who had trained as an organist but never had the opportunity to play in a church, plays in Canterbury Cathedral for a huge ceremony before D-Day.

The gender politics of the film are extraordinary, and Carolyn Dinshaw has explored the queerness of the film and of Colpepper's behaviour.[6] Chaucer, history and the past are for men, according to Colpepper – although the film shows that the character who is most interested in what he has to say and in the history of the land is in fact Alison. The film is fascinated by ideas of nation and place. It imagines Englishness as fundamentally rural – something that the Londoner Chaucer would have found hard to understand. Indeed, Chaucer was a figure of modernity in his own time: son of a merchant, himself a customs' officer, fascinated by science and new ideas, experimenting with forms, he lived at the heart of change and was energized by it. His world was urban, and it was also, as I have written about extensively elsewhere, profoundly European and grounded in travel, multilingualism and exchange.[7] The idea of England promoted in *A Canterbury Tale* is anti-cities. London is despised: indeed, the opening shot does not trace the route of Chaucer's pilgrims, from London to Canterbury – instead it traces the more rural route from Winchester to Canterbury, a route which does not go near the metropolis. The film is punctuated with beautiful images of wheat fields, forests and rivers, as well as picturesque village houses, and lingering shots of Canterbury Cathedral. Alison speaks with horror of living in a closed-in urban street as she had to do before the war, and plaintively asks, 'Why should people who love the country have to live in big cities?' Throughout the film, going to the movies is disparaged (rather self-defeatingly, perhaps) as an activity that takes people away from seeing real life and things that matter.[8] What they should be doing, Colpepper says, is lying on the earth and looking up at the sky (FIGURE 7.4).

Englishness is also defined through cultural differences with Americans – and, indeed, one of the functions of films made at this time was to educate American soldiers about life in the UK to 'orient' them. Great stress is placed on the differences between British and American uniforms and, in particular, on the importance of tea-drinking to the British, as the film makes it clear that drinking coffee first thing in the morning is not acceptable, and that 'good' Americans quickly learn about how much tea goes into a pot. The audience is told that only tea-drinkers – China, Russia and the UK – have been able to resist the Nazis. The vision of Englishness is hilariously rigid.

7.4
In a scene from Powell and Pressburger's *A Canterbury Tale*, Alison meets Thomas Colpepper (the disturbing Glueman) in the fields, and they contemplate the beauty of the English countryside and the paths that medieval pilgrims used to tread.

A radically different view of Englishness is suggested in the more recent BBC adaptation of 'The Man of Law's Tale' (2003).[9] Chaucer's Tale is about the expansion of Christianity into England, and about the clash of three religions – Christianity, Islam and paganism. The heroine Constance, sometimes seen as an allegory for the church, is the daughter of the emperor of Rome. She marries first the Sultan of Syria and then the king of Northumbria. Both marriages are threatened by her mothers-in-law: the Sultaness causes her son and his followers to be killed; King Alla's mother in Northumberland forges letters to engineer Constance being sent away in a boat with her child. Earlier, Constance had been wrongly accused of murder and saved by divine intervention. In the end, Constance, Alla and their son are reunited in Rome and their son becomes the emperor; Constance has also effected mass conversions in Northumbria, and has been protected by God throughout the tale.

The BBC adaptation turns this into a story about the contemporary British nation and its relationship to immigration. Constance is a refugee from Nigeria who has fled sectarian violence. She was a victim of people-traffickers, trying to reach the UK on a boat, and then cast off alone on a small vessel (FIGURE 7.5). The story is radically changed, but quite a few elements are retained: Constance converts locals and is resented for this; she is falsely accused of murder; the real murderer is discovered because of the ramifications of swearing on a Bible; her mother-in-law betrays her and forges a communication (now an email rather than a letter); her husband (Alan) comes to search for her and her baby back in their home country. England is depicted in both versions as a place defined by its relationship with the sea; liminal encounters on the shore are symbolically central to understanding how a nation is defined through encounters with others. Indeed both versions do suggest – in some ways – that immigrants should be welcomed, rather than suspected, and that they can enrich English/British culture.

The Man of Law, however, suggests that while England and Rome can be united, Islam is not assimilable into European hegemony. The BBC adaptation, in contrast, emphasizes the idea that England is inherently a place of wide cultural mixing. Constance's evil stepmother was herself an immigrant from Iran decades earlier; the couple who take Constance in are a white man and a black woman; the church she attends has a very mixed congregation. The story ends with a mixed-race marriage and child. The adaptation largely avoids talking about Islam – we are told that Constance had a Muslim father and a Christian mother, but compared with Chaucer's version there is very little about Islam. The modern adaptation also has an uncomfortable relationship with Christianity: Alan's frustration

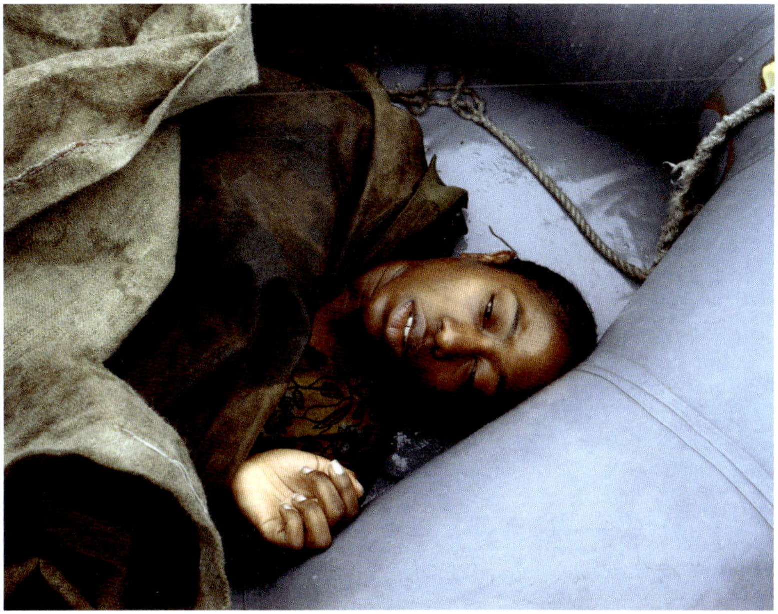

with Constance's blind faith, his refusal to convert, and the seemingly obvious wrongness of her belief that God will save her (rather than lawyers and Alan's commitment) is very different from the tone of the original. England is not presented as a fundamentally Christian country, as it is by the Man of Law – it is presented as a place of ongoing religious diversity, though also a place of racism and horrifying systems of detention. As the *Refugee Tales* was to do a few years later (discussed in the next chapter), the BBC adaptation uses Chaucer as a way to talk about cultural mixing and immigration, and to question the narrow ideas of Englishness presented in earlier responses, such as *A Canterbury Tale*.

7.5
In the BBC 2003 adaptation of 'The Man of Law's Tale', Constance is depicted as a Nigerian refugee, fleeing sectarian violence, who arrives in the UK on a small boat. 'The Man of Law's Tale' has been particularly influential on refugee responses to Chaucer in the *Refugee Tales* collections too.

Variety

The BBC adaptations were made as six stand-alone one-hour films, using different directors and casts. The principle of aesthetic variety is also central to Jonathan Myerson's animated *Canterbury Tales* (1998). The tales are presented in three half-hour episodes, each covering three or four complete tales, plus snatches of other tales, and a liberal amount of framing material from the 'General Prologue' and the link passages in the *Tales*. The use of multiple different animation studios, techniques and practitioners allows Myerson to create a richly textured work, one which pays creative homage to the aesthetic experiments of *The Canterbury Tales* itself. The focus on the frame narrative also allows Myerson to focus on the relationship between tellers and tales, and the idea of listening to multiple voices.

More than any other version, the animated *Tales* aims to recreate the world of the pilgrims. We start in the Tabard Inn, and in between each tale we return to the pilgrims and see and hear them talking and arguing together and commenting on the tales. These linking sections often contain bits of 'General Prologue' descriptions (in Chaucer's voice) focusing on the pilgrim who is about to tell the next tale, and we also hear snatches of other tales. All the way through, then, we are reminded that each tale is being told by a specific individual with a biased perspective, and that each tale is a part of a bigger whole, a piece of the jigsaw.

This emphasis on the idiosyncratic perspective of each teller is made particularly clear in the dazzling Miller–Reeve sequence. In *The Canterbury Tales*, the first tale, the Knight's, is followed by the Miller's – which parodies 'The Knight's Tale' – and the Reeve then decides that 'The Miller's Tale' (which was

about a carpenter, the Reeve's profession) was aimed at him. The Reeve then tells a tale about a miller to take revenge on the pilgrim Miller. His tale takes the same basic plot as the Knight's and Miller's – a patriarch, and two men fighting over women – and makes it yet more disturbing. While the marriage in 'The Knight's Tale' is coerced, the sex is legally and socially acceptable; in 'The Miller's Tale' it is adulterous, and in the Reeve's it is rape. The link between the Knight's and Miller's tales – so fundamental in *The Canterbury Tales* as it sets up the radical levelling of the voices of different classes – is completely broken in the animated version, as 'The Knight's Tale' comes second and the Miller's and Reeve's are the ninth and tenth tales. However, the link between the Miller's and Reeve's tales, and the idea that their tales reflect their own preoccupations and that they are told in relation to each other's tales, are made even stronger.

7.6
A scene from the animated *Canterbury Tales*, directed by Jonathan Myerson. This scene from 'The Canon's Yeoman's Tale' is filmed in stop motion, a technique that involves moving models and objects, and therefore gives a more three-dimensional and realistic impression in comparison with other techniques.

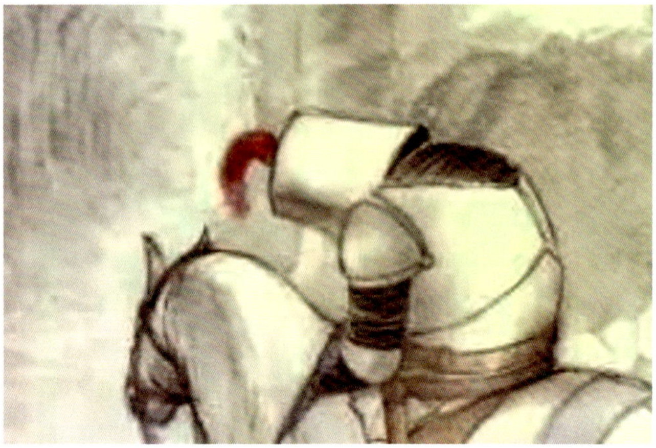

7.7
A scene from 'The Wife of Bath's Tale', in Myerson's animated *Canterbury Tales*. This tale is drawn in pencil animation, creating a very different look for this romance in comparison with the stop motion used for the Pardoner, Canon's Yeoman, Miller and Reeve, for instance.

In an innovative move, the two tales are interlaced. We move from a scene of 'The Miller's Tale' to a scene of 'The Reeve's Tale', to the Miller and Reeve arguing, to 'The Miller's Tale' again, to the Miller and Reeve arguing, back to 'The Reeve's Tale', and so on. At one point Chaucer says 'Don't blame me' in a close echo of a narratorial comment in 'The Miller's Prologue', as the different layers of reality – frame and tales – blur together. As the tales move to their fast-paced climaxes, we shift more quickly between one and the other, and we see hands pulling one picture down to replace it with the other tale. The effect is to demonstrate the crucial importance of viewpoint and perspective, to remind us not to think of texts – poems or films – as authoritative, but to be aware of diversity of opinion.

This focus on diversity also comes through in the visual aesthetics of the animated tales. The frame sections are all made in stop motion, an animated film-making technique whereby models and objects are physically moved and manipulated between individual frames. These parts of the story thus look three-dimensional, and this technique is also used for the tales that have a claim to contemporary 'realism' – the

Pardoner's, Miller's, Reeve's and Canon's Yeoman's (FIGURE 7.6). These stories are all set in the present moment, in England or Flanders (i.e. fairly locally) and do not involve pagan gods or the supernatural. The other tales use various different styles: 'The Wife of Bath's Tale' is drawn in pencil animation (FIGURE 7.7); 'The Nun's Priest's Tale' and 'The Franklin's Tale' are in thick-line animation – with visible, heavy, black borders around objects and characters. 'The Franklin's Tale' is drawn in block colours and is simply drawn and animated (FIGURE 7.8). The tales are visually striking: images of the colour palette of 'The Nun's Priest's Tale', of the giant gods encircling the world in 'The Knight's Tale', or of the hectic laboratory of 'The Canon's Yeoman's Tale' are memorable indeed. As we shift between tales, and between tale and frame, the audience is conscious of stylistic change, of the various ways in which a tale can be told. This mimics *The Canterbury Tales*, which are told in a wide variety of poetic forms, including rhyme royal, rhyming couplets, tail rhyme and prose, and also in a range of genres, including

7.8
A scene from 'The Franklin's Tale' in Myerson's animated *Canterbury Tales*. This tale is drawn in thick-line animation, with heavy black borders. The stylized aesthetic is heightened by the use of a limited colour palette, and block colours.

romance, fabliau, beast fable and saint's life.[10] The aesthetics of the animation does the same kind of work as the focus on the teller–tale relationship: we are reminded of the subjectivity of narration and of response, and of the extraordinary variety of forms and styles available to writers, animators and other artists. In the final chapter of this book we will see how a contemporary poet (Patience Agbabi) responded to Chaucer's formal variety by herself playing with an exceptionally wide range of old and new poetic forms.

Endings

Film and television adaptations usually tend to depict an arrival at Canterbury itself, in a break from what Chaucer himself did. Chaucer was supremely comfortable with uncertainty, openness and unfinishedness – or perhaps he was deeply uncomfortable with certainty, closure and conclusion. His pilgrims do not reach Canterbury, but are left forever suspended on the borders of their destination. However, Pasolini brings the pilgrims to Canterbury Cathedral. *A Canterbury Tale* has a long, final section in the streets and Cathedral. Myerson depicts a two-way pilgrimage whereby the pilgrims not only get to Canterbury and spend time in the streets and Cathedral, but also get back to the Tabard Inn; in this he follows in the footsteps of scribes/editors such as the copyist in charge of the Alnwick manuscript, who inserted the 'Canterbury Interlude', featuring the pilgrims' arrival at Canterbury, and turned them round and back to London. The urge for completion was also evident in the actions of the scribes and poets who finished off some tales, such as the Cook's, and inserted other tales, such as the Plowman's, as we saw earlier in this book. Indeed, it is really interesting to note that Pasolini finished off 'The Cook's Tale', and Myerson finished 'The Squire's Tale' (although he left Sir Thopas in its interrupted, 'unfinished' state).

Many writers and directors, then, remain somewhat reluctant to embrace the radical openness and scruffiness of Chaucer's text. But – perhaps paradoxically – these creative responses and interventions also themselves bear witness to that openness, as writers do not see Chaucer's texts as untouchable, preserved in a fixed state. On the contrary, adaptors take up the implicit challenge of Chaucer's open, diverse texts to try out new interpretations and possibilities. I hope there is more to come.

32 . Chaucer (2527)

Bod. 660

Bod. 686

Whan that april with his shoures swote
The drouth of march hath perced the rote
And bathed euery veyne in swich licour
Of which vertu engendred is the flour
When zepherus eke with his swete breth
Inspired hath in euery holt and heth
The tendre croppes and the yong sonne
Hath in the Ram his half cours y ronne
And smale fowles maken melodye
That slepeth al nyght with open ye
So priketh hem nature in her corages
Than longen folk to gon on pilgrimages
And palmeres to sechen straunge strondes
To ferne halwes couth in sondry londes
And specialy from euery shires ende
Of Engelond to Caunterbury they wende
The holy blisfull martir for to seke
That hem hath holpen when they were seke
Befel that in that seson on a day
In Suthwerke at the taberd as y lay
And redy to wende on my pilgrimage
To Caunterbury with ful deuoute corage
At nyght was comen into that hostrye
Wel nye a twenty in a companye
Of sondry folk by aventure y falle
In felawship and pilgremes were they alle
That toward Caunterbury wold þei ryde
[The c]hambres and stables weren wyde
And wel were esed at the beste
And shortly whan tyme was to reste
So had y spoken with ham euerychone
That y was of here felawship anone
And made forwarde erly for to ryse
To take oure wey ther as y you devyse
But natheles while y haue tyme and space
Or that y further in this tale pace
Me thinketh it acordeth to reson
To tel you al the condicion
Of ech of hem so as it semed me

A.
C.7.11

8
CHAUCER IN THE TWENTY-FIRST CENTURY

Marion Turner

Chaucer still has an extraordinary power to inspire writers. In the twenty-first century a very wide range of authors – performance poets, lyric poets, playwrights, novelists, short-story writers, and some completely unclassifiable wielders of the pen – have written texts overtly responding to Chaucer's work, especially to *The Canterbury Tales*. Some of the most well known of these authors include Zadie Smith (*The Wife of Willesden*), Patience Agbabi (*Telling Tales*), Caroline Bergvall (*Alisoun Sings*) and Marilyn Nelson (*The Cachoeira Tales*).[1] An impressive roster of literary titans has contributed to the Chaucerian *Refugee Tales* volumes edited by David Herd and Anna Pincus: Ali Smith, Bernadine Evaristo, Abdulrazak Gurnah, Jackie Kay, Helen MacDonald, Kamila Shamsie, Ian Sansom, Philippe Sands, Shami Chakrabarti and Monica Ali, among many others.[2]

Pilgrimage

In order to begin to explore why Chaucer's texts are not only still read and loved but are also dynamic prompts for creativity in the twenty-first century, I will return to the beginning. The extraordinary opening lines of the 'General Prologue', lines which introduce the idea of the pilgrimage, have always haunted readers and writers (FIGURE 8.1). Most famously, T.S. Eliot

8.1
A beautiful manuscript image of the opening lines of *The Canterbury Tales*, elaborately decorated with scrolls and foliage, and an author figure enclosed in the opening letter 'W'. These lines have been an inspiration for myriad poets across time. Oxford, Bodleian Library, MS. Bodl. 686, fol. 1r.

inverted them to craft the opening of his masterpiece, *The Waste Land*: 'April is the cruellest month, breeding / Lilacs out of the dead land, mixing / Memory and desire, stirring / Dull roots with spring rain.' A hundred years ago, Chaucer's lines were the springboard for one of the key texts of modernism. Today, they continue to inspire new adaptations and versions that speak to the contemporary moment, often by meditating on the idea of movement, diaspora and journeys of many kinds.

Here are the original lines – the first sentence of *The Canterbury Tales*:

Whan that Aprille with his shoures soote
The droghte of March hath perced to the roote,
And bathed every veyne in swich licour
Of which vertu engendred is the flour;
Whan Zephirus eek with his swete breeth
Inspired hath in every holt and heeth
The tendre croppes, and the yonge sonne
Hath in the Ram his half cours yronne,
And smale foweles maken melodye,
That slepen al the nyght with open ye
(So priketh hem Nature in hir corages),
Thanne longen folk to goon on pilgrimages,
And palmeres for to seken straunge strondes,
To ferne halwes, kowthe in sondry londes;
And specially, from every shires ende
Of Engelond, to Caunterbury they wende,
The hooly blisful martir for to seke,
That hem hath holpen whan that they were seeke.

(lines 1–18; p. 23)

(When April with his sweet showers has pierced the drought of March to the root, and has bathed every vein in such liquid, from the power of which the flower is born; when the West Wind also with his sweet breath has inspired the tender crops in every wood and field, and the young sun has run his half course in Aries, and small birds, that sleep all the night open-eyed, sing melodies – as Nature encourages them in their hearts – then, people long to go on pilgrimages, and pilgrims to seek strange shores, to distant shrines, known in various countries, and especially, from every shire's end of England, they go to Canterbury to seek the holy blissful martyr who has helped them when they were sick.)

This eighteen-line sentence does many things: it sets the scene for the pilgrimage in the spring, a time of natural fertility and a time when the end of Lent and the beginning of the Easter season encouraged spiritual growth; it incrementally narrows our focus, moving us from universal cycles of life to human life to England to the individual body of the saint; it emphasizes the life-giving, miraculous powers first of the breath of life, symbolized by the west wind (Zephirus), and then of the body of Thomas Becket; through its cadences and formal patterning ('Whan… Whan… Thanne…') it mimics the idea of cyclicality – both seasonal and liturgical – *and* the idea of teleology; and it crystallizes a concept of desire around an urge to travel, to move through the landscape.

The first volume of *Refugee Tales* (FIGURE 8.2) draws closely on these lines throughout its Prologue. I quote part of it here:

Now longen folk to goon
On this pilgrimage.

In June not April
And with the sweet showers far behind us
Though with the birds singing
And people sleeping
With open eye
And what we long for
Is to hear each others' tales
And to tell them again
As told by some hath holpen
Walking
So priketh hem nature
Not believing the stories
Our officials tell.
...
As the young sun rises
Woken in their homes
People are picked up and detained,
Routinely and
Arbitrarily
In every holt and heeth
Under the sun while
Smale fowles maken melodye
And why we walk is
To make a spectacle of welcome.[3]

These lines oscillate between direct quotation/allusion to the 'General Prologue' lines – 'longen folk'; 'sweet showers'; 'open ye'; 'hath holpen'; 'priketh hem nature'; 'young sun'; 'in every holt and

heeth'; 'smale fowles maken melodye' – and jarring reminders of the reality of the refugee experience today: 'Not believing / the stories our officials tell'; 'Woken in their homes / People are picked up and detained.' The idea of the desire for movement, the longing to walk, is juxtaposed with reminders about policies that criminalize movement.

In the concept of the *Refugee Tales* project more generally, this focus on movement and liberty is also contrasted with indefinite detention, enforced unlimited staying still. Mixing Middle English quotation with modern English also draws the reader's attention to history – the history of language change. Perhaps for some, this polyglot reading experience might remind them that the history of the English language is a history first of immigration and subjugation and then of colonizing; that

8.2
The covers of *Refugee Tales*, from 2016–21. There are now four volumes in this series, a project inspired by *The Canterbury Tales* that brings together well-known poets and refugees to highlight refugees' stories and to campaign for an end to indefinite detention. *Refugee Tales*, vols I–IV, edited by David Herd and Anna Pincus.

English is embedded in other languages, in interactions between peoples, in movements between countries.[4] The lines quoted above end with a clear agenda – to make a spectacle of welcome; to tell asylum seekers that they are seen and wanted. And that spectacle of welcome also involves listening – 'what we long for / Is to hear each other's tales' – just as *The Canterbury Tales* is a text that is, above all else, about the importance of listening to multiple tales and points of view, placing marginal voices on the same level as voices of authority.

In *The Cachoeria Tales*, Marilyn Nelson uses the opening of the 'General Prologue' to develop a contemporary idea of pilgrimage that engages overtly with enforced movement, with the African diaspora that scattered peoples across the Atlantic through the slave trade:

> When April rains had drenched the root
> of what March headlines had foreseen as drought,
> I invited my extended family –
> with artificial spontaneity –
> to join me on some kind of 'pilgrimage.'
> A fellowship gave me the privilege
> of offering to cover their airfare
> and several nights in a hotel somewhere.
> Thinking of a reverse diaspora,
> I'd planned a pilgrimage to Africa.
> Zimbabwe, maybe Senegal:
> some place sanctified by the Negro soul.[5]

The opening couplet ostentatiously mimics Chaucer but the lines then move away from the language of the *Tales*, except for the repeated references to pilgrimage. Those opening lines, with their focus on contrast – April / March; rain / drought;

life / death – also set the tone for the subsequent lines, which continue to circle around paradoxes and juxtapositions ('artificial spontaneity' 'reverse diaspora'). The rhyming couplet structure (which itself imitates Chaucer's style) also encapsulates the idea of pairs and contrasts – root / drought; diaspora / Africa. Like *Refugee Tales, The Cachoeira Tales* interrogates the idea of travel, underpinned by the most monstrous and brutal movement of people through abduction into chattel slavery, and overlaying this with contemporary experiences of travel and movement in many manifestations – including as a search for origins, for identity, for community.[6] There are fundamental parallels with the Chaucerian idea that the search for 'straunge strondes' (foreign shores) can be healing, can help pilgrims 'whan that they were seeke' (when they were sick).

Patience Agbabi's remix – as she describes it – of *The Canterbury Tales* opens with Harry Bailly's grime version of the beginning of the 'General Prologue'.[7] The seasonal focus of the original, taken up in *Refugee Tales* and *The Cachoeira Tales,* fades here, as April is reconceptualized as a woman and the fertility of nature becomes the sexual allure of this object of desire:

> When my April showers me with kisses
> I could make her my missus or my mistress
> But I'm happily hitched – sorry home girls –
> Said my vows to the sound of the Bow Bells
> Yet her breath is as fresh as the west wind,
> When I breathe her, I know we're predestined
> To make music; my muse, she inspires me,
> Though my mind's overtaxed, April fires me,
> How she pierces my heart to the fond root
> Till I bleed sweet cherry blossom en route[8]

The lines draw very closely on Chaucer's lines: the 'April showers'; 'breath'; 'west wind'; 'pierced my heart to the fond root'. They also explore the crucial theme of desire and the theme of inspiration – breathing life and creative power into the world, or into a person. Changing the focus onto the individual – a woman rather than the season – radically changes the scope of the lines, however, shifting them onto interpersonal relations rather than cosmic forces. There is a different kind of intimacy about these lines. The route is not the route of the Pilgrims' Way, or the route to find 'some place sanctified by the Negro soul'; it is a route to sexual fulfilment, a pilgrimage to a sexual consummation that promises to literalize the images of overspilling 'shoures' and 'licour' in Chaucer's lines. And the masculine April of Chaucer's version has been transposed into a woman, although she keeps the penetrative force of Chaucer's dominant month, piercing Harry's heart as Chaucer's April pierced the drought of March. The lines are balanced between homage and inversion. And the Prologue is framed explicitly as a 'Grime Mix', announcing its connection to contemporary forms and rhythms, a text for its own moment that always acknowledges its past.

It is striking that all of these examples bring together a pilgrimage into the past – to English canonical poetry – and the cultural mixing of modernity. Chaucer's French- and Italian-inspired text meets the experience of refugees from all over the world (*Refugee Tales*); the forced migrations of slaves and the lives of their descendants (*The Cachoiera Tales*); and the genres of rap and grime that have emerged from black culture (*Telling Tales*). A figure at the head of the English canon – but a poet who was, in fact, living at the heart of global trade systems and was a multilingual traveller – is a starting point for different poets to think about the journeys that many people across time have made and have been compelled to make.[9]

Form

Agbabi's lines reveal her fascination with form. The lines are ten-syllable rhyming couplets, like Chaucer's, and Agbabi also imitates Chaucer by playing with so-called 'perfect rhymes' in which a word is rhymed with the same sound ('seke' / 'Seeke'; 'me' / 'me'; 'root' / 'route'). Unlike Chaucer's lines, however, these ten-syllable lines are not iambic. Chaucer's pentameters move fairly regularly in a rough iambic metre – unstressed–stressed. Agbabi's do not. There are many anapaests (unstressed, unstressed, stressed, e.g. 'Said my vows to the sound') and lines often end with spondees (two stressed syllables, e.g. 'kisses', 'mistress', 'home girls', 'Bow Bells'). If you hear Agbabi performing the poem (and there is a recording freely available on YouTube), the rhythms are clear and represent a kind of overlaying of rap and grime beats onto the ten syllable line (FIGURE 8.3).[10] The lines move fast, and can be most fully appreciated through performance – which is also true of Chaucer's poetry, written in a culture in which poetry was usually read out loud in groups, and in which even when people read alone they often did so aloud.[11]

Agbabi's *Telling Tales* more generally demonstrates that Chaucer's formal variety has inspired her to remix his poetry through formal experiment. Harry declares in the Prologue:

> From the grime to the clean-cut iambic,
> Rime-royale, rant or rap, get your slam kick.

8.3
Patience Agbabi, Nigerian-British poet, whose version of *The Canterbury Tales*, *Telling Tales*, was published in 2014. Unusually, Agbabi's version includes adaptations of every Tale in a very wide range of poetic forms.

Chaucer was a master of many different genres and styles. Within *The Canterbury Tales* there are romances, saints' lives, penitential tracts, bawdy fabliaux, beast fables, confessions, miracle stories and homilies. Most tales are told either in rhyming couplets or in rhyme royal (a form invented by Chaucer, and inspired by Boccaccio, and which follows the rhyme pattern ABABBCC). One tale is in a popular form known as tail rhyme, and two are in prose; another is in eight-line stanzas. Outside the *Tales*, Chaucer also wrote four dream vision poems, complaints, a long five-book romance, a translation of a philosophical tract and another translation of a romance, and many short lyrics. Some of his poems use octosyllabic (eight-syllable) lines but most are decasyllabic (ten-syllable). He was the first poet in English to write in an early version of the iambic pentameter. Chaucer experimented with formal prologues as modes of framing sections of text; he stretched what the tale-collection form was capable of; he set genres side by side to expose their limitations; he played with juxtaposing elaborate French vocabulary with plainer Old English words; and he thought seriously about the new forms being used in Italy and adapted them to his own vernacular.[12]

In her own version of the *Tales*, Agbabi too makes variety and experiment central to her technique. She adapts every one of the *Canterbury Tales*, including those often avoided by translators such as the antisemitic 'Prioress's Tale' and the prose 'Parson's Tale' which deals with the seven deadly sins. Throughout the text, Agbabi deploys an exceptionally wide range of forms, frequently switching line length, rhythmic pattern, rhyme scheme and verse form.

'The Tale of Melibee', for instance, becomes a specular poem ('Unfinished Business'): that is, a mirror poem in which the whole poem acts as a palindrome and can be read from end to beginning or beginning to end.[13] This very complicated formal structure allows Agbabi to showcase a crucial theme of the text – how an urge for revenge can be transformed and inverted as it becomes an acceptance of reconciliation. The central lines demonstrate how this is done:

> None of them, even Joe, has the right to live.
> How can I forgive?
> How can I forgive
> none of them? Even Joe has the right to live.

It is a brilliant mirroring of form and content. A similarly close connection between form and content is evident in 'The Man of Law's Tale' ('Joined-Up Writing'), told as a crown of sonnets. It is a seven-sonnet sequence, in which the last line of each sonnet is repeated as the first line of the next, and the last line of the final sonnet takes us back to the first line of the first sonnet in the sequence. The Tale is told from the point of view of the old mother-in-law who is endlessly circling around her past crimes in her memory, and can find no way of moving on from them or rebuilding her relationship with her son: the circular, repetitive structure mimics the movement of a mind stuck in regretful stasis.

Some of Agbabi's formal innovations explore the boundaries of poetry. Her version of 'The Monk's Tale', for instance, draws on texting culture. Chaucer's version of this tale consists of a series of mini-tragedies, told in eight-line verses (a form not used elsewhere in the *Tales*). The Monk says he has a hundred of these stories to tell, but he is cut off after seventeen as the pilgrims find his stories too boring and depressing. Indeed, he tries to impose the same pattern on every story and his tale has no sense of progress, or moving forward. Agbabi's version is called '100 chars' and is by monkey@puzzle. The pun on 'characters' – as figures in a story or individual letters or symbols to type – sets out how this tale will proceed. It is told in verses each of which contains exactly a hundred characters, including spaces. The last verse, for instance, reads like this:

> his fon buzzN n beepN d pulse of our
> dull predictiv lyfs long aftr d medics
> pronouncd him past tense

The connection is explicitly made between dull stories and dull form, when the teller writes about 'dull predictiv lyfs' – the 'predictiv' nods towards predictive texting, while the 'lyfs' reminds us of the boring subject matter of the Monk's endless tragedies. Comically, the spelling of 'lyfs' could be read either as written incorrectly due to quick typing on a phone, or as quoting Middle English. And the final words – 'past tense' – remind us that the tale is about death, and that it is about the past, while also signalling that the tale itself is over.

In *A Double Sorrow: Troilus and Criseyde*, Lavinia Greenlaw similarly produces a free and imaginative translation that consciously responds to Chaucer's formal experiments and concerns. In *Troilus and Criseyde*, Chaucer used rhyme royal (described above). Greenlaw writes in her introduction that she was interested in Chaucer's use of a form that is imperfect, that suggests circularity as well as development, 'progression without conclusion'.[14] While Greenlaw's poem is also written in seven-line stanzas – one to a page – the stanzas vary both from each other and from Chaucer's stanza in many ways. Some are separated into five plus two, or four plus three, or two plus four plus one, or three plus two plus two lines, making obvious some of the possibilities for dividing sense units inherent within rhyme royal itself. Line length and rhyme scheme are also varied greatly, in a way that is ostentatiously different from Chaucer's verse form. For instance, the whole of the elaborately patterned seven stanza proem to Book III becomes one stanza, in free verse, with shortening lines so that the final line is only two words, and two syllables, 'Seize it'.[15] It is obvious on every page that Greenlaw understands that for Chaucer, as for all great poets, form and content are inseparable. To try to grasp what he is doing involves intense engagement with the *how* of the poem, with the extraordinary power of poetry to do things through form. Her response involves a creative remaking of a form (rhyme royal) that Chaucer himself pioneered.

One of the most inventive contemporary interpreters of Chaucer, Caroline Bergvall, overtly meditates on form in her creative free adaptation of the Wife of Bath. *Alisoun Sings* is a truly idiosyncratic text: part prose, part poetry; interweaving Middle English, standard English and contemporary slang; juxtaposing anecdotes from Caxton with pop-song lyrics; drawing widely on the histories of feminism and political activism; it is entirely *sui generis*. One of Bergvall's preoccupations is form in all its meanings:

> Indeedy, glorious is this forest of forms yet now so ravaged & alien, how are one to know in troth which one to inhabit & pursue, which one be a real possibility, which oon a dated morpho-karmic entity. Survival depends on passing through all sorts of vital forms camouflaging to heal, masking to reveal, passing to shine through, camouflaging to seduce.[16]

The lines themselves use different forms of speech – from fairly formal English ('Survival depends on passing through all sorts of vital forms'), to casual ('Indeedy'), to grammatically incorrect ('how are one to know'), to Middle Englush ('oon') to archaic ('in troth'). A few lines later, Bergvall makes explicit reference to Atalanta (and the section is also titled Atalanta) and to Philomela – women whose physical form was changed as they metamorphosed into a lion and nightingale respectively. The section ends with a reference to 'the worlde reveled in a seventeen sillable plop' – the faux medieval spelling followed by a reference to the Japanese poetic form of the haiku. Overall, the section puts a magnifying glass onto form in all its meanings, encouraging us to think about bodies, physical forms, language forms, spelling and the forms of words, literary and generic forms, and formal differences across time and place. Thinking *with* Chaucer enables and encourages many writers to foreground the endless possibilities of form.[17]

Character

Alisoun Sings also bears witness to many contemporary writers' fascination with Chaucerian character. Authors across time have lined up to declare Chaucer the master of character writing. Dryden, for instance, wrote in his 'Preface' to the *Fables* that he could see before him 'all the Pilgrims in the Canterbury Tales, their Humours, their Features, and the very Dress, as distinctly as if I had supp'd with them at the Tabard in Southwark', going on to say that Chaucer 'has taken into the Compass of his Canterbury Tales the various Manners and Humours (as we now call them) of the whole English Nation, in his Age. Not a single Character has escap'd him.' He famously summed up his view on Chaucer's characters with the words:

'Tis sufficient to say according to the Proverb, that here is God's Plenty.'[18]

There is no doubt that over the centuries the Wife of Bath is the character who commanded the most fascination, admiration, loathing, amusement, identification and creative responses from Chaucer's readers. I've written elsewhere about her journey through scribal commentary, early modern ballads, texts by writers such as Shakespeare, Pope, Gay, Voltaire, Percy MacKaye, James Joyce, Vera Chapman, and many others. In the twenty-first century too, she has continued to dominate creative responses to Chaucer's texts.[19]

Bergvall, for example, focuses her book on Alison of Bath. She imagines herself as a kind of vessel through which Alison's voice can speak. In the 'Preface', Bergvall writes about hearing her voice, adding that

> For years from then on it will be my stubborn task to listen for this voice, and transcribe or compose what she says, and keeps on saying, and try to get what it is it wants from me. All my attention and skills now tuned to the depths like a vast sensory receptor whenever the veils of time draw thin.[20]

The Wife of Bath is here explicitly imagined as an independent voice, outside of Bergvall's mind and outside of her own text, an inspirational, muse-like figure.[21] But she is also profoundly of this world, able to talk explicitly about sexual violence, contemporary politics, popular culture, misogyny and much more.

Another particularly innovative recent adaptation of 'The Wife of Bath's Prologue and Tale' is Zadie Smith's play *The Wife of Willesden*, which was premiered and published in November 2021 (FIGURE 8.4). It is a faithful version of 'The Wife of Bath's

Prologue and Tale', with the Prologue – and the Wife of Bath herself – transposed from the fourteenth century to twenty-first-century North London, and the tale that she tells relocated from Arthurian Britain to eighteenth-century Jamaica. Alison becomes Alvita, and the relevance of the concerns of the Wife of Bath in the present day are made clear:

> And if Alvita does make you nervous
> It's worth remembering – though I'm sure you know –
> When wives spoke thus four hundred years ago
> You were all shocked then. The shock never ends
> When women say things usually said by men...[22]

The character of Alison/Alvita is presented as in some ways transcending time, although she is also very much rooted in her own moment and frequently talks about contemporary culture – the Book of Wicked Wives becomes a selection of modern women-hating books by men such as Jordan Peterson and Warren Farrell. The play also engages with the difficulty of putting the univocal Prologue format onto the stage by bringing in other speakers, for instance to voice the authorities that oppress Alison, or to act out scenes that she describes, so that much of the play becomes a visualization of her mind, her imagination, her memory. And because (in the second part of the play) she is acting out the tale, it is impossible to forget that this tale is closely connected to the Wife's own concerns. When immersed in reading *The Canterbury Tales*, it is possible to forget that each tale is told by a particular pilgrim – but that becomes impossible in this staged version, where the same actors inhabit Prologue and Tale. Indeed, the barriers between Prologue and Tale come down at the end of the Tale, when the rapist/'Young Maroon' changes

into one of Alvita's husbands; and the loathly lady/bride becomes Alvita herself. The Wife's own character and life thus take over even more than they do in the original. This is a play that has to be carried by an extraordinary actor – Clare Perkins dominated the stage in the Kiln season in winter 2021. More than any of Chaucer's other characters, the Wife of Bath continues to be remade and reinvigorated in a huge range of texts today.

8.4
Claire Perkins stars as Alvita, the Wife of Willesden, a contemporary version of Alison, the Wife of Bath. This play, by Zadie Smith, premiered in the Kiln Theatre in north-west London in autumn 2021.

New Directions

In the twenty-first century, Chaucer is also finding his way into new media. There are wonderful cartoon versions of Chaucer – including a series by a graphic artist and doctoral student, Kristen Haas Curtis (FIGURE 8.5), who is drawing a

8.5

Kristen Haas Curtis, a medievalist and artist, uses the original Middle English in her cartoon version of 'The Nun's Priest's Tale'. The simple, striking colour palette is used to great effect: the nightmare is all in shadowy blue; and the consistent use of red subtly refers to the hen Pertelote's claim that Chauntecleer, the rooster, has bad dreams because of an excess of red bile.

graphic account of the process of writing a thesis about the reception of the Wife of Bath. A recent project that I worked on developed a Web-based interface using drama and artificial intelligence to allow readers/players to enter the Tabard Inn and talk to responsive versions of Chaucer's pilgrims (FIGURE 8.6).[23] This kind of innovation allows writers to introduce Chaucer's characters to new audiences and to use contemporary technologies to prompt creative responses to the texts, empowering students to influence the texts and to privilege their own interests and readings. There are even elaborate three-dimensional pop-up versions of Chaucer's writings (FIGURE 8.7). Chaucer himself was an innovator. He was interested in science and the new, as evidenced by his writing *A Treatise on the Astrolabe* for his son. He read new poetry in Tuscan before anyone else in England was aware of it, and developed new literary forms in English in response. His generic and formal range was extraordinary – and many of his texts were explicitly responses to other people's writings. The plethora of creative responses being generated by his own texts today is a fitting tribute to the openness and variety of Chaucer's writings and to his own fascination with experiment and novelty.

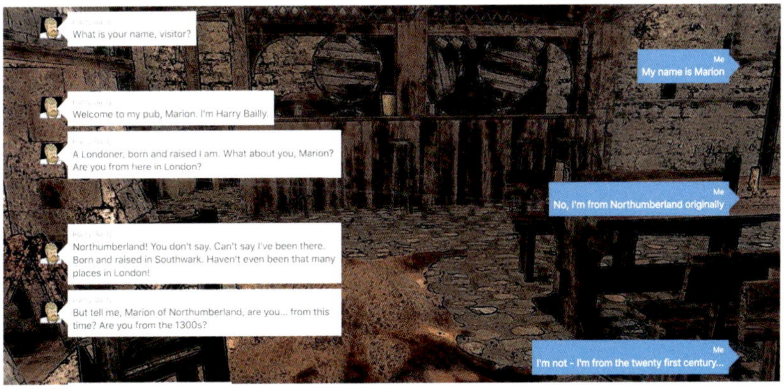

8.6
A screenshot from 'Virtual Chaucer', an interactive experience in which the player/reader talks to the pilgrims. Here, Marion introduces herself to Harry Bailly in the Tabard Inn. Virtual Chaucer was the result of a collaboration between the University of Oxford, Creation Theatre and Charisma AI, an interactive storytelling platform.

IS AWAY HIS STUDENT LODGER, NICHOLAS, SEDUCES HIS YOUNG WIFE, ANISOUN. ANOTHER STUDENT, ABSOLON, ALSO DESIRES HER AND WOES HER BY SINGING LOVE SONGS UNDER HER WINDOW.
TO GET JOHN OUT OF THE WAY, NICHOLAS TELLS HIM THAT A NOAH-LIKE FLOOD IS ON ITS WAY. TO SAVE HIMSELF FROM DROWNING JOHN MUST SLEEP IN A BARREL HANGING FROM THE CEILING.
WHEN THE WATERS RISE JOHN MUST CUT THE ROPES AND LET THE BARREL FLOAT AWAY.

8.7
Paul Johnson's incredible pop-up version of 'The Miller's Tale', featuring three-dimensional scenes of the rooms and spaces of the tale, in a riot of exuberant colour. *Serenade to Chaucer*, 2018. Oxford, Bodleian Library, Rec. a.45.

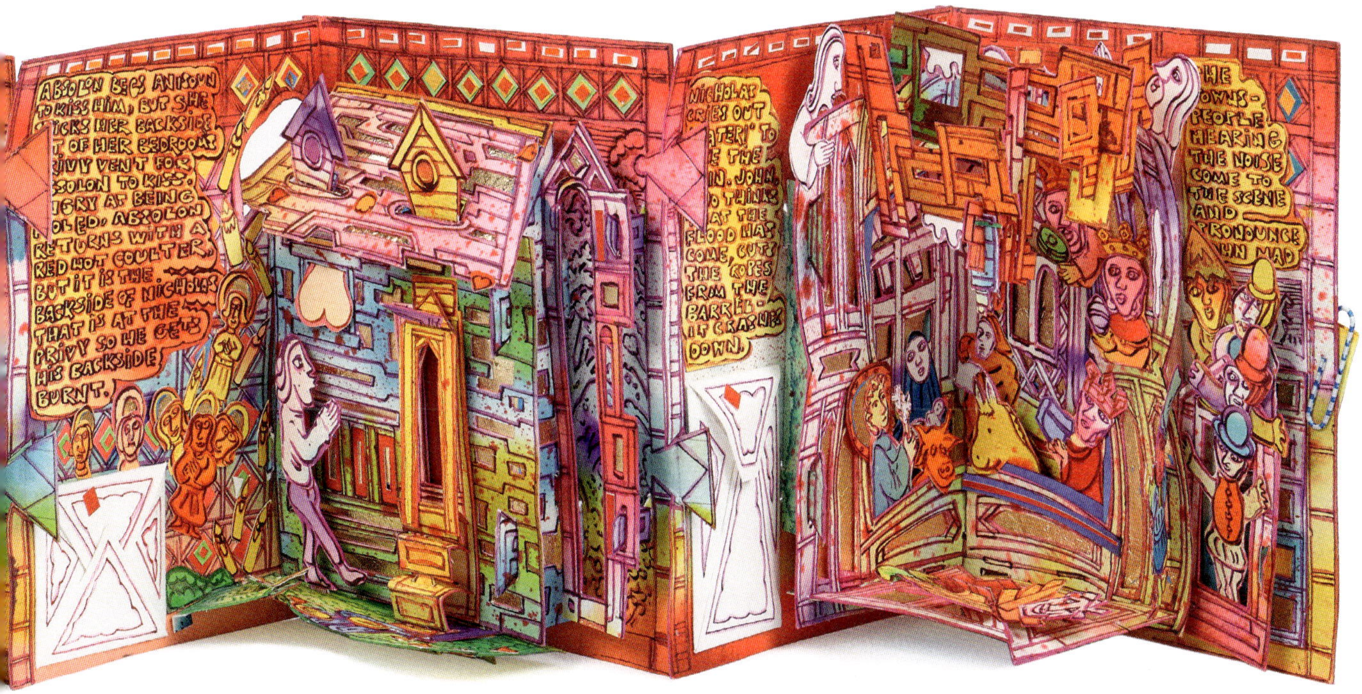

Dates of composition of Chaucer's major works c.1370–1400

c. 1370:	*The Book of the Duchess* (Chaucer's earliest surviving poem)
1380s:	*The Parliament of Fowls*
1380s:	*The House of Fame*
1380s:	versions of some *Canterbury Tales*, including 'The Knight's Tale' and the 'The Second Nun's Tale'
1380s:	*Boece* (translation of Boethius's *Consolation of Philosophy*)
c. 1385:	*Troilus and Criseyde* (Chaucer's major, five-book romance)
c. 1386:	*Prologue to the Legend of Good Women* (F-version) and *Legend of Good Women*
c. 1391:	*A Treatise on the Astrolabe*
c. 1394:	*Prologue to the Legend of Good Women* (G-version)
c. 1387–1400:	*The Canterbury Tales* (Chaucer's most famous work)

Key early manuscripts and printed editions 1400–1600

c. 1400:	the Hengwrt Chaucer (Aberystwyth, National Library of Wales, Peniarth MS. 392D) (the earliest extant manuscript of the *Tales*)
c. 1400–1405:	the Ellesmere Chaucer (San Marino, Huntington Library, MS. EL 26 C 9) (the most famous manuscript of the *Tales*)
c. 1400–1425:	the Corpus *Troilus* (Cambridge, Corpus Christi College, MS. 61)
c. 1450:	Oxford, Bodleian Library, MS. Fairfax 16 (compilation of many poems by Chaucer and others)
1476/7:	Caxton's first edition of *The Canterbury Tales* (the first printed version of the *Tales*)
1483:	Caxton's second edition of *The Canterbury Tales*
c. 1490:	Scottish Chaucer: Oxford, Bodleian Library, MS. Arch. Selden. B. 24

CHRONOLOGY

Selected major texts, editions, translations and adaptations

1498: Wynkyn de Worde, *The Canterbury Tales* (print)

1526: Richard Pynson, *The Canterbury Tales; Troilus and Criseyde, House of Fame* (print)

1532: William Thynne, *The Workes of Geoffrey Chaucer* (the first time an English author's writings were published as a collected 'works')

1561: John Stow, *The Works of Geoffrey Chaucer* (print)

1598: Thomas Speght, *The Workes of our antient and lerned English poet, Geffrey Chaucer* (print)

Selected adaptations, editions and translations c. 1600–1900

c. 1600: *The Wanton Wife of Bath* (ballad)

1602: Thomas Speght, *The Workes of our ancient and learned English poet, Geffrey Chaucer* (influential, major, expansive edition)

1639: Francis Kynaston, *Amorum Troili et Creseidae Libri Quinque* (Latin translation of *Troilus and Criseyde*)

1700: John Dryden, *Fables ancient and modern* (creative translations) (very influential translations that circulated widely in England and abroad)

1713: John Gay, *The Wife of Bath* (play)

1715: Alexander Pope, *The Temple of Fame* (poem)

1722: John Urry, *The Works of Geoffrey Chaucer* (edition)

1763: Voltaire's version of 'The Wife of Bath's Tale' in French (one of the earliest translations of Chaucer on the Continent)

1775: Thomas Tyrwhitt, *The Canterbury Tales* (edition)

1803: William Godwin, *Life of Geoffrey Chaucer* (biography)

1804: Maria Edgeworth, *The Modern Griselda* (novel)

1833: Charles Cowden Clarke, *Tales from Chaucer* (children's version) (widely read version, and the beginning of a major trend for children's Chaucer)

1859: Edward Burne-Jones makes the Prioress wedding cabinet for William and Jane Morris

1868: founding of the Chaucer Society; beginning of the *Six-Text Print*, ed. Frederick Furnivall (an important marker in scholarly work on Chaucer)

1877: Mary Haweis, *Chaucer for Children: A Golden Key*

1894: Walter Skeat, *The Complete Works of Geoffrey Chaucer* (edition)

1896: William Morris, 'The Kelmscott Chaucer' (famous, beautifully illustrated medievalist version of Chaucer's texts)

Selected adaptations, editions and translations 1900–present

1913–25: translations of some of the *Tales* into Chinese by Sun Yuxiu and Lin Shu (marks Chaucer's global reach in the twentieth century)

1917: Kenji Kaneko, *Kantaberi Monogatari* [カンタヘリ物語], first Japanese translation of the *Tales*

1940: John Manly and Edith Rickert, *The Text of the Canterbury Tales* (edition) (major edition co-edited by a female scholar)

1944: *A Canterbury Tale*, directed by Michael Powell and Emeric Pressburger (film)

1952: Nevill Coghill, *The Canterbury Tales* (translation) (very popular and influential translation)

1957: William Auld and Reto Rossetti, Esperanto *Canterbury Tales* in *Angla Antologio*

1968: *Canterbury Tales*, by Nevill Coghill and Richard Hill (West End musical)

1972: *I racconti di Canterbury*, directed by Pier Paolo Pasolini (film) (one-sided, well-known film of some of the Tales)

1980: Ivan Kashkin and Osip Borisovich Rumer, *Kenterberiĭskie rasskazy, Canterbury Tales* translated into Russian with lithographs by Sergey Barkhin

1985: David Wright, *The Canterbury Tales* (translation)

1987: *The Riverside Chaucer*, first edition (remains the principal edition of Chaucer's works for students and scholars)

1994: Nazmi Ağıl, *Canterbury Hikâyeleri*, translation of the *Tales* into Turkish

1998: Jonathan Myerson's animated *Canterbury Tales* (Oscar-nominated and BAFTA-winning short films)

2003: BBC adaptations of six *Canterbury Tales* (TV)

2005: Marilyn Nelson, *The Cachoeira Tales* (adaptation set in the USA and Brazil)

2006: Damdiny Bi͡ambaa, *Dėėdsiĭn ülgėr: Mongol Angli khėlėėr*, Mongolian translation of the 'Squire's Tale'

2009: Lük Bey/Luk De Ryck, *Verhalen voor Canterbury*, Belgian comic book adaptation of selected *Tales*

2009: Alireza Mahdipour, translation of selected *Canterbury Tales* into Persian poetry

2013: José Francisco Botelho, *Contos da Cantuária* (translation of the *Tales* into Brazilian Portuguese)

2014: Patience Agbabi, *Telling Tales* (major modern version of all the *Tales*)

2014: Lavinia Greenlaw, *A Double Sorrow: Troilus and Criseyde*

2016: David Herd and Anna Pincus, eds, *Refugee Tales* (first volume of several; ongoing)

2019: Caroline Bergvall, *Alisoun Sings*

2021: Zadie Smith, *The Wife of Willesden* (very successful contemporary play closely based on the Wife of Bath's Prologue and Tale)

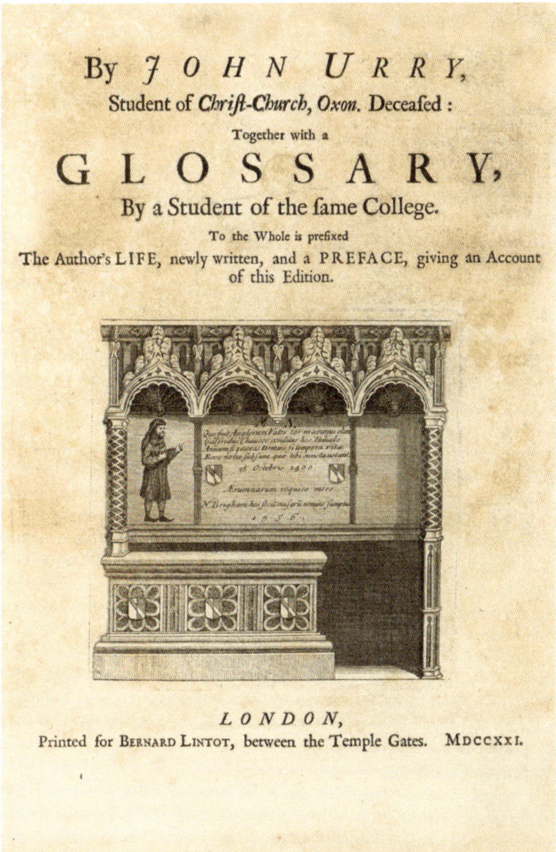

By *JOHN URRY*,
Student of *Chriſt-Church*, *Oxon.* Deceaſed:
Together with a
GLOSSARY,
By a Student of the ſame College.
To the Whole is prefixed
The Author's LIFE, newly written, and a PREFACE, giving an Account of this Edition.

LONDON,
Printed for BERNARD LINTOT, between the Temple Gates. MDCCXXI.

An image of Chaucer's tomb, depicted in 1721. The monument itself, still visible today in Poets' Corner in Westminster Abbey, was erected in 1556. Chaucer was buried in the Abbey when he died in 1400, not because he was a poet but because he lived in the Abbey's precincts. John Urry, *The Works of Geoffrey Chaucer*, 1721. Oxford, Bodleian Library, Douce C subt. 252, title page.

INTRODUCTION

1. Throughout this book, unless indicated otherwise, Chaucer citations are from Geoffrey Chaucer, *The Riverside Chaucer*, 3rd edn, gen. ed. Larry D. Benson, Oxford University Press, Oxford, 2008.
2. Lavinia Greenlaw, *A Double Sorrow: Troilus and Criseyde*, Faber & Faber, London, 2014.
3. For further discussion, see Marion Turner, *The Wife of Bath: A Biography*, Princeton University Press, Princeton NJ, 2023. For Skelton's lines, see John Skelton, 'Phyllyp Sparowe', in *The Complete English Poems*, ed. V.J. Scattergood, Penguin Books, Harmondsworth, 1983, pp. 71–105, lines 614–627. For the fate of the ballad, see Edward Arber (ed.), *A Transcript of the Register of the Company of Stationers of London, 1554–1640*, London, 1875–77, vol. 2, p. 831.
4. Marion Turner, *Chaucer: A European Life*, Princeton University Press, Princeton NJ, 2019.
5. G.K. Chesterton, *Chaucer*. Faber & Faber, London, 1934, pp. 9, 15.

CHAPTER 1

1. A.I. Doyle and M.B. Parkes, 'The Production of Copies of the *Canterbury Tales* and the *Confessio Amantis* in the Early Fifteenth Century', in M.B. Parkes and Andrew G. Watson (eds), *Mediaeval Scribes, Manuscripts and Libraries: Essays Presented to N.R. Ker*, Scolar Press, Aldershot, 1978, pp. 163–203.
2. John M. Bowers, 'The House of Chaucer & Son: The Business of Lancastrian Canon-Formation', *Medieval Perspectives* 6, 1991, pp. 135–43; Simon Horobin, 'Thomas Hoccleve: Chaucer's First Editor?', *Chaucer Review*, vol. 50, no. 3–4, 2015, pp. 228–50; Linne R. Mooney, 'Chaucer's Scribe', *Speculum* 81, 2006, pp. 97–138; Lawrence Warner, 'Scribes, Misattributed: Hoccleve and Pinkhurst', *Studies in the Age of Chaucer* 37, 2015, pp. 55–100.
3. Martha Carlin, 'Thomas Spencer, Southwark Scrivener (d. 1428): Owner of a Copy of Chaucer's Troilus in 1394?', *Chaucer Review*, vol. 49, no. 4, 2015, pp. 387–401.
4. John M. Bowers (ed.), *The Canterbury Tales: Fifteenth-Century Continuations and Additions*, Medieval Institute Publications, Kalamazoo MI, 1992.
5. Both Plowman's tales are available in online editions: d.lib.rochester.edu/teams/text/dean-six-ecclesiastical-satires-plowmans-tale-introduction; d.lib.rochester.edu/teams/text/bowers-canterbury-tales-fifteenth-century-ploughmans-tale.
6. Julia Boffey and A.S.G Edwards, 'Bodleian MS Arch. Selden. B. 24 and the "Scotticization" of Middle English Verse', in Thomas A. Prendergast and Barbara Kline, *Rewriting Chaucer: Culture, Authority, and the Idea of the Authentic Text, 1400–1602*, Ohio State University Press, Columbus OH, 1999, pp. 166–85; T.S. Miller, 'Chaucer Abroad, Chaucer at Home: MS Arch. Selden B. 24 as the "Scottish Ellesmere"', *Chaucer Review*, vol. 47, no. 1, 2012, pp. 25–47.
7. Seth Lerer, *Chaucer and His Readers*, Princeton University Press, Princeton NJ, 1993.
8. Nicola McDonald, 'Chaucer's *Legend of Good Women*, Ladies at Court and the Female Reader', *Chaucer Review*, vol. 35, no. 1, 2000, pp. 22–42, and 'Games Medieval Women Play', in Carolyn P. Collette (ed.), *'The Legend of Good Women': Context and Reception*, D.S. Brewer, Cambridge, 2006, pp. 176–97.
9. Stephen Partridge, '*Glosses in the Manuscripts of the Canterbury Tales: An Edition and Commentary*', Ph.D. dissertation, Harvard University, Cambridge MA, 1992.
10. Kenneth Clarke, *Chaucer and Italian Textuality*, Oxford University Press, Oxford, 2011, pp. 130–51.
11. Susan Schibanoff, 'The New Reader and Female Textuality in Two Early Commentaries on Chaucer', *Studies in the Age of Chaucer* 10, 1988, pp. 71–108.
12. For more discussion, see Marion Turner, The Wife of Bath: A Biography, Princeton University Press, Princeton NJ, 2023.
13. Robert A. Pratt, 'The Order of the Canterbury Tales', *PMLA*, vol. 66, no. 6, 1951, pp. 1141–67.
14. See Horobin, 'Thomas Hoccleve'.

CHAPTER 2

1. 'Chaucer, Geoffrey: *The Canterbury Tales*', Christie's, Lot 998506, 7 July 1998, www.christies.com/en/lot/lot-998506.

NOTES

2. On Speght's Chaucer, see, most recently, Megan Cook, *The Poet and the Antiquaries: Chaucerian Scholarship and the Rise of Literary History, 1532–1635*, University of Pennsylvania Press, Philadelphia PA, 2019, pp. 100–129. For summary discussions of Chaucer's early printed editions, see Paul G. Ruggiers (ed.), *Editing Chaucer: The Great Tradition*, Pilgrim, Norman OK, 1984.
3. Quotations of Caxton's *Recuyell* come from W.J.B. Crotch (ed.), *The Prologues and Epilogues of William Caxton*, Oxford University Press, Oxford, 1928, p. 6. For a discussion of Caxton's career on which this chapter relies, see Seth Lerer, *Chaucer and His Readers: Imagining the Author in Late Medieval England*, Princeton University Press, Princeton NJ, 1995, pp. 147–75.
4. On *Sammelbände* of Caxton's books, see Alexandra Gillespie, 'Caxton's Chaucer and Lydgate Quartos: Miscellanies from Manuscript to Print', *Transactions of the Cambridge Bibliographical Society*, vol. 12, no. 1, 2000, pp. 1–25; and Gillespie, 'Poets, Printers, and Early English *Sammelbände*', *Huntington Library Quarterly* , vol. 67, no. 2, 2004, pp. 189–214.
5. Alexandra Gillespie, *Print Culture and the Medieval Author: Chaucer, Lydgate, and their Books, 1473–1557*, Oxford University Press, Oxford, 2006, p. 30.
6. Alexandra Gillespie, 'Are *The Canterbury Tales* a Book?', *Exemplaria*, vol. 30, no. 1, 2018, p. 72.
7. On the *Tales*' diverse orders, see Robert J. Meyer-Lee, 'Abandon the Fragments', *Studies in the Age of Chaucer*, vol. 35, no. 1, 2013, pp. 47–83.
8. On the possibilities for circulation created by Pynson's three editions, see Martha Driver, 'Woodcuts and Decorative Techniques', in Vincent Gillespie and Susan Powell (eds), *A Companion to the Early Printed Book in Britain, 1476–1558*, D.S. Brewer, Cambridge, 2014, pp. 118–20. On the *House of Fame* in manuscript, see Julia Boffey and A.S.G. Edwards, 'The Early Reception of Chaucer's *House of Fame*', in Isabel Davis and Catherine Nall (eds), *Chaucer and Fame: Reputation and Reception*, D.S. Brewer, Cambridge, 2015, pp. 87–9.
9. Kathleen Forni, *The Chaucerian Apocrypha: A Counterfeit Canon*, University Press of Florida, Gainesville FL, 2001.
10. On Stow's inclusion of the *Siege*, and his edition's impact on Elizabethan poetry, see Jeff Espie, 'Literary Paternity and Narrative Revival: Chaucer's Soul(s) from Spenser to Dryden', *Modern Philology*, vol. 114, no. 1, 2016, pp. 39–58; Espie, '(Un) couth: Chaucer, *The Shepheardes Calendar*, and the Forms of Mediation', *Spenser Studies*, vol. 31, no. 1, 2018, pp. 243–71; and Espie, 'Spenser, Chaucer, and the Renaissance *Squire's Tale*', *Spenser Studies*, vol. 33, no. 1, 2019, pp. 133–60.

Quotations from, and references to, early printed editions draw directly from the following texts, listed in chronological order and cited parenthetically by signature number in the chapter text.

Whan that Apprill with his shouris sote, William Caxton, Westminster, 1476/7, STC 5082.

Boecius de consolacione philosophie, William Caxton, Westminster, 1478, STC 3199.

Canterbury Tales, William Caxton, Westminster, 1483, STC 5083.

The book of fame made by Gefferey Chaucer, William Caxton, Westminster, 1483, STC 5087.

Canterbury Tales, Richard Pynson, London, 1492, STC 5084.

The boke of Chaucer named Caunterbury tales, Wynkyn De Worde, London, 1498, STC 5085.

The interpretacion of the names of goddis and goddesses, Wynkyn De Worde, London, 1498, STC 17005.

The noble and amerous auncyent hystory of Troylus and Cresyde, Wynkyn De Worde, London, 1517, STC 5095.

The boke of Canterbury tales, Richard Pynson, London, 1526, STC 5086.

The boke of fame, made by Geffray Chaucer, with dyuers other of his workes, Richard Pynson, London, STC 5088.

The boke of Troylus and Creseyde, Richard Pynson, London, 1526, STC 5096.

The workes of Geffray Chaucer, Thomas Godfrey, London, 1532, STC 5068.

The workes of Geffray Chaucer, Richard Grafton, London, 1542, STC 5069.

The workes of Geffray Chaucer, Nicholas Hill, London, 1550, STC 5071.

The woorkes of Geffrey Chaucer, John Kingston, London, 1561, STC 5076.

The workes of our antient and lerned English poet, Geffrey Chaucer, Adam Islip, London, 1598, STC 5078.

The workes of our ancient and learned English poet, Geffrey Chaucer, Adam Islip, London, 1602, STC 5080.

CHAPTER 3

1. For a truly comprehensive discussion of Chaucerian poetic influence in theory and practice, see Tom Mason and David Hopkins, *Chaucer in the Eighteenth Century: The Father of English Poetry*, Oxford University Press, Oxford, 2022.
2. John Dryden, *Fables ancient and modern, Printed for Jacob Tonson*, London, 1700, 'Preface', C5r.
3. Ibid., 'Preface', C7v.
4. Ibid.
5. Ibid., Dr.
6. Dryden, *Fables*, p. 536.
7. Ibid., p. 252.
8. Ibid., p. 242.
9. John Milton, *Paradise Lost*, ed. Gordon Teskey, Norton, New York, 2005, 9:351–352, p. 206.
10. Alexander Pope, *The Works of Alexander Pope*, ed. John Butt, Routledge, London, 1992, p. 172.
11. Ibid., p. 188.
12. Ibid., p. 189.
13. Caroline Spurgeon, *Five Hundred Years of Chaucer Criticism (1357–1900)*, Oxford University Press, and Kegan Paul, Trench, Trübner, Frowde, London, 1922 (1908–10), part 4, p. 542; Betsy Bowden, *The Wife of Bath in Afterlife: Ballads to Blake*, Lehigh University Press, Bethlehem PA, 2017, p. 47.
14. Bowden, The *Wife of Bath in Afterlife*, pp. 2, 6.
15. John Gay, *The Wife of Bath. A Comedy*, B. Lintot, London, 1713, p. 3.
16. Ibid., p. 59.
17. *The Canterbury Tales of Chaucer, Modernis'd by several hands*, 3 vols, Printed for J. and R. Tonson, London, 1741, 1, p. 31.
18. For Chaucerian editing in the first half of the century, see William L. Alderson and Arnold C. Henderson, *Chaucer and Augustan Scholarship*, University of California Press, Berkeley CA, 1970, and the essays in Paul G. Ruggiers, ed., *Editing Chaucer: The Great Tradition*, Pilgrim, Norman OK, 1984.
19. *The Works of Geoffrey Chaucer*, ed. John Urry, B. Lintot, London, 1722, p. 5. *The Canterbury tales of Chaucer*, ed. Thomas Tyrwhitt, 4 vols, T. Payne, London, 1775–8, vol. I, p. 20.
20. *The Works of Geoffrey Chaucer*, ed. Urry, p. 32.
21. *The Canterbury tales of Chaucer*, ed. Tyrwhitt, vol. I, p. xx.
22. Ibid., vol. I, p. vi.
23. See Daniel Cook, *Thomas Chatterton and Neglected Genius, 1760–1830*, Palgrave, London, 2013, ch. 2.

CHAPTER 4

1. *The Works of Geoffrey Chaucer Now Newly Imprinted*, ed. F.S. Ellis, Kelmscott Press, London, 1896 [the Kelmscott Chaucer].
2. *A Six-Text Print of Chaucer's Canterbury Tales in Parallel Columns*, ed. Frederick Furnivall, 8 vols (in 4), Chaucer Society first series 1, 14, 15, 25, 30, 31, 37, 49; second series 3, Chaucer Society, London, 1868–77.
3. Charles Cowden Clarke, *The Riches of Chaucer: in which his impurities have been expunged; his spelling modernised; his rhythm accentuated; and his obsolete terms explained*, 4th edn, Macmillan, London and New York, 1896.
4. Ibid., p. vii. This sentence actually appeared in the much earlier first edition, Effingham Wilson, London, 1835; the 'Preface to the First Edition' was reprinted in subsequent editions.
5. Clarke, *The Riches of Chaucer*, p. 175.
6. Mary Eliza Haweis, *Chaucer for Children: A Golden Key*, Chatto & Windus, London, 1877, p. x.
7. Ibid., p. xiii.
8. Charles Cowden Clarke, *Tales from Chaucer, In Prose. Designed chiefly for the use of young persons*, Effingham Wilson, London, 1833.
9. On Chaucer and/as children's literature, see further my 'Infantilizing the Father: Chaucer Translations and Moral Regulation', *Studies in the Age of Chaucer* 22, 2000, pp. 93–114, and Velma Bourgeois Richmond, *Chaucer and Children's Literature: Retellings from the Victorian and Edwardian Eras*,

McFarland, Jefferson NC, 2004.

10. Thomas Tyrwhitt, *The Canterbury Tales of Chaucer*, 4 vols, T. Payne, London, 1775; a fifth volume with a glossary appeared in 1778.

11. W. Lipscomb, *The Canterbury Tales of Chaucer; Completed in a Modern Version*, 3 vols, Oxford and London, 1795, vol. 1, p. vi.

12. William Godwin, *Life of Geoffrey Chaucer, The Early English Poet: Including Memoirs of his Near Friend and Kinsman, John of Gaunt, Duke of Lancaster: with Sketches of the Manners, Opinions, Arts and Literature of England in The Fourteenth Century*, 2 vols, Richard Phillips, London, 1803, vol. 1, p. 248.

13. R.H. Horne, *The Poems of Geoffrey Chaucer, Modernized*, Whittaker & Co., London, 1841, pp. xxx, v, x.

14. Thomas Babington Macaulay, *The History of England from the Accession of James II*, Longman, Brown, Green, and Longmans, 1849, vol. 1, p. 17.

15. Ibid., vol. 1, pp. 18–19.

16. Godwin, *Life of Geoffrey Chaucer*, vol. 1, pp. 389, 395.

17. Arthur Burrell, *Chaucer's Canterbury Tales for the Modern Reader*, J.M. Dent, London, 1908.

18. Michelle R. Warren, '"The last syllable of modernity': Chaucer in the Caribbean', *postmedieval: a journal of medieval cultural studies* 6, 2015, pp. 79–93, p. 87.

19. P.R. Stephensen, 'The Foundations of Culture in Australia' (1935) in *The Writer in Australia: A Collection of Literary Documents, 1856 to 1964*, ed. John Barnes, Oxford University Press, Melbourne, 1969, pp. 204–44, p. 211.

20. Clarke, *Tales from Chaucer*, p. iii.

21. *The Complete Works of Geoffrey Chaucer: Edited from Numerous Manuscripts*, ed. Walter W. Skeat, 7 vols, Clarendon Press, Oxford, 1894–97, vol. 1, p. liii.

22. Haweis, *Chaucer for Children*, p. 4.

23. Mary Eliza Haweis, *Chaucer for Schools*, Chatto & Windus, London, 1881, p. x.

24. Mary Eliza Haweis, *Tales From Chaucer*, George Routledge and Sons, London, 1887, pp. 16, 90.

25. F.J. Furnivall, 'Introduction', in F.J. Harvey Darton, *Tales of the Canterbury Pilgrims: Retold from Chaucer & Others*, Wells Gardner, London, 1904, p. vi.

26. On the place of Chaucer in the early university teaching of English, see D.J. Palmer, *The Rise of English Studies: An Account of the Study of the English Language and Literature from its Origins to the Making of the Oxford English School*, Oxford University Press, London, 1965, esp. pp. 23, 25, 26, 115, 128, 146; see also Chris Baldick, *The Social Mission of English Criticism, 1848–1932*, Clarendon Press, Oxford, 1983.

CHAPTER 5

1. E. Talbot Donaldson, *Speaking of Chaucer*, Norton, New York, 1970, pp. 9, 103. See also discussion in Carolyn Dinshaw, *Chaucer's Sexual Poetics*, University of Wisconsin Press, Madison WI, 1989, pp. 13–14, 30.

2. John Matthews Manly and Edith Rickert, *The Text of the Canterbury Tales*, University of Chicago Press, Chicago IL, 1940, p. viii. For discussion of Rickert, see Elizabeth Scala, 'Scandalous Assumptions: Edith Rickert and the Chicago Chaucer Project', Medieval Feminist Forum 30, 2000, pp. 27–37, and Scala, '"Miss Rickert of Vassar" and Edith Rickert at The University of Chicago (1871–1938)', in Jane Chance (ed.), *Women Medievalists and the Academy*, University of Wisconsin Press, Madison WI, 2005, pp. 127–45; Sylvia Tomasch, 'Editing as Palinode: The Invention of Love and the Text of the Canterbury Tales', *Exemplaria*, vol. 16, no. 2, 2004, pp. 457–76.

3. C.H. Beeson, George La Piana and J.S.P. Tatlock, 'Report of the Committee on the Award of the Haskins Medal', *Speculum*, vol. 17, no. 3, 1942, pp. 453–4.

4. For a study of women and medievalism in the nineteenth century, see Clare Broome Saunders, *Women Writers and Nineteenth-Century Medievalism*, Palgrave Macmillan, London, 2009.

5. Maria Edgeworth, *The Modern Griselda*, 2nd edn, corrected, J. Johnson, London, 1805.

6. Ibid., p. 66.

7. Thomas Gisborne, *An Enquiry into the Duties of the Female Sex*, 4th edn, T. Cadell Jr and W. Davies, London, 1799, p. 6. See discussion in Alison Ganze Langdon, 'The More Things Change: Maria Edgeworth's "The Modern Griselda"', *The Year's Work in Medievalism* 28, 2012, pp. 2–9.

8. 'The Modern Griselda; a Tale by Miss Edgworth', *Annual Review* 3, 1804, pp. 553–4.

9. Eleanora Louisa Hervey, 'Griseldis, with her Children', *The Athenaeum* 1179, 1 June 1850, pp. 583–4.

10. Eleanora Louisa Hervey, 'Griselda', in *Our Legends and Lives: A Gift for All Seasons*, Trübner and Co., London, 1869, pp. 223–4.

11. Renee Ward, 'Giving Voice to Griselda: Radical Reimaginings of a Medieval Tale', *Studies in Medievalism* 26, 2017, pp. 87–116. Ward also helpfully prints the poems in full.

12. Mary Eliza Haweis, *Chaucer for Children: A Golden Key*, Chatto & Windus, London, 1877.

13. Ibid., p. 83.

14. Ibid.

15. Ibid., p. 82.

16. See discussion in Sian Echard, *Printing the Middle Ages*, University of Pennsylvania Press, Philadelphia PA, 2008, pp. 126–61, and Mary Flowers Braswell, 'The Chaucer Scholarship of Mary Eliza Haweis (1852–1898)', *Chaucer Review*, vol. 39, no. 4, 2005, pp. 402–19.

17. Haweis, *Chaucer for Children*, p. 109.

18. Kathleen Davis, *Periodization and Sovereignty: How Ideas of Feudalism and Secularization Govern the Politics of Time*, University of Pennsylvania Press, Philadelphia PA, 2008.

19. See Voltaire, and Sylvain Menant, *Contes En Vers Et En Prose*, Bordas, Paris, 1992, vol. 1, pp. 331–46.

20. For further discussion of Beauclerk, see Betsy Bowden, *The Wife of Bath in Afterlife: Ballads to Blake*, Lehigh University Press, Bethlehem PA, 2017, p. 206, and Marion Turner, *The Wife of Bath: A Biography*, Princeton University Press, Princeton NJ, 2023, p. 198.

21. See Stephanie Trigg, *Congenial Souls: Reading Chaucer from Medieval to Postmodern*, University of Minnesota Press, Minneapolis MN, 2001.

CHAPTER 6

1. Jonathan Hsy, *Trading Tongues: Merchants, Multilingualism, and Medieval Literature*, Ohio State University Press, Columbus OH, 2013; Marion Turner, *Chaucer: A European Life*, Princeton University Press, Princeton NJ, 2019.

2. Louise Bennett, *Jamaica Labrish: Jamaica Dialect Poems*, ed. Rex Nettleford, Sangster's Book Stores, Kingston, Jamaica, 1966, pp. 218–19.

3. Arthur Thomas Quiller-Couch (ed.), *The Oxford Book of English Verse 1250–1900*, Oxford University Press, Oxford, 1900.

4. Lian Zhang, 'Chaucer in China: A History of Reception and Translation', *Chaucer Review*, vol. 55, no. 1, 2020, pp. 1–31, pp. 6, 8–9; Candace Barrington and Jonathan Hsy, 'Global Chaucers', in *Medieval Afterlives in Contemporary* Culture, ed. Gail Ashton, Bloomsbury, London, 2015, pp. 147–56, p. 151.

5. Kenji Kaneko, *Kantaberi Monogatari* [カンタベリ物語], Toado-shoten, Tokyo, 1917; Koichi Kano, 'Preamble to the First Japanese Translation of *The Canterbury Tales*: A Social Mirror and a Cultural Bridge', *Literature Compass*, vol. 15, no. 6, June 2018, pp. 1–8, p. 4.

6. Alireza Mahdipour, 'The Translator Writes Back', *Literature Compass*, vol. 15, no. 6, June 2018, pp. 1–8, 3, 7; Barrington and Hsy, 'Global Chaucers', pp. 149–50.

7. Raúl Ariza-Barile, 'The Mexican Chaucer: Philology South of the Border', *Literature Compass*, vol. 15, no. 6, June 2018, pp. 1–11; José Francisco Botelho, *Contos da Cantuária*, Companhia das Letras, São Paulo, 2013.

8. José Francisco Botelho, 'Old Janus Drinking From His *Guampa*: A Brazilian Re-creation of *The Canterbury Tales*', *Literature Compass*, vol. 15, no. 6, June 2018, pp. 1–12, p. 8; Barrington and Hsy, 'Global Chaucers', p. 150.

9. Megan Cook and David Hadbawnik, '"His Latin Stile Hath Englisht Thee": Kynaston's 1635 *Troilus and Criseyde*', *Global Chaucers* (blog), 4 November 2014; Barrington and Hsy, 'Global Chaucers', pp. 12–13.

10. The first book to describe Esperanto was published in Russian, commonly known as *Unua Libro* (First Book); L.L. Zamenhof, Международный язык [*Dr Esperanto's International Language*], Warsaw, 16 July (O.S. 14 July), 1887.

11. William Auld and Reto Rossetti, *Angla Antologio 1000–1800*, Universala Esperanto-Asocio, Rotterdam, 1957, p. 9.

12. Ibid., p. 30.

13. Brantley L. Bryant (@LeVostreGC), twitter.com/LeVostreGC/status/665232642070065152; David J. Peterson (@Dedalvs), twitter.com/Dedalvs/status/665227907329978368.

14. Ouyang Yu, *The Kingsbury Tales: A Novel*, Brandl & Schlesinger, Blackheath NSW, 2008; Jonathan Hsy, *Antiracist Medievalisms: From "Yellow Peril" to Black Lives Matter*, Arc Humanities Press, Leeds, 2021, pp. 128, 130–32; Caroline Bergvall, *Meddle English: New and Selected Texts*, Nightboat, New York, 2011; Julian Talamantez Brolaski, *Of Mongrelitude*, Wave, Seattle WA, 2017; Hsy, *Antiracist Medievalisms*, pp. 111–14; Jos Charles, *feeld*, Milkweed, Minneapolis MN, 2018.

15. Grace Skidmore, 'Highlighting the Autolithographic Soviet Chaucer', *Global Chaucers* (blog), 15 September 2020; Aleksandr Abramovich Anikst (ed.), *Kenterberiĭskie rasskazy*, Moscow, 1980, with poetry translation by Ivan Kashkin and

Osip Borisovich Rumer and illustrations by Sergey Barkhin.

16. Zhang, 'Chaucer in China', p. 10; Candace Barrington and Jonathan Hsy, 'Editors' Introduction: Chaucer's Global Orbits and Global Communities', *Literature Compass*, vol. 15, no. 6, June 2018, pp. 1–12; Hsy, *Antiracist Medievalisms*, pp. 115–32; Heather Blurton, 'Retelling the *Prioress's Tale*: Antisemitism, Racism, and Patience Agbabi's *Telling Tales*', *Chaucer Review*, vol. 56, no. 4, 2021, pp. 397–412.

17. R.M. Lumiansky, *The Canterbury Tales of Geoffrey Chaucer*, Simon & Schuster, New York, 1948, p. xxiii; Greg Wilsbacher, 'Lumiansky's Paradox: Ethics, Aesthetics and Chaucer's "Prioress's Tale"', *College Literature*, vol. 32, no. 4, Fall 2005, pp. 1–28.

18. Charles Cowden Clarke, *Tales From Chaucer Told For Young People*, illus. Arthur Szyk, Heritage Press, New York, 1947.

19. Michael Gibbs Hill, *Lin Shu, Inc.: Translation and the Making of Modern Chinese Culture*, Oxford University Press, Oxford, 2012; Candace Barrington, 'Chaucer in China (2): Reading Lin Shu', *Global Chaucers* (blog), 8 November 2013.

20. Charlotte C. Morse, 'Popularizing Chaucer in the Nineteenth Century', *Chaucer Review*, vol. 38, no. 2, 2003, pp. 99–125.

21. Masui Michio, *Kantaberi monogatari: Zen'yaku* [カンタベリ-物語: 完訳], 3 vols, Iwatami-Shoten, Tokyo, 2011–12; *The Works of Geoffrey Chaucer Now Newly Imprinted*, ed. F.S. Ellis, Kelmscott Press, London, 1896.

22. Jonathan Hsy and Candace Barrington, 'Translations and Adaptations, Listed by Country', *Global Chaucers* (blog), updated March 2022.

23. Lük Bey [pen name of Luk De Ryck], *Verhalen voor Canterbury*, Bonte magazine, 2009; *The Canterbury Tales* (iPad app, 2010); Shing Yin Khor, *The Canterbury Ghosts*, 2018, shingkhor.com/new-divinations; Shing Yin Khor (@sawdustbear), twitter.com/sawdustbear/status/1047169670858432512; Kristen Haas Curtis, 'Canterbury Ghosts: Discussing Adaptation with Shing Yin Khor', *COMMode: Canonicity, Obscenity, and the Making of Modern Chaucer* (blog), 28 July 2021, updated 8 September 2021.

24. Peter Cook, *Sir Gawain and Finger-licious Stories* (DVD); Peter Cook, 'Features in American Sign Language Storytelling', *Storytelling, Self, Society*, vol. 7, no. 1, 2011; Edna Edith Sayers, 'Experience, Authority, and the Mediation of Deafness: Chaucer's Wife of Bath', in *Disability in the Middle Ages: Reconstructions and Reverberations*, Ashgate, Farnham and Burlington VT, 2010, pp. 81–92; Jonathan Hsy, 'Symptom and Surface: Disruptive Deafness and Medieval Medical Authority', *Journal of Bioethical Inquiry* 13, 2016, pp. 477–83; Jill Bradbury et al., 'Response to Carol L. Robinson, 'Go Ask Alisoun: Geoffrey Chaucer and Deafland (deafness as authority)', *Literature Compass*, vol. 6, no. 1, 2019, e12503.

25. Jonathan Fruoco, 'Chaucer en français: The Problem of Retranslaton', *Global Chaucers* (blog), 29 December 2020; Stephanie Downes, 'Chaucer in Nineteenth-Century France', *Chaucer Review* , vol. 49, no. 3, 2015, pp. 352–70.

26. Louise D'Arcens, 'The Thunder After the Lightning: Language and Pasolini's Medievalist Poetics', *postmedieval* 6, 2015, pp. 191–9, pp. 196, 193.

27. Frederick M. Biggs, 'The Miller's Tale and *Heile van Beersele*', *Review of English Studies*, vol. 56, no. 226, September 2005, pp. 497–523; Barrington and Hsy, 'Global Chaucers', pp. 152–3.

28. Carmel Jordan, 'Soviet Archaeology and the Setting of the *Squire's Tale*', *Chaucer Review*, vol. 22, no. 2, Fall 1987, pp. 128–40.

29. Jack Weatherford, *Genghis Khan and the Making of the Modern World*, Crown Publishers, New York, 2004, pp. xxiv, 239–40; Adrian Barlow, 'Mongolia: Chaucer and Chinggis Khaan', *Adrian Barlow's Blog*, 15 June 2012.

30. Damdiny Bi͡ambaa, *Dėėdsiĭn u̇lgėr: Mongol Angli khėlėėr* [*The Squire's Tale: In Mongolian and English*], Ulaanbaatar, 2006.

CHAPTER 7

1. For discussions of screen adaptations of Chaucer, see Kathleen Coyne Kelly and Tison Pugh (eds), *Chaucer on Screen: Absence, Presence, and Adapting the Canterbury Tales*, Ohio State University Press, Columbus OH, 2013.

2. Louise D'Arcens, 'The Thunder after the Lightning: Language and Pasolini's Medievalist Poetics', *postmedieval*, vol. 6, no. 2, 2015, pp. 191–9.

3. Both the BBC adaptations and Myerson's version are discussed in Kathleen Forni, *Chaucerian Afterlife: Adaptations in Recent Popular Culture*, McFarland, Jefferson NC, 2013, ch. 3.

4. See Martin Greene, 'The Dialectic of Adaptation: The Canterbury Tales of Pier Paolo Pasolini', *Literature/Film Quarterly*, vol. 4, no. 1, 1976, pp. 46–53, and Carol L. Robinson, 'Celluloid Criticism: Pasolini's Contribution to a Chaucerian Debate', in Leslie J. Workman (ed.), *Medievalism in Europe*, Boydell & Brewer, Woodbridge, 1994, pp. 115–26.

5. On the Wife of Bath across time, see Marion Turner, *The*

Wife of Bath: A Biography, Princeton University Press, Princeton NJ, 2023.

6. Carolyn Dinshaw, *How Soon Is Now? Medieval Texts, Amateur Readers, and the Queerness of Time*, Duke University Press, Durham NC, 2012.

7. Marion Turner, *Chaucer: A European Life*, Princeton University Press, Princeton NJ, 2019.

8. See Tison Pugh, 'Chaucerian History and Cinematic Perversions in Michael Powell and Emeric Pressburger's 'A Canterbury Tale', in K.C. Kelly and T. Pugh (eds), *Chaucer on Screen: Absence, Presence, and Adapting the 'Canterbury Tales'*, Ohio State University Press, Columbus OH, 2016, pp. 111–29.

9. For further discussion, see Kathleen Davis, 'Time, Memory, and Desire in the BBC Man of Law's Tale', in Kelly and Pugh (eds), *Chaucer on Screen*, pp. 239–48.

10. As Steve Ellis notes, Myerson's version does, however, move away completely from Chaucer's poetic brilliance. See *Chaucer at Large*, University of Minnesota Press, Minneapolis MN, 1999, pp. 121–40, pp. 139–40.

CHAPTER 8

1. Zadie Smith, *The Wife of Willesden*, Penguin Random House, London, 2021; Patience Agbabi, *Telling Tales*, Canongate, London, 2014; Caroline Bergvall, *Alisoun Sings*, Nightboat Books, New York, 2019; Marilyn Nelson, 'The Cachoeira Tales', in *The Cachoeira Tales and Other Poems*, Louisiana State University Press, Baton Rouge LA, 2005, pp. 11–54.

2. There are currently four *Refugee Tales* volumes, all edited by David Herd and Anna Pincus and published by Comma Press, Manchester. The authors mentioned here feature as follows: Ali Smith and Abdulrazak Gurnah in volume I (2016); Jackie Kay, Kamile Shamsie and Helen MacDonald in volume II (2017); Monica Ali, Ian Sansom and Bernadine Evaristo in volume III (2019); and Philippe Sands and Shami Chakrabarti in volume IV (2021). For more information about the project, see www.refugeetales.org/about.

3. *Refugee Tales*, pp. v–vii.

4. On place, Chaucer and the *Refugee Tales*, see Helen Barr, 'Stories of the New Geography: The Refugee Tales', *Journal of Medieval Worlds*, vol. 1, no. 1, March 2019, pp. 79–106.

5. Nelson, *The Cachoeira Tales*, p. 11.

6. David Wallace, 'New Chaucer Topographies', *Studies in the*

Age of Chaucer 29, 2007, pp. 3–19; Kathleen Forni, *Chaucer's Afterlife: Adaptations in Recent Popular Culture*, McFarland, Jefferson NC, 2013, p. 111.

7. On grime, see Sasha Frere-Jones, 'True Grime: A Genre's Magic Moment', *The New Yorker*, 13 March 2005, www.newyorker.com/magazine/2005/03/21/true-grime.

8. Agbabi, *Telling Tales*, p. 1.

9. Marion Turner, *Chaucer: A European Life*, Princeton University Press, Princeton NJ, 2019.

10. www.youtube.com/watch?v=-U-ozgjZfjQ

11. Joyce Coleman, *Public Reading and the Reading Public in Late Medieval England and France*, Cambridge University Press, Cambridge, 2005.

12. See Marion Turner, 'Form', in Frank Grady (ed.), *The Cambridge Companion to the Canterbury Tales*, Cambridge University Press, Cambridge, 2020, pp. 1–20.

13. 'Unfinished Business' and 'Joined up Writing' are foci of discussion in Jonathan Hsy and Candace Barrington, 'Queer Time, Queer Forms: Noir Medievalism and Patience Agbabi's *Telling Tales*', in David Hadbawnik (ed.), *Postmodern Poetry and Queer Medievalisms: Time Mechanics*, De Gruyter, Berlin, 2022, pp. 159–77.

14. Lavinia Greenlaw, *A Double Sorrow: Troilus and Criseyde*, Faber & Faber, London, 2014, p. xii.

15. Ibid., p. 93.

16. Caroline Bergvall, *Alisoun Sings*, Nightboat Books, New York, 2019, p. 13.

17. On Bergvall, see David Hadbawnik, 'Speak Like a Child: Caroline Bergvall's Medievalist Trilogy', in Hadbawnik (ed.), *Postmodern Poetry and Queer Medievalisms*, pp. 179–204.

18. John Dryden, *Fables ancient and modern*, Jacob Tonson, London, 1700 [unnumbered pages].

19. Marion Turner, *The Wife of Bath: A Biography*, Princeton University Press, Princeton NJ,2019.

20. Bergvall, *Alisoun Sings*, p. vii.

21. See also Bergvall's comments in 'The Language Of Alisoun: In Conversation with Caroline Bergvall', nightboat.org/the-language-of-alisoun-in-conversation-with-caroline-bergvall.

22. Smith, *The Wife of Willesden*, p. 12.

23. www.virtual-chaucer.com.

At the end of this stunning, tiny, Russian Chaucer, there is a pull-out illustration of all the pilgrims riding on their horses, with castles and countryside as their backdrop. *Kenterberiĭskie rasskazy*, 1980. Oxford, Bodleian Library, 27976 g.2.

CHAPTER 1

John M. Bowers (ed.), *The Canterbury Tales: Fifteenth-Century Continuations and Additions*, Medieval Institute Publications, Kalamazoo MI, 1992.

A.I. Doyle and M.B. Parkes, 'The Production of Copies of the *Canterbury Tales* and the *Confessio Amantis* in the Early Fifteenth Century', in M.B. Parkes and Andrew G. Watson (eds), *Mediaeval Scribes, Manuscripts and Libraries: Essays Presented to N.R. Ker*, Scolar Press, Aldershot, 1978, pp. 163–203.

Seth Lerer, *Chaucer and His Readers: Imagining the Author in Late Medieval England*, Princeton University Press, Princeton NJ, 1993.

Thomas A. Prendergast and Barbara Kline, *Rewriting Chaucer: Culture, Authority, and the Idea of the Authentic Text, 1400–1602*, Ohio State University Press, Columbus OH, 1999.

Marion Turner, *The Wife of Bath: A Biography*, Princeton University Press, Princeton NJ, 2019

CHAPTER 2

Megan L. Cook, *The Poet and the Antiquaries: Chaucerian Scholarship and the Rise of Literary History, 1532–1635*, University of Pennsylvania Press, Philadelphia PA, 2019.

Joseph A. Dane, *Who Is Buried in Chaucer's Tomb? Studies in the Reception of Chaucer's Book*, Michigan State University Press, East Lansing MI, 1998.

Alexandra Gillespie, *Print Culture and the Medieval Author: Chaucer, Lydgate, and their Books, 1473–1557*, Oxford University Press, Oxford, 2006.

James Simpson, 'Chaucer's Presence and Absence, 1400–1550', in Piero Boitani and Jill Mann (eds), *The Cambridge Companion to Chaucer*, Cambridge University Press, Cambridge, 2004, pp. 251–69.

CHAPTER 3

William L. Alderson and Arnold C. Henderson, *Chaucer and Augustan Scholarship*, University of California Press, Berkeley CA, 1970.

Betsy Bowden, *The Wife of Bath in Afterlife: Ballads to Blake*, Lehigh University Press, Bethlehem PA, 2017.

Tom Mason and David Hopkins, *Chaucer in the Eighteenth Century: The Father of English Poetry*, Oxford University Press, Oxford, 2022.

Paul G. Ruggiers (ed.), *Editing Chaucer: The Great Tradition*, Pilgrim Books, Norman OK, 1984.

Caroline Spurgeon, *Five Hundred Years of Chaucer Criticism (1357–1900)*, Oxford University Press, and Kegan Paul, Trench, Trübner, Frowde, London, 1922 (1908–10).

CHAPTER 4

Siân Echard, *Printing the Middle Ages*, University of Pennsylvania Press, Philadelphia PA, 2008.

Steve Ellis, *Chaucer at Large: The Poet in the Modern Imagination*, University of Minnesota Press, Minneapolis MN, 2000.

David Matthews, *The Making of Middle English 1765–1910*, University of Minnesota Press, Minneapolis MN, 1999.

FURTHER READING

Stephanie Trigg, *Congenial Souls: Reading Chaucer from Medieval to Postmodern*, Minneapolis: University of Minnesota Press, 2002.

CHAPTER 5

Jane Chance (ed.), *Women Medievalists and the Academy*, University of Wisconsin Press, Madison WI, 2005.

Carolyn Dinshaw, *Chaucer's Sexual Poetics*, University of Wisconsin Press, Madison WI, 1989.

Clare Broome Saunders, *Women Writers and Nineteenth-Century Medievalism*, Palgrave Macmillan, London, 2009.

Renee Ward, 'Giving Voice to Griselda: Radical Reimaginings of a Medieval Tale', *Studies in Medievalism*, vol. 26, 2017, pp. 87–116.

CHAPTER 6

Candace Barrington and Jonathan Hsy (eds), 'Resources', *Global Chaucers* (blog).

Candace Barrington and Jonathan Hsy (eds), 'Special Issue: Chaucer's Global Compaignye', *Literature Compass*, vol. 15, no. 6, June 2018.

Jonathan Hsy, *Antiracist Medievalisms: From 'Yellow Peril' to Black Lives Matter*, Arc Humanities Press, Leeds, 2021.

Jonathan Hsy, *Trading Tongues: Merchants, Multilingualism, and Medieval Literature*, Ohio State University Press, Columbus OH, 2013.

Susan E. Phillips, 'Chaucer's Language Lessons', *Chaucer Review*, vol. 46, no. 1–2, 2011, pp. 39–59.

Shyama Rajendran, 'Undoing "the vernacular": Dismantling Structures of Raciolinguistic Supremacy', *Literature Compass*, vol. 16, no. 9–10, September–October 2019.

Denise Ming-yueh Wang, 'Chaucer's English and Multilingualism', *Medieval and Early Modern English Studies*, vol. 22, no. 2, 2014, pp. 1–27.

CHAPTER 7

Kathleen Coyne Kelly and Tison Pugh (eds), *Chaucer on Screen: Absence, Presence, and Adapting the Canterbury Tales*, Ohio State University Press, Columbus OH, 2013.

Kathleen Forni, *Chaucerian Afterlife: Adaptations in Recent Popular Culture*, McFarland, Jefferson NC, 2013.

Leslie J. Workman (ed.), *Medievalism in Europe*, Boydell & Brewer, Woodbridge, 1994.

CHAPTER 8

Helen Barr, 'Stories of the New Geography: The Refugee Tales', *Journal of Medieval Worlds*, vol. 1, no. 1, March 2019, pp. 79–106.

David Hadbawnik (ed.), *Postmodern Poetry and Queer Medievalisms: Time Mechanics*, De Gruyter, Berlin, 2022.

David Wallace, 'New Chaucer Topographies', *Studies in the Age of Chaucer* 29, 2007, pp. 3–19.

www.refugeetales.org.

Jeff Espie is Director of Vice-Presidential Communications at the University of Toronto Mississauga. Before moving into university administration, he earned an MSt from the University of Oxford and a PhD from the University of Toronto and published articles on medieval and early modern literary history in *Modern Philology*, *Literary Imagination*, *English Literary Renaissance*, and elsewhere. His 2019 analysis of Spenser and Senecan tragedy won the essay prize from the *Review of English Studies*.

Alexandra Gillespie is Principal of the University of Toronto Mississauga, Vice-President of the University of Toronto, and Professor of English and Medieval Studies. Her research spans from the poetics of Chaucer's *Canterbury Tales* to the global development of early book technologies, from scientific approaches to book history to literary theory and philosophy. On these topics she has published more than forty articles, six co-edited volumes and one monograph, including *Print Culture and the Medieval Author* (2006), and led several international collaborations, including as co-primary investigator on a Mellon-funded project about *The Book and the Silk Roads*.

Jonathan Hsy is Professor of English at George Washington University, and he is the founding co-director of Global Chaucers and contributor to *The Chaucer Encyclopedia*, *A New Companion to Chaucer*, and Open Access Companion to The Canterbury Tales. He is the author of *Antiracist Medievalisms: From 'Yellow Peril' to Black

Lives Matter (2021), *Trading Tongues: Merchants, Multilingualism, and Medieval Literature* (2013) and co-editor of *A Cultural History of Disability in the Middle Ages* (2020).

David Matthews is Professor of Medieval and Medievalism Studies at the University of Manchester. He is a past editor of *Studies in the Age of Chaucer*; recent books are *Subaltern Medievalisms: Medievalism 'from below' in Nineteenth-Century Britain* (2021; co-edited with Mike Sanders) and *Medievalism: A Critical History* (2015). He is currently working on the fates of medieval literature in the sixteenth century.

Adam Rounce is Associate Professor in English Literature at the University of Nottingham. He has written extensively on various seventeenth- and eighteenth-century writers, including Dryden, Pope and Johnson. He is co-editor of *Irish Political Writings after 1725* (2018) in the ongoing Cambridge University Press edition of the writings of Jonathan Swift, and the author of *Fame and Failure* (2013).

Marion Turner is the J.R.R. Tolkien Professor of English Literature and Language at the University of Oxford. She is the author of numerous books and articles about medieval literature, especially Chaucer, including the prize-winning biography *Chaucer: A European Life* (2019), *Chaucerian Conflict* (2007) and *A Handbook of Middle English Studies* (2013). Her most recent book is *The Wife of Bath: A Biography* (2023). She curated the exhibition *Chaucer Here and Now*.

Iamque domos patrias Scithice post aspera gentis
Prelia laurigero &c

Heere bigynneth the knyghtes tale

Whilom as olde stories tellen vs
Ther was a duc þt highte Theseus
Of Atthenes he was lord and gouernour
And in his tyme swich a conquerour
That gretter was ther noon vnder the sonne
fful many a riche contree hadde he wonne
What with his wysdom and his chiualrie
He conquered al the regne of ffemenye
That whilom was ycleped Scithia
And wedded the queene ypolita
And broghte hire hoom with hym in his contree
With muchel glorie and greet solempnytee
And eek hir faire suster Emelye
And thus with victorie and with melodye
Lete I this noble duc to Atthenes ryde
And al his hoost in Armes hym bisyde
And certes if it nere to long to heere
I wolde yow haue toold fully the manere
How wonnen was the regne of ffemenye
By Theseus and by his chiualrye
And of the grete bataille for the nones
Bitwixen Atthenes and Amazones
And how asseged was ypolita
The faire hardy queene of Scithia
And of the feste þt was at hir weddynge
And of the tempest at hir hoom comynge
But al that thyng I moot as now forbere
I haue god woot a large feeld to ere
And wayke been the oxen in my plough
The remenant of the tale is long ynough
I wol nat letten eek noon of this route
Lat euery felawe telle his tale aboute
And lat se now who shal the soper wynne
And ther I lefte I wol ageyn bigynne
This duc of whom I make mencioun — Narrat
Whan he was come almoost vn to the toun
In al his wele and in his mooste pryde
He was war as he caste his eye aside
Where that ther kneled in the weye
A compaignye of ladyes tweye and tweye

PICTURE CREDITS

© Ashmolean Museum, University of Oxford, WA1939.2: 0.1, 4.2

© Ashmolean Museum, University of Oxford, WA1920.3: 4.7

Courtesy of Candace Barrington: 6.2; 6.3

BBC Photo Archive: 7.1, 7.5

Courtesy of José Francisco Botelho: 6.4

Marc Brenner/Kiln Theatre: p. 10, 8.4

British Library, London © British Library Board. All rights reserved/Bridgeman Images: 1.11

The Governing Body of Christ Church, Oxford: 1.5, 1.7

By kind permission of Comma Press, cover designs by David Eckersall: 8.2

Kristen Haas Curtis: 8.5

Photo Lyndon Douglas: 8.3

Everett Collection Inc./Alamy: 7.3, 7.4

Hangook University of Foreign Studies Press, 2007: 6.3

The Huntington Library, San Marino, California: p. 220, 1.2, 1.3, 9.3

© Paul Johnson: 8.7

By permission of Llyfrgell Genedlaethol Cymru/National Library of Wales: 1.1, 1.4

Merton College – By permission of The Warden and Fellows of Merton College Oxford, photo by Colin Dunn / Scriptura Ltd: 2.1

The Parker Library, Corpus Christi, Cambridge: 1.10

Photo 12/Alamy: 7.2

Courtesy of S4C and Christmas Films: 7.6

Courtesy of S4C and Christmas Films/Beryl Productions: 7.7

Courtesy of S4C and Christmas Films/Picasso Pictures: 7.8

Courtesy of Shing Yin Khor: 6.8

By permission of the President and Fellows of St John's College, Oxford, A.2.5: 2.4, 2.8

www.virtual-chaucer.com: 8.6

Published by Yushokan: 6.2

The opening of 'The Knight's Tale' from the gorgeous Ellesmere Chaucer, *c.* 1400. Readers are reminded of the importance of the teller by the insertion of beautiful miniatures at the start of each tale. San Marino, Huntington Library, MS. EL 26 C 9, fol. 10r.

INDEX

First published in 2023 by Bodleian Library Publishing
Broad Street, Oxford OX1 3BG
www.bodleianshop.co.uk

ISBN: 978 1 85124 615 1

The production of this book was supported by a generous grant from the British Academy and the Leverhulme Trust.

Publisher: Samuel Fanous
Managing Editor: Susie Foster
Editor: Janet Phillips
Picture Editor: Leanda Shrimpton
Designed and typeset by Dot Little at the Bodleian Library in 12/16 Adobe Jenson
Printed and bound by Gomer Press Limited on 150gsm Arctic Matt paper

FSC www.fsc.org MIX Paper from responsible sources FSC® C114687

WORLD LAND TRUST™ www.carbonbalancedprint.com CBP2275

British Library Catalogue in Publishing Data
A CIP record of this publication is available from the British Library